A Wa Warning:
End-times Prophecy Survey of the Great Reset

Dr. D.A. Kelly, Sr.

Cadmus Publishing
www.cadmuspublishing.com

Published by Cadmus Publishing
www.cadmuspublishing.com
Port Angeles, WA

ISBN: 978-1-63751-205-0

I dedicate this book to my Lord and Savior Jesus Christ. I forever love you and thank you.

Acknowledgement

I would like to first, thank my wonderful parents, JoJo and Alice Bess. You have never left my side, despite my past. You have shown me what unconditional love looks like. And that family is everything; like JoJo said, "when everyone else leaves you, family will be there to pick you up." I love you two. To my beloved 5 children: Alicia, DJ, Shekinah, Devon, and Elijah; and my 7 grandchildren (my own United Nations and growing) I'm so proud of you all. To my grandchildren who are my inspiration; remember to continue to glorify God in all you do; write your name on people checks; and put your name on a building. To my younger grand-babies, I love you guys beyond your imagination. I pray for the Lord to guide you to be a: Doctor, Lawyer, or Indian Chief. It is my prayer that you all read this book, and share aspects therein with your children's children. Teach them the values of life that's only through Jesus Christ, the Eternal Son of God. Know Him. Love Him. Serve Him and one day, be with Him. I love you all from the deep chambers of my beating heart, from generation to generations. God Bless you!

To my beautiful and smart sisters: Shanee (Chris) and Chevon (June), and my niece, Keanna and AJ, my nephew. I'm extremely proud of you and love you dearly. Shanee and Chris thank you for your support with this ministry. You two mean so much to me. I would like to thank you for the tough, and honest feedback and critique: Minister Jenkins, Minister Duncombe, Michael Raby for the editing, Charlie from Brooklyn, Minister Graham. And thanks to Rev. Carney, Minister Joey and Mother Day. Lastly, I cannot forget to thank my haters! I can't forget about you.

God Bless you all.

Stay prayed up. Word up. So the Devil won't mess you!

TABLE OF CONTENTS

DR. D.A. KELLY, SR

Introduction

I have never thought in my lifetime, I would witness such a horrendous train of events such that has occurred since 2020. What was so alarming was the dramatic hustle to change the world due to COVID-19 crisis, followed by this insufferable bending of the backbone to our illustrious Republic in matters inherent to our constitutional rights. We see an embrace of lawlessness with an increase in violence in our major cities, perpetrated in the effort to destabilize our country, leaving some believers to think all we can do is shake our heads in disbelief. There are certain global elites seduced by the flirtation of experiments aligned with trans-humanism. We all ought to be real concerned about the direction these corrupt people are shifting the weight of the country to lean away from Christ.

Like many, though, I never imagined bearing witness to the wanton disregard for life of the innocent with open-armed celebrations with things which were once taboo. I see it like this – taking a soiled shirt, then turning it inside out as if it is freshly clean. The shirt is still funky-filthy. Every day there is something new, from the indoctrination of elementary children on sexual immorality to talks of eliminating single-family homeownership. Perhaps most of us may interpret day-to-day news as overwhelming, for it may even seem that every "new issues" has whipped passed us at warp speed. These compounding issues have ignited a fire in my heart, and ushered me towards Bible prophecy. I'm excited and most grateful that the Lord has granted me the discernment and the ability to decrypt these events into substantive evidence for my research to warn those who are willing to understand the signs of the time. Each day, I see an enormous dark cloud of danger, hovering over the horizon, drawing closer like an approaching Middle Eastern sandstorm.

For those unfamiliar with sandstorms, I'll explain. In 2008, I deployed as a company commander to Bagram Air Base in Afghanistan. One afternoon in April, I was touring the company area of operation with the outgoing commander. It appeared to be business as usual, with Airmen and Soldiers walking around in various uniforms, signifying whether they were on – or off-duty. As the outgoing commander drove, I noticed the sun had dimmed and a reddish smog had appeared.

"Roll up your window," the outgoing commander said.

As soon as I finished rolling up my window, our vehicle was bombarded with millions of tiny grains of sand. Visibility was limited, much like that of a heavy rainfall. I was amazed by this man's ability to recognize the signs of an imminent sandstorm.

I was completely unfamiliar with the conditions of Afghanistan sandstorms, and it was not something briefed during my short stay in Manas Air Base, Kyrgyzstan. Even though I identified the changes, I had no understanding of their meaning. Without the commander's understanding and warning, I would have been blasted in the face with stinging sand. I learned from this experience and passed on that knowledge: how to identify an approaching storm; places to shelter; and measures to protect oneself, if caught in the storm.

Even now, I can see a formation of a dark-reddish calamity cloud approaching in our direction. It is due to these unusual experiences that Jesus Christ has granted me that ability to discern these perilous times as a watchman on-duty with years of studying eschatology (end-times prophecy) and much prayer. I must emphasize: I'm not a prophet, nor do I intend to set dates nor predict times or the like. To do so would be foolish, and it would recklessly discredit my call to action. So, I must reiterate with great urgency, it is my duty to blow the trumpet of warning and educate whoever will hear the warnings within the short time before the Rapture of the Church. Therefore, I have taken the time to process and create a tapestry of current events to show the signs of an apocalyptic cloud bursting towards us.

A Watchman's Warning

When I lived in Germany, I had many opportunities to visit Nuremburg, a metropolitan city rich in historical significance. I was able to visit Das Zeppelinfeld, which was also known as "Hitler's Stadium," and saw quite a bit of medieval architecture. Throughout the city, areas were still encircled by high, ancient brick walls. Many of the walls had watch towers, and some of the gates contained sentinel posts. A sentinel post is an alcove on the outside of a city's gates, usually on the upper level of the wall. Watch towers and sentinel posts were present in most communities throughout history. The men assigned to these posts were the militaristic early warning system for their communities, hundreds of years before satellites were placed in space for the job. Indeed, this duty required trust and capability, as these men became all that stood between the adversary and a community's people.

The Bible is rife with examples of watchmen, including 2 Samuel 18:24, 2 Kings 9:17, and Isaiah 21:6-9. The Hebrew word, "saphah," is used 40 times in the Old Testament in its verb form, signifying someone taking the position of watchman to care for the common people.

For instance, within the book of Ezekiel, Ezekiel received a mandate from God to:

> "…speak to the children of thy people, and say unto them, when I bring the sword upon a land, if the people of the land take a man of their coast, and set him up for their watchman: if when he seeth the sword come up on the land, he blow the trumpet, and warn the people…" (33:3)

In fact, Ezekiel's feet moved with due diligence to obey the One True Living God. He embraced this enormous opportunity to warn an indifferent class of people to take the hard right over the easy wrong, repent or else. This man of God was eyeball-to-eyeball with folks not willing to listen to God. Some Preacher! It's probably safe to say by twenty-first century standards, these people were out of their minds. We can imagine the level of anxiety that may have tugged at Ezekiel's emotions. I'm not at all saying he was scared, but there may have been a Hebrew variant of "Good grief, come on people!" If you look back at Ezekiel 3:5&7, God told Ezekiel:

> "For thou art not sent to a people of a strange speech and of a hard language but to the house of Israel…but the house of Israel will not hearken unto thee, for they will not hearken unto me: for all the house of Israel are imprudent and hard hearted."

The prophet had girded himself for the impossible mission, even though the house of Israel was a rebellious house, as noted in verse nine. God wasn't concerned about Israel's behavior at the moment; instead,

He commanded Ezekiel: "And go, get thee to them of the captivity, unto the Children of thy people, and speak unto them, and tell them. Thus saith the Lord God whether they will hear, or whether they will forbear," (Ezek. 3:11). If you will, take a moment and consider this from a different perspective – Ezekiel did not have a choice to opt out of God's plan. Some of us would reject this claim, even suggest that we all have the liberty to choose right over wrong or wrong over right. An emphatic no! We do not. Here is why: whenever we are sold out for pleasing God, all other options are off the table. Further, to neglect the responsibility that accompanies the watchman's call gives birth to consequences and repercussions none of us want to reap. When God draws us, we should not allow anything to discourage us from satisfying our Lord. On the contrary, let's hypothetically say Ezekiel went on to pull a Jonah, where inaction and silence would have been deafening. However, look at the consequences stated when Ezekiel was told, "When I say unto the wicked, Thou shalt surely die: and thou givest him not warning, nor speakest to warn the wicked from his wicked way, to save his life; the same wicked man shall die in his iniquity; but *his blood* will I require at *thine hand*" (Ezek. 3:18). The consequence for disobedience is having the wicked's blood on our hands. Do you want to pay for someone else's sin? I don't!

What does it profit us to follow God's Word to warn the wicked? It simply separates us from any accountability of such deterioration of moral imperative. Jesus emphasizes: "All that the Father giveth me shall come to me… no one can come to me, except the Father which hath sent me draws him; and I will raise him up at the last day" (John 6:37(a) & 44). Likewise, "wherefore the rather, brethren, give diligence to make your calling and election sure: for if ye do these things, ye shall never fall" (2 Pet. 1:10). Any refusal to follow through with a call entrusted to us is a "fall." This is the reason why I emphasize that we "neglect not the gift that is in thee, which was given thee by prophesy, with the laying on of the hands of the presbytery", and it behooves us to "take heed unto thyself, and unto the doctrine; continue in them: for in doing this though shalt both save thyself, and them that hear thee" (1 Tim. 4:14 & 16). Again, God came upon Ezekiel with a word to "blow the trumpet, and warn the people" (Ezekiel. 33:3). God has given me a trumpet to blow and a tower to stand watch. I must obey Him.

Trumpet Significance

In the book of Joshua, this great leader called upon the priests, ordering them to gather seven priests to take up seven horns (shophar) fashioned from rams. What is interesting about these animals is that they were used as actual battering rams for breaking down gates and walls. Throughout the Bible, these shophars were used as instruments for: signaling people to move (Josh. 6:6, 9, 20), preparing for battle or attack (Judges 7:16-22; 2 Sam. 6:15; Job 39:24-25), assembling for religious celebration (Psalms 81:3, Num. 10:10; 2 Chr. 29:27-28), warning of incoming danger (Neh. 4:18-20), calling people to repentance (Ezek. 33:3-16), warning of invasion (Amos 3:6), and royal coronations (2 Kings 9:13).

When we refer to the Joshua account, God armed him with the best strategy to siege Jericho without firing a shot. The Lord says, "And ye shall compass the city, all ye men of war, and go round about the city once. This shalt thou do six days" (Joshua 6:3). For six long days, the priests were focused, determined to go around the city in the presence of the Lord.

The seventh day required a little bit more effort on the part of the priests. The Lord ordered:

"Ye shall compass the city seven times, and the priests shall blow with the trumpets. And it shall come to pass, that when they make a long blast with the ram's horn, and when ye hear the sound of the trumpet, all the people shall shout with a great shout; and the wall of the city shall fall down flat," (Joshua 6:4-5).

The purpose of the trumpet is to inspire the people to respond in unison, so that the stronghold will weaken so that the walls "fall down flat." In the same context, we, who are called to the watchman's post, are armed with a trumpet (our mouth), backed by the full authority of God to proclaim His righteous plan. Keep in mind, not everyone is built for the assignment to boldly cut down the fragile curtain of deception, or to gather the intestinal fortitude to faithfully "tar and feather" wicked schemes, and the lies of the enemy. Some are not even willing to escort unwanted attention to those issues-at-large. Finally, a watchman's actions should inspire others to make life-changing decisions. It is by the guidance of the Holy Spirit, who will strengthen you to handle the weight of any issue by empowering you to stand on godly truths, that we can stand tall. What say you? What direction are you going to take at the intersection of coward and courage? Whichever choice you make has an actual risk attached to it.

CHAPTER 1

THE KEY TO BIBLICAL INTERPRETATION

2020 started off with the greatest tragedy, thus far, of the 21st century, the COVID-19 crisis. Every nation around the world, in some shape or form, was affected economically, politically, and spiritually. I believe in giving credit where credit is due. I like to use the idiom, Chinese Communist Party (CCP) Virus, which has unfortunately destroyed many dreams by infecting over 160 million people and killing nearly 5 million more innocents and counting. As a result, fear is a scorching heat that has melted the hearts and minds of millions of Americans, leaving so many floating adrift on rafts of shattered hopes in a raging river of confusion. Just like another catastrophe, the terrorist attacks on September 11, 2001, where two commercial aircraft leveled the Twin Towers, killing thousands of people in the name of Islam. I remember after the fall of the Towers people started to ask, out of curiosity, if these events were signs defining the end of the world?

An enormous interest pertaining to end-times prophecy has consumed people to seek a connection between current and future Biblical events, ranging from calamities to blessings. Strangely, though, out of the

66 books of the Bible, The Revelation of Jesus Christ, is often neglected by readers, as are the books of the Minor Prophets. I believe this is due in part to the difficulty some may have in understanding the prophetic language which graces the pages. Secondly, those who diligently read these books tend to be unfamiliar with the proper methods governing biblical interpretation. In fact, there is a scientific method and theory to biblical interpretation of a scriptural text called "hermeneutics." I know of a number of believers who neglect Revelation because it is "hard to understand" or, that it is "too scary" to read. What I do not understand is that these are the same people, once a large scale calamity manifests, who dust off their Bible from the trunk of their car and turn to Revelation with the expectation that an answer will jump off the pages. There is nothing exactly wrong with this approach, considering it is the Bible they use to search for answers. An important point here is we do not know what we do not know. What we don't understand, we do not like. What we do not like is neglected. Does this sound familiar? Well, I truly believe our Lord and Savior, Jesus Christ, has assigned me this task to apply color between the lines, to help others, to understand what is staged before their eyes: if not, "how shall they hear without a preacher" (Rom. 10:14)? When I was writing this chapter, I believe the Holy Spirit led me to explore with the reader the following biblical precepts:

1. Bible composition

2. Biblical doctrine

3. Interpretation method

By this reason alone, I have the moral imperative to respectfully provide the reader with a basic explanation respectfully before we dive further into this book. You will see many of these terms and doctrines throughout this book.

Bible Composition

It is necessary to establish some foundation on the basis of the infallibility and authority of all Scriptures. In 66 AD, prior to martyrdom, apostle Paul wrote in 2 Timothy 3:16 how: "all Scriptures is given by inspiration of God, and is profitable for doctrine, for reproof, for correction, for training, for instruction in righteousness." In general, he wanted to provide his readers with the assurance to the authenticity of Scriptures, thus pointing specifically to the equity between the Old Testament Scriptures and the New Testament. It was essential to give deference to each covenant, as these are testimonies to the full richness of the whole council of God. It is very important for us, students of God's Word, to study to show ourselves approved unto God, by adding to our faith daily. These testimonies are the body of progressive revelation that was graciously "breathed out" by 40 authors over a period of 1,600 years and written in three different languages.

Previously, I mentioned, the Bible is composed of 66 books that are broken-down as:

- 39 Old Testament books

- 27 New Testament books

- 1,189 chapters

- 31,109 verses

- One-fourth of the Bible is prophecy

- "God" appears in 3,893 verses

- "Lord" appears in 6,749 verses

Biblical doctrine

I believe it is important to note that Biblical doctrine is definitely one of the widely controversial topics within Christendom. It is one thing to be a scrupulous learner, but another to reject topics due to ignorance and fear. For this reason, it is necessary for me to define certain terms as we continue to mature in the process of our spiritual growth. Now, the "introductory formula" which governs us on matters pertaining to Christian life or articulates warnings expressed through illustrations and applications are known as doctrines. For instance, the teaching on God's grace is considered the "Doctrine of Grace." A teaching of the End Times is the "Doctrine of Eschatology." A Teaching on the life and ministry of Jesus Christ is called the "Doctrine of God the Son" or "Christology," with many more doctrines yet to list. You get the point. You do not have to be intimidated when hearing the term "doctrine" being used as a nomenclature to label some tenet of study. Unfortunately, the word theology, which means the science of God, has been viewed negatively. It seems that people immediately get defensive as if it is a gateway to something insidious. We are called to explain the biblical relevance to those whom are misguided and ignorant of the facts. The late theologian R.C. Sproul wrote it is common that:

> "The modern Christian tends to ignore or decry the importance of the right doctrine. Tired of endless disputes, Christians today embrace the idea that what really matters is right relationship, nor right doctrine. The idea that one is more important than the other is faulty premise; both right relationships and right doctrine matter." [1]

There is nothing more important than practicing right doctrine to avoid biblical error. If we are not careful, it is easy "to be earnest, eloquent, and knowledgeable in Scripture and yet preach it either inaccurately or in less than its full truth."[2] Many churches today are avoiding the uncut "meat" of the Bible doctrine (1 Cor. 3:2). Instead, these ministries would rather hide the "meat" of the Word and keep the people on a 2% "milk" diet. We are being held to a higher standard as stewards of God's Word, which is why it is crucial for us to "study to shew thyself approved unto God a workman that needest not to be ashamed…" (2 Tim. 2:15). We are commanded to "rightly divide the Word" before tackling the mission of interpreting prophecy. "Knowing this first, that no prophecy of the Scripture is of any private interpretation" (2 Pet. 1:20). What this Scripture means, in most cases, is that one cannot just cherry pick a single Scripture and appoint our personal meaning to it. What held then holds now. It is extremely dangerous to spontaneously interpret the meaning of a text without diligently investigating what the author had meant, at that moment, to the author's original audience. We cannot interpret Scripture through our American cultural lens in the place of ancient culture. It is easy to find yourself within a danger zone when thinking Scripture may be meaning one thing, while in context, it was intended to mean something else. Contextual criticism is everything. This is why it behooves us to correctly apply the appropriate hermeneutical method as an "interpretive key."[3] someone might complain, "these things being presented are rather technical, man!" It is very technical. Here is why; you may find yourself thinking a Scriptural passage means one thing, in essence – there is a whole different meaning. Once you have broken-through a threshold of misinterpretations, you have now entered into a dangerous posture as being labelled as some false-teacher or false whatever. The technical part comes with utilizing additional reference material such as: exhaustive concordance, commentaries, biblical history, language, and word study dictionaries to aide you through your search for true contextual meaning.

Remember, for those of us whom are called to operate in the gift as a watchman, it is not easy. We who are called to witness must dig into the very fabric of the word. Anything that is good, doesn't always come easy. If it was easy, everybody and their momma would be doing it, but God has chosen us to be His mouthpiece to a dying world that is thirsty for the Living Water. Therefore, for the purpose of pleasing God, let us apply the appropriate hermeneutics, that is "the science of interpretation."[4] As a "science," this suggests there are rules which govern how one might interpret Scriptures within the "specific genres," such as parables, allegories, and apocalyptic. [5]

Understand this: interpreting prophecy is a challenge if we don't know the "why." Let's explore some of the special literary forms to answer the "why" and then transition into the "how." The word, "prophecy," derives from the Greek word, *propheteia*, and translates to the "inspired declaration of divine will and purpose," "a prediction of something to come."[6] Indeed, it was the prophets who were bearers of the two designations: Fore-telling (telescoping) and Forth-telling (megaphone) in prophecy. A fore-teller is a prophet who would receive a Word from God that would manifest in the future. In the Old Testament, prophets were men, and prophetess were women; both were called by God to deliver His divine plan, purpose, and future. We can understand this as it evolved in the New Testament, where John the Baptist was known as the last Old Testament prophet because he came in the spirit and power of Elijah (Lk. 1:17). Just like all the prophets preceding himself, this preacher proclaimed Jesus Christ and the Second Coming.

The prophet Zechariah prophesied of the time when Jesus would find a young colt and ride into town, and it was fulfilled in John 12:14-15, the Prophet writes, "Rejoice greatly, O daughter of Zion; shout, O daughter of Jerusalem: behold, thy King cometh unto thee; he is just, and having salvation; lowly, and riding upon an ass, and upon a colt the foal of an ass" (Zech. 9:9). In 2 Peter 1:21, the apostle Peter explained that apostolic witness was hinged on the prophetic assertion by men whom God had approved. He wrote to his audience, "for the prophecy came not in old time by the will of man: but holy men of God spake as they were moved by the Holy Ghost." In John, the Jews sought to kill Jesus not only for breaking the Sabbath, but for asserting God was His Father. Nevertheless, in John 5:46, Jesus answered and said to the Pharisees: "For had ye believed Moses, ye would have believed me: *for he wrote of me*. But if ye believe not His writings, how shall ye *believe my words?*" (emphasis added). Jesus' message is about faith. These men were quick to point Jesus to with whom their faith rested; in fact, Moses was speaking about Jesus.

Notably, the first five books of the Bible, known as the "Pentateuch," were written by Moses as evidence about the Savior. Without the first eleven chapters in the book of Genesis, there would not have been an Israel or an everlasting covenant between God and man in the form of salvation. Most importantly, there would not have been Jesus Christ. Because of God's divine plan, things were set in motion for the scenes of His everlasting plan. Just think – to offer His creation "the Way" to be made right with God, He came down from Heaven in the form of God-Man. The Messiah. Christ Jesus. His only Begotten Son. Our Savior.

Finally, a Forth-teller is a "megaphone" for the Lord – he faithfully proclaims prophecy (the Word of God) whether past, present or future. Also, those called to this ministry had the duty to call the wicked to righteousness. They were despised, reviled, hated, slandered, lied upon, beaten, and martyred for the purpose of obedience to proclaiming God's Word. Both were commonly practiced by Old Testament prophets, Jesus, and the Apostles.[7] Even today, pastors, evangelists, teachers, and watchmen are forth-telling the Word of God, which is the Bible. I do not believe prophets exist today. Here is why: prophets spoke a special revelation breathed from God which was delivered to the Church once and for all. This was confirmed by Jude, saying: "it was needful for me to write unto you, and exhort you that ye should earnestly *contend* for the faith which was *once* delivered unto the saints" (Jude 1:3, emphasis added).

Jude is telling his audience "to carry on the struggle" for the faith "after" the special revelation was delivered to the saints once and for all.[8] The word "delivered" (Greek: paradotheisē) is an undefined (aorist) participle. Therefore, this means the helping verb, *after*, will modify the main verb, *delivered*. For the saints of God are instructed "after" the Scriptures, as we know them, has been delivered to the saints (holy people, Christians) once and for all. We are to strive or fight for the Word of God through the remainder of our lives. There are no new special revelations which follow after the first-century church. Finally, the Apostle Paul validates this claim as the Church is "built upon the foundation of the apostles, and prophets, Jesus Christ himself being the Chief corner stone" (Eph. 2:20). Jesus Christ is the foundation of our salvation that was built upon His works on the Cross. Nothing else can be done to further what has already been sealed and delivered. The bottom line is the Bible is our source to the divine revelation that is enveloped within God's Word, as it is our instructions for holy living.

Interpretation Methods

We can find apocalyptic character in various passages in the books of Daniel 9-12 and Revelation 4-21. For instance, half of Daniel has already been fulfilled with the historical characters of Kings Nebuchadnezzar, Darius, and Cyrus. While the later portion of the book focuses on future events, such as the Seventy Weeks (The Great Tribulation). Someone may ask the question, "how can one fully gain an accurate depiction of future events when there are so many arrows pointing in so many directions in different sources without getting confused?" Let's say people open up Revelation and explore Chapter 12, the Beast's dogged attempt to destroy the Nation of Israel. Immediately one becomes lost in the figurative language, not truly understanding what is to be taken as literal. Let's explore some of the methods which can help you better understand biblical hermeneutics. Biblical interpretation is not an easy task, considering if you never had proper training to know when to view certain bible passaged literally or figuratively, thus knowing when to compare Scripture to capture the author's intended meaning.

In short order, I will provide you with four methods which will aid you in determining the "why" and the "how" through our Biblical interpretation. I remember in seminary, Dr. Paul Benware's book, *Understanding*

End-Times Prophecy was one of my required textbooks for an eschatology course that was simple to consume. Many of the methods still standout in my professional endeavors. I believe each of these methods are user-friendly, not as technical as other Biblical Interpretation material. As dispensational pre-millennialists, we are to apply a literal approach when interpreting Scriptures.[10] All considered historical events need to be interpreted in accordance with the author's intention.[11] When Scriptures are spiritualized or allegorized (embellished), the integrity of the passage is compromised, thus the reader is set to do eisegesis, which is reading into the text. In their book, *Hermeneutics*, Henry A. Virkler and Karelynne G. Ayayo explained: "The meaning of Scripture is to be found in a careful study of words and of the culture and history of its writers."[12] If I had said: "during the CCP virus, most states instituted a nationwide shut-down." We would interpret this statement as being literal. Another instance is: "Iran has threatened to destroy Israel for years." You would not allegorize this statement, as this would also be taken literally. In the New Testament accounts, it was Jesus or the Apostles who spoke about historical-cultural accounts, such as: Moses, Abraham, the Israelites' Red Sea experience, or manna during the wilderness. They understood each one to be real people and real events, while at the same time providing history a place of relevancy within the scope of the New Covenant. When a passage asserts: "If we confess our sins, He is faithful and just to forgive us our sins, and to cleanse us from unrighteousness," we are to, by faith, trust Christ will accomplish this task literally (1 Jn 1:9). We all are sinners by nature. Therefore, if we come boldly before the Throne of Grace with a contrite heart and confess our iniquities, it is as the Word of God teaches us, our faithful Lord will forgive and cleanse us of our sins. Amen! Most Christians believe a literal translation is important, specifically when searching for a Bible translation that is "word-for-word" verses "thought-for-thought" (embellishment).[13]

There are many books that suggest different methods of interpreting prophecy. I would say, a large portion of prophecy is written in *signs* and *symbols*. When you are confronted by signs and symbols in writings, "[c]ompare prophecy with prophecy."[14] It is likely you may not fully understand the Tribulation events, such as in Daniel or Zechariah 14:1-21. However, if you were to take those books and cross-reference them with Ezekiel 38-39, Matthew 24-25, 1 Corinthians 15:51-53, 1 Thessalonians 4:13-18, or Revelation, eschatological framework will become clearer. Then, you are less likely to experience interpretation error. Daniel 11:36 provides details pertaining to the future antichrist, known as "the little horn" whom "shall speak marvelous things against the God of gods." Compare this passage to Revelation 13:5-6, which apostle John envisioned and wrote: "And there was given unto him a mouth speaking great things and blasphemies…[a]nd he opened his mouth in blasphemy against God, to blaspheme His name, and His tabernacle and them that dwell in heaven." All you would need to do then is read the remainder of that chapter to better understand the nuts and bolts of the prophecy's events. One thing about prophecy is that there is a major distance between the time it was prophesized and its fulfillment. In some instances, there may be an 800 year span that separates the two. In order to articulate the origin of meaning, the passages are to be "interpreted in light of time intervals."[15]

I remember many years ago, there was a burning desire in my heart to create El Shaddai Outreach International Ministry (ELSOIM) with locations in several major cities. We would be a force-multiplier ministry, which meant, not being segregated to only one ministry function as preaching. However the "force-multiplier" meant providing several programs: consulting, pastoral care, teaching in different churches in diverse locations, community development with employees and so on. I prayed about it, therefore assumed this was a sign for me to "execute and devise" a plan to incorporate and submit for our 501(c)3 immediately. Nope! It did not happen that way. We did incorporate, and I preached all over the place and had several consulting opportunities, but my military career accelerated at Mach speed. I commanded a company while assigned to the 101st Airborne Division during a deployment, I had the opportunity to preach three times during Sunday and weekday services. Also, during that same deployment, I witnessed a Muslim woman receive the water baptism during an outside, evening service at the chapel. It was freezing cold, but she wanted Jesus and that water. My point is this: during the moment ELSOIM occupied my mind, I did not think decades would stand between that image of ELSOIM Group and reality. Nevertheless, I used this example to illustrate how many Old Testament prophets did not realize the signs God gave them was something set to happen in the future, like a thousand years later. When Isaiah spoke about the virgin birth of Jesus, the Messiah, he did not know how long this would be until it came to pass (Isaiah 9:6).

Throughout the Bible, it is common to find obstacles in the language which appears to be figurative, which tends to leave the reader confused and unable to articulate the implied meaning of the verse. To overcome this obstacle is to "interpret figurative language scripturally."[16] At times in the Gospels, Jesus spoke figuratively. Take, for example, John 6:35, 48 & 51, when He declared: "I am the Bread of Life," and "I am the Living Bread which cometh down from Heaven." It is obvious Jesus is not telling people He is a giant loaf of banana-nut bread which can be consumed physically – although Catholics believe this literally. It would be absurd to even imply such a thing. We are to interpret this passage as Jesus speaking figuratively of Himself, during a time when God sent manna down from Heaven to sustain the Israelites during their forty-year wilderness experience (Exodus 16:4, 5). Take, for instance, 1 Corinthians 10: the Apostle Paul is explaining to the Church of Corinth, even though the Israelites ate the physical food (manna) and drunk physical water (from a rock), both were provided by God supernaturally in their time of need. Manna was a type of bread that was consumed to sustain the Israelites, just as Christ is the Bread which came down from Heaven supernaturally as our spiritual food and drink. He is indeed, the One who sustains believers supernaturally. Likewise, Jesus said to the Samaritan woman at Jacob's' well: "Whosoever drinketh of this water shall thirst again: But whosoever drinketh of the water that I shall give him shall never thirst; but the water that I shall give him shall be in him a well of water springing up into everlasting life" (John 4:13-14). At the conclusion, we were baptized in Christ Jesus, as well as communing with Him daily through His Word. I want to encourage you to practice these methods and eventually, with much prayer, the Holy Spirit will open your mind so the process can be made smoother. Lastly, here is a simple test: if someone was to tell you how their spouse is "plucking their last nerve like a banjo," how would you interpret this language?

CHAPTER 2

SYSTEMATIC THEOLOGY: UNLOCKING BIBLICAL PROPHECY

The basic trouble with the church today is her unworthy concept of God...Our religion is weak because our [view of] God is weak... Christianity at any given time is strong or weak depending on her concept of God.

A.W. Tozer[1]

I once heard a man of God emphasize that the Word of God is the textbook of our Savior. Throughout the Bible, there is a multitude of evidence which validates how the authors of the Bible were inspired by God. They were an extension of His finger to write into history the greatness of His glory. The last words of King David was: "The Spirit of the Lord spake by men, and his word was in my tongue" (2 Samuel 23:2). He was in awe that God would use someone like himself as a mouth piece. Both Apostles Paul and Peter, respectively, reaffirm David's sentiments, stating, "all Scriptures is given by inspiration of God, and is profitable for doctrine, for reproof, for correction, for instruction in righteousness," and "[f]or the prophecy came not on old time by the will of man: but holy men of God spake as they were moved by the Holy Ghost" (2 Timothy 3:16, 2 Peter 1:21).

The last two years have spurred a curiosity about the religious climate in America towards Christianity, the Bible, and eternal expectations. A growing number of Americans do not believe or accept orthodox theological views of Christianity. For instance, 71% of Americans believe the Bible is the Word of God, while 55% believe the Bible is 100% accurate in all that it teaches.[2] What about those calling themselves Christians when the same questions are posed to them? Only 32% of Catholics, 36% of mainline Protestants, and 67% of Black Protestants believe the Bible is 100% accurate.[3] Only 18% of Evangelicals and 20% of Black Protestants believe the Bible is helpful, but not literally true.[4] Since January 2021, the number of Americans "who never use the Bible" has decreased to 29%, the lowest since 2016.[5] Just over half of Americans (54%) believe the Scriptures provide the essential tools to live a wholesome life.[6] Interestingly, only 48% of Americans "read, listen to, or pray with their Bible three to four times a year."[7]

Systematic theology is simply a standardized methodical structure in studying God, His divine governance, Creation, and divine plan packaged in the form of Biblical doctrines. There are ten doctrines, I believe, which have an eschatological connection. As you take your time to explore the production of specific Biblical information, you will eventually mature in your appreciation of theological and sociological perspectives in prophecy. Below, several important doctrines are explained.

Doctrine of Divine Inspiration

In the last chapter, I shared with you the meaning of "Revelation," which involves the unveiling or uncovering of evidence that God has made available to humanity through His divine nature. We know humans are fallible and sinful. We, in our limited understanding, cannot fathom the mysteries of God in totality. In Job 11:7-8, Zophar expresses how God's counsel is unsearchable: "Canst thou by searching find out God? Canst thou find the Almighty unto perfection? It is as high as heaven; what canst thou do? Deeper than hell; what canst thou know?"

In Isaiah 48:3, God convinced the people, as He "declared the former things from the beginning; and they went forth out of my mouth." This insinuates that the Word did not come from anyone other than the Lord. He continued furthered, stating, "and I shewed them; I did them suddenly, and they came to pass." God did this because He is all-powerful and mighty in His glory. "I, even I, have spoken" is the ingredient of inspiration for man to move in His perfect will.

Doctrine of the Trinity (Triune God)

Imagine there in front of you is as glass of ice-cold water. If I were to ask you what this glass of water would be used for, you might say something, such as life sustainment, drinking, cleaning, cooking, bathing, et cetera. What about ice? What is its purpose? You might state it is to refrigerate foods, make ice-cream, cool the environment, or for healing purposes. The main ingredient of ice is water that has been reduce in temperature. What is steam? It is water that has been heated to its boiling point, and it is good for increasing humidity in a room, cooking, and pressing clothes. When all is said and done, we can agree that water in its various forms has three distinct states, which accomplish different things. Similarly, as you explore the idea of the Trinity, the composition of the Triunity of God is revealed, in His plurality as God the Father, God the Son and God the Holy Spirit. He is one God with three distinct persons and functions. The term "person" does not, in anyway, suggest a limitation within the governance of the Godhead.[8] It is only codified by the divine nature of an omnipotent God. Seven in ten Americans believe that there is One God in three distinct persons.[9]

A key challenge to this Trinitarian view is people are not finding the Trinity in their Bible. Due to an indifference of understanding, people have used this excuse to reject the doctrine. Consider this, just because the word, "trinity," is not written in your Bible does not negate the significance of its contextual relevance. In fact, there are other terms in Christian theology you will not find written within your Bible, yet maintain its importance, such as "atheist," "rapture," and "Bible." Do we toss the baby out with the bath water? Of course not. The first place we can find the evidence of a plural pronoun (*us* and *our*) that supports the Triunity of God is in Genesis 1:26, "And God said, Let *us* make man in *our* image, after *our* likeness…" In the LXX (Septuagint; the Greek translation of the Old Testament), the Greek word, "poiēsomēn," translates to "Let *us* make or Let *us* by doing something."[10] Indeed, this exhortation is proof that the Godhead is completely one as expressed in the shema (shuh-MAH) of Deuteronomy 6:4, which asserts: "Hear, O Israel: The Lord our God is *one* Lord." The Hebrew word, "'ehad," is a common term that is defined as *one*; also, the phrase "man is become as *one of us*" refers back to the triunity of God, thus illustrating a prolific execution of His divine plan for mankind (Genesis 3:22).[11] Even in the New Testament, we can see this plurality of the Godhead adorn the pages of the Gospels, while marching to the rhythm of our Heavenly Father.

For instance Jesus furthered this doctrine by saying,

Believe me that I am in the Father, and the Father in me: or else believe me for the very works' sake…[e]ven the Spirit of truth; whom the world cannot receive, because it seeth him not, neither knoweth him: but ye know him; for he dwelleth with you, and shall be in you." (John 14:11, 17).

According to Christ, the triunity is with us as well. Those who are in Christ Jesus, saved by grace through faith, are granted the Holy Spirit, and are thereby secured with the Holy Trinity. Amen! As evidence of God's promise, I understand this doctrine can be difficult to grasp. This is why "we walk by faith, not by sight" (2 Corinthians 5:7). "So then faith cometh by hearing, and hearing the word of God" (Romans 10:17). In a way, you could say that listening is our main sense in our walk with God.

We need to replicate the same level of faith as Paul and Barnabas had after returning to Antioch from evangelizing Darbe. They were all about the Father's business of "confirming the souls of the disciples, and exhorting them to continue in the faith" (Acts 14:22a). Look at their actions: "and when they were come and had gathered the church together, they rehearsed all that God had done with them, and how he had opened the door of faith unto the Gentiles" (Acts 14:27). I encourage you to tell others about the Trinity and how the Lord has opened the door of faith to them, as it is His will for us in Christ Jesus to increase in Him.

Doctrine of the Virgin Birth of Christ

The virgin birth is one of the most important doctrines that many people struggle to accept as a literal, historical event. Many are incredulous because of the scientific challenges which rest upon the idea of the birth of a child by a virgin without any human initiator. Consider in this day and age, if a woman was to claim to be pregnant without having sex, people would think she is a lunatic. The question is rather, did this really happen? Yes, it did happen! Those who stumble are right, it is impossible to believe when they are devoid of a Christian worldview. I'm not just speaking about the unchurched, but those of the household of faith whom observe this historical event as fictitious or even as figurative. Let's call it for what it is. Basically, that fraternity of thinkers is calling God the Father a liar. Anyone who makes such accusations against the Word of God disavows biblical truth. Believers are sanctified through truth. Before the Passion, Jesus' intercessory prayer to the Father, on the behalf of His disciples, said: "Sanctify them through thy truth: *thy word is truth*" (John 17:17, emphasis added). The Word of the Lord is truth! Even Muslims believe in the virgin birth. They are not believers of Christ crucified, yet it is in their Quran. If you ever get into a conversation with a Muslim, they will, with excitement, witness to you about the virgin birth. Thus, it is beneficial to explore the basis of the miraculous work of the Holy Spirit.

Miraculous Work in the Old Testament

The first anticipation of the virgin birth is expressed in Genesis 3:15, as the first messianic prediction, known as the *protoevangelium*. What is so amazing about this piece of antiquity is the stage is already being set for Satan to receive a three-gallon "can of whip-Cross." Oh yeah, we are talking about some Holy Ghost mixed-martial arts, where Satan's head will be wounded by the bottom of Christ's foot. I like to inject some humor to depict how I imagine God might have responded. Something like this:

"Satan, you're trippin'. You know you messed up. You know… you messed…up." He makes this assertion while slowly chewing on some grapes and nuts. "Since you did all this mess, you're going to sliiide on your belly. That's right! Guess what your diet is going to be?"

In a low basso voice, Satan responds, "Ahh, ahhhh, berries and cherries?"

God listens and gives him a stink-face. "Nahhhh. D…U…S…T. Dust! You will do this all the days of your life." God squats down with His hands on His knees, getting eyeball to eyeball with Satan in his serpent form, and says, "And I will put enmity between thee and the woman, and between *thy seed* and *her seed;* it shall bruise *thy head* and thou shalt bruise *his heel*" (v. 15, emphasis added). After 6,000 years, Satan is still confused, fueled with envy and strong hatred towards God and His people.

We begin this epic path to salvation with this prophecy as an indictment on Satan to be bruised under the heel of the woman's seed, as it related to the Second Coming of Christ, our Lord. For the time draws nigh as He is coming very soon and will quickly establish His everlasting Kingdom here on earth.

In the LXX, God told Satan, "You will (Gk. tēreō) *lie in wait for* and *will observe* the Seed of the woman, Jesus Christ." The most interesting part of the context is that Satan will observe in high-definition Jesus' heel making contact against his (Gk. kephalēn) head.[12] Amazingly, Satan will have to wait until that specific date and patiently watch as he is being crushed by the omnipotent God. The seed of Satan are those who consciously set themselves as an enemy against the seed of woman. The Bible states their future is in the lake of fire with their father, Satan, the Beast, and the False Prophet. This design thus denotes a *spiritual progeny*; although neither the woman nor Satan, who is spirit, can produce seed. Men, of course, are the only ones capable to produce seed. The seed of the woman are the elect (Isaiah 45:4; Matthew 24:22; Mark 12:22; Romans 8:33) and the Children of God (1 John 3:2), both of whom are joined together through faith (Romans 8:17). The Apostle Paul addresses this by saying: "But when the fullness of the time was come, God sent forth his Son, *made of a woman*, made under the law" (Galatians 4:4). "The Greek word translated 'fullness' is *plērōma*, indicating that Christ came at the perfect time."[13] Why did God use a virgin to give birth to His seed as the Giver of Life? In Jeremiah 22:30, we get a glimpse into the curse imposed upon the line of David. The last king in this line was Coniah (Jehoiachin), who served for only three months, with whom God expressed his disapproval and asserted: "Thus saith the Lord. Write ye this man childless, a man that shall not prosper in his days: for no man of his seed shall prosper, sitting upon the throne of David, and ruling any more in Judah" (v. 30). What was ironic after being deposed as king was that God appointed Zedekiah to govern after him. However, he died before Coniah passed away in Babylon. It is recorded that Coniah had seven sons, and it was made clear his seed would never elevate to the level of the King of Judah. When you examine the genealogy of Christ, Joseph, the husband of Mary, was a descendent of "Jechonias as begat Salathiel; and Salathiel begat Zorobabel... and Jacob begat Joseph the husband of Mary, of whom was born Jesus, who is called Christ" (Matthew 1:12, 16). It is because of this ancestral connection that Joseph was accepted through the generational curse. Even the Bible teaches us that children pay for the sins of their fathers (Deuteronomy 5:9). However, Jesus was not subject to this curse, because He is the beloved son of David through Mary.

Like a juicy soap-opera, these dramatic scenes are exclusive to the New Testament books of Matthew, Luke, and Galatians. In Luke 1:26-37, the angel, Gabriel, had greeted Mary with this awkward news, explaining how she will become pregnant by the Holy Spirit. For one, she was in her tender years, between 12 and 13. At this point, it is necessary to dive into a historical-cultural analysis of the matrimonial law. In doing so, I believe it will afford us an opportunity to travel through time having a front row seat at the foot of their conversation. It is important to note that a father had the authority to marry off his 12-year-old daughter. As terrifying as it may sound, this was the custom during ancient times.

It is rather complicated to understand this system with its many moving parts, while attempting to avoid becoming partisan and judgmental. A look at the morality of an ancient culture from a modern, Western worldview can be difficult. Today, for couples to marry, there must be consent between the husband and wife. Back then, this union was arranged by the families, along with the community perception playing a major role in the matchmaking. For the young man, it was his responsibility to be vocal and state the acquisition (Hb. quiyan) of the woman, something to the effect: "this woman is to be my wife before God."[14] To say "I'm going to marry whoever" is not good enough. In this day and age, a man and woman can engage in secret without any witnesses, then announce to the world on Twitter or Facebook their engagement. People would consider this valid. Not so in the ancient. In order for this union to be official, two witnesses had to be present for legal purposes, in accordance to their customs.

For men, we know once you find that "good" woman, it will definitely cost you. I remember my fifth grade teacher, Ms. Bullock. She used to tell the class: "No woman wants a dumb man. You want to be a doctor, lawyer or an Indian chief." As you can tell, the propagation of this idea is different from generation to generation and from culture to culture.

How much different was their matrimonial program compared to the Western customs? The engagement was called the betrothal, similar to today's engagement. The time span between a betrothal and the actual marriage ceremony was one year. Similarly, you can recognize how many couples in the West wait at least one year before their marriage ceremony. However, the "betrothed woman is called *wife*, can become a widow, be put away by divorce and punished with death for adultery."[15] In contrast, in the West, we address the significant other as fiancée; a wife is only reserved for marriage. As for death, there is no significant designation for the death of one's fiancée. If one or the other fornicates with someone, there is no remedy other than to leave the relationship. Adultery is only for married people. Fornication is sexual immorality singles engage in. In death, the only thing that might benefit the surviving "significant other" is a life insurance policy.

The ancient man was required to provide his bride with a marriage contract prior to the betrothal. Joachim Jeremias, a professor at the University of Gottingen, provides details about the dynamics of the marriage contract:

The basic importance of this marriage contact consisted of legal ruling of all financial matters between the two parties. Its main dispositions were: (a) Establishing what the bride's father was to pay – the marriage portion (goods of usufruct, i.e. goods which remain in the ownership of the wife while the husband has the right of usufruct), and the dowry (goods of reserve stock, i.e., goods which become the property of the husband, but the equivalent of which must be guaranteed to the wife in case of divorce). (b) Established the written marriage bond (ketubbah, i.e. the sum which revert to the wife in case of separation or the death of her husband).[16]

Prior to being betrothed, young girls were sheltered and unexposed to the debauchery we are accustomed to in the 21st century. Single females, particularly, were accustomed "not to go out at all."[17] Certain duties may have permitted her to move unaccompanied, like fetching water at noon.[18] Nevertheless, "a woman must not be alone in the fields... [for] it was not customary even in the country for a man to converse with a strange woman."[19] Depending on the family's religious affiliation, she might have been obligated to wear head and face coverings, so no one could recognize her.[20]

I believe Gabriel's message to Mary was a bit overwhelming, after considering the historical-cultural reality. Then Mary responds and asks, "How shall this be, seeing I know not a man?" I can imagine, based on the level of surprise, both Joseph and Mary were at the corner of Shock and Awe. We can imagine a young man's eagerness to "know" his wife, but finds out that someone else had beat him to it, or so he thought. Although Scripture is silent about Joseph's direct thoughts, however, one can only imagine the emotional burden he felt. According to the law, he was obligated to give her a *get* (divorce papers), thus putting her away.

The Bible does provide some evidence that Joseph did flirt with the idea of quietly divorcing Mary instead of making a public spectacle. Subsequently, God intervened by sending an angel to dissuade this imminent divorce. In the end, Mary accepted her place as the most famous woman in history, and Joseph accepted her as his wife.

Filled with joy, Mary was eager to lift her voice and sing praises, which have become known as the *Magnificent*, to her beloved God, the Father. She acknowledged God's mercy is forever present from generation to generation. I imagine that day being a cool day brightened by a blue sky and smells of myrrh dancing in the wind, with Mary singing:

My soul doth magnify the Lord,
And my spirit hath rejoiced in God my Saviour.
For hath regarded the low estate of his handmaiden: for,
Behold, from henceforth all generations shall call me blessed.
For He that is mighty hath done to me great things;
And holy is his name. And His mercy is on them that fear Him
From generation to generation. He hath shewed strength with His arm;
He has scattered the proud in the imagination of their hearts.
He hath put down the mighty from their seats, and exalted them
Of low degree. He hath filled the hungry with good things;
And the rich He hath sent empty away.
He hath helped His servant Israel, in remembrance of His mercy;
 As He spake to our fathers, to Abraham, and to his seed forever.
-Luke 1:46-55

Doctrine of Sin

Oh, sirs, if ungodliness is evil, why do you so much practice it?
And if goodness is good, why do you so little practice it?
Either take Christ in your lives or cast Him out of your lips!
Either obey His commandments more or else call Him Lord no more!
Either get oil in your lamps or cast away your lamps.
To be a professor of piety and a practice of iniquity
Is an abomination unto the Lord.
Some would not seem evil and yet would be so!
Others would seem to be good and yet are not so!
Either be what you seem or else be what you are.
There are many who blush to confess their sins
Who never blushed to commit their sins.

-William Dyer[21]

I view sin as the pork of humanity that smells and tastes good, but is detrimental to our spiritual, mental, and physical health. It is the universal disease that does not only involves actions engulfed in transgressions, but also actions that draw a divide between man and God. I define it simply as any act that opposes the righteousness of God, which severs the relationship between God and man. In Ephesians, Paul wanted to re-mind the church in Ephesus how Christians once walked in the flesh, and were, by nature, sinful like the rest of mankind "among whom also we all had our conversation in times past in the lusts, of our flesh, fulfilling the desires of the flesh and of the mind; and were by nature the children of wrath, even as other" (2:3). American theological views are shocking in that 67% believe everyone sins, but that most people are "by nature good."[22] Considering this view among different groups in Christianity, Evangelicals were the lowest at 54%, 64% of Black Protestants, and the Catholics ranked the highest at 79%.[23]

Everybody on this side of Heaven will suffer from this disease. In Job, the Bible states a "man that is born of a woman is of few days and full of trouble" (14:1). No one can run or hide, because "[t]he heart is deceitful above all things, and desperately wicked" (Jeremiah 17:9).

No matter who you are – great or small, young or old, wealthy or poor – all are attracted to sin. "If we say that we have no sin, we deceive ourselves and the truth is not in us" (1 John 1:8). "Wherefore, as by one man sin entered into the world, and death by sin; and so death passed upon all men, for that *all have sinned*" (Romans 5:12, emphasis added). Some are more prone to do evil than others, yet rest assured, there is no one free from the devices of the enemy, as seen in John, Chapters 24 and 25. A wise man once said, "a man is a free agent to operate within his own power of self-determination...that God is the creator of all moral beings who are the author of sin in their lives." A person seeking his own self-interest usually develops some moral injury. The late Elder Day sung a song that resonates with me that says, "It's nobody fault but mine. It's nobody fault but mine. If I die and my soul be lost, it's nobody fault but mine."[24] I tell people that there is no wrong way to do right. Sin is nobody's fault, but my own fault, if I decide to remain in the marketplace of sin. Gratefully, I know somebody who is willing to forgive anybody, and He is "the Lamb of God, which taketh away the sins of the world" (John 1:29). "For we wrestle not against flesh and blood, but against principalities, against powers, against the rulers of the darkness of this world, against spiritual wickedness in high places" (Ephesians 6:12). It is important to note the significance for our examination into the origin of sin, so that we can define with clarity the tactical schemes used by the enemy.

Original Sin

"Now the serpent was more subtle than any beast of the field which the Lord God had made. And he said unto the woman, Yea, hath God said, Ye shall not eat of every tree of the garden?... And the eye of them both were opened, and they were naked: and they sewed fig leaves together, and made themselves aprons" (Genesis 3:1, 7).

In Genesis, the serpent is immediately described as the "more subtil[e]" (Gk.; phronimos), which translates to being "more wise."[25] Notwithstanding, being the wisest of all the beasts of the field subsequently made it an excellent target. One factor suggest that due to Satan's ability to clothe himself in the façade of a serpent, his scheme made the process more accommodating to possess and dominate, through the serpent's wisdom. Science calls this psychological manipulation. Before I go any further, I will define "subtle" as wise, cunning, sophisticates, charming, nice, evasive, and insidious (proceeding inconspicuously, but harmfully).[26]

At this point, we are taking a broader look into the design that contribute to the Great Deception which gave birth to sin. Did you know that deception was the first attack on man to blind him from the truth of God's Word? The scheme was devise to have man become insensitive to sin. Satan understands his time is drawing close to the fulfillment of the protoevangelium. You better believe he is determined to take as many human beings with him as possible. Are you one of those whom he has snatched up on his collision course with Hell?

Unfortunately, the diabolic modification of the serpent became the first demonic possession recorded in history. Have you ever been deceived? How many times have you crashed and failed at the testing of your faith? At the end of that hardship, did you look like a real dummy? I believe we all have experiences a similar "issuation" – a situation that derives from numerous problems – in some shape or form. At best, Satan's plan had to be disguised well to stealthily inflict mind-bending techniques on the woman. Before he could enact his plan, there was a need for a creature that appeared gentle to the eye and evoked soft feelings in the heart, such as "cute," cuddly," or maybe a bit "funny looking" (like the GEICO gecko). Regardless, the type of animal had to be equipped with the ability to desensitize the effects, but insidious enough to conceal the evil being committed. Think about it. Satan is methodical and extremely diligent. In fact, this is the same strategy being used today against us. He is charming, evasive, sophisticated and insidious. Temptation, even though it's not sin within itself, definitely will arrive in some innocent form to manipulate us and destabilize our discernment, so we become spiritually and faithfully inert.

I will never forget an ex-church leader who started out very professional, engaged in the management of the church operations. He was very polite, respectful, and appeared to be interested in the day-to-day operations. When I preached, the individual would be very helpful with a number of things, such as providing the necessary props or providing pastoral support for our guest speakers. After about three months, we began to notice how subtle he was about the little things around the church. First, it was rearranging nonessential furniture. O.K., not a big deal. Then, it evolved into disposing of brand-new teaching material that was never used. When confronted about his behavior, he would be dismissive and speak disparagingly to two of the other preachers. It wasn't long before some of the elders began to depart, because of being falsely accused of petty offenses. One day, an explosion of strife and discord disrupted everything. No matter how many complaints were raised, nothing was ever done. I remember the emotional turmoil after he falsely accused several of our pastoral staff of stealing. Moreover, he set up circumstances to entrap people in compromising situations. Nevertheless, Satan will inject an insidious influence to a church to help the church fall away. Evil is evil. Similarly, it is here within Satan's craftiness, that he would point out to Adam and Eve that nakedness was the by-product of their disobedience. They had no clue about what shame was, nor did they understand how their actions would change the world to accommodate sin. In Genesis 3:8-9, God searches for them even after knowing what had occurred, "and they heard the voice of the Lord God walking in the garden in the cool of the day: and Adam and his wife hid themselves from the presence of the Lord God amongst the trees of the garden." Then, God asked them a rhetorical questions: "And the Lord God called unto Adam, and said unto him, Where art thou?" God walked in the cool of the day calling out, "Adam, where are you?"

Did you notice God called for Adam, but not Eve? He was not happy at all. In God's Creation order, He created man first. Adam was ordained with stewardship over the Earth. Then it was found that man should not be alone, and so God made Eve. Eve was made to be a help meet, but Adam held the responsibility. It was not until Adam and Eve were in the presence of God that they become cognizant of the state of their sinfulness. God is holy and righteous; being in His presence is like shining a light in the dead of darkness. Sin in the vicinity of God is like a red stain on a bleach-white outfit. There is no ducking and hiding when God calls; there is an automated response. Now, there will be times God will honor our liberty and not press us, but there will also be a time during the Day of the Lord when every knee will bow and tongue confess Jesus Christ is Lord. All because of some slick-tongue word-play that got the world in the condition it is in now.

God had simply told Adam and Eve to eat from any tree in the garden, except from the tree of knowledge of good and evil (Genesis 2:17). Both man and his wife walked around the garden in their birthday suits without worrying about sunburn. There was no one around to body shame them. I believe the majority of Americans would refuse to walk around in a swimming suit, let alone without clothes. Even the animals were friendly. Gazelles had no worries of becoming two racks of smoked baby-back ribs. The serpent once walked on its hind legs and spoke like the gecko on the GEICO commercials (without the British accent).

Satan's deception of Eve gave birth to death. In an instant, everything in the garden was given an expiration date. Man, beast, and the planet were adjudicated a death sentence. The Apostle John said, "And I saw a new heaven and new earth: for the first heaven and the first earth were passed away; and there was no more sea" (Revelation 21:1). The Earth is dying. What the wicked call "climate change" is the result of man's depravity. For this very reason, the Great Flood occurred during Noah's day, a result of the rapid decay of the firmament (the ozone layer) associated with a dying planet.

When a child is born, it starts to die at the same time. God created man in His image, to live eternally before sin was introduced. My point is that Adam died at the ripe old age of 930 years. It was after the Flood, however, that man began to die at a younger age. The oldest living person in the 21st century is over 110 years old. Death opened the door to toil – vines instantly developed thorns. Adam had to sweat when he worked for a living. I don't know about you, but I do not like to have sweat dripping from my eyebrows. Women, you have Eve to thank for painful child birth and the often burdensome menstrual cycle. Finally, we all have witnessed the product of sin that has migrated all throughout our lives. In Matthew 24:8, Jesus teaches His disciples and explains, "all these are the beginning of sorrows." It was because of sin that famines, pestilence, earthquakes, and flood will wax worse and worse. The worse man becomes, the worse the world's calamities will become in intensity and frequency. It is because of the sin that the Tribulation will take the spotlight prior to the Second Coming. During all of the birth pangs felt from 2020 on, remember, these are the culmination of the first Adam's disobedience, while the Last Adam will judge this world, establishing His Everlasting Kingdom.

Doctrine of Salvation

In a Lifeway Research survey, Protestant pastors were asked, "if a person is sincerely seeking God, he/she can obtain eternal life through religions other than Christianity – pluralism?"[27] It is shocking the number of pastors who believe salvation can be obtained outside of Jesus Christ. The study showed twelve percent of pastors believe that salvation can be obtained through other religions, with only three percent were unsure.[28] Now, consider the number of people being led astray by these spiritually-inert pastors. "A few heads nodding or an occasional 'Amen' does not indicate everyone believes Christianity is the only way."[29] However, 48% of Americans believe salvation can be earned by doing "enough good things."[30] Among Christians, 70% of Catholics believe in a "works-oriented" salvation with 46% of Pentecostals, 44% of mainline Protestants, and 41% of Evangelicals.[31] One in five Christians follow the heresy "that God will let all people into heaven."[32] Now, we can understand why there is such a sharp departure from sound biblical doctrine.

The word "salvation" comes from the Greek stem, *sotēr* (Hb. verb, *yasa*), meaning "Savior" and "Deliverer." *Sotēria* derives from the Greek word that means "salvation" and "deliverance." The word translates as *Yeshuah* in Hebrew, to mean "God is with us" or "Immanuel." Most notably, Yeshuah is the same name Mary was told to name our Savior, Christ Jesus (Luke 1:22-23). "Salvation" can be defined as God's divine plan to rescue His creation from the sting of death by forgiveness of one's sins and granting eternal life.

Salvation in the Old Testament

Salvation certifies Yahweh, the proper name of God, as the protector of His people against the dangers of bondage (Exodus 14:13), enemies (Judges 2:18, 1 Chronicles 16:35; Psalms 119:155; Isaiah 45:15-17), and unforgiveness (Psalms 51:12, 17).[33] It was demonstrated through Israel's deliverance from bondage in Egypt: "[a]nd Moses said unto the people, Fear ye not, stand still, and see the *salvation* of the Lord, which he will shew to you today: for the Egyptians whom ye have seen today, ye shall see them again no more forever" (Exodus 14:13, emphasis added). As a protector, God will go before and fight the enemy of His people. In Deuteronomy 21:4, the Bible gives an account "for the Lord your God is he that goeth with you, to fight for you against your enemies, to *save* you" (emphasis added). David prayed for cleansing, asking God to "[r]estore unto me the joy of thy salvation; and uphold me with thy free spirit" (Psalms 51:12). Salvation was spoken as a sign of the coming Savior, born of a virgin, in Isaiah 7:14, "[t]herefore the Lord himself shall conceive, and bear a son, and shall call his name Immanuel." Further, "[f]or unto us a child is born, unto us a son is given: and the government shall be upon his shoulder: and his name shall be called Wonderful, Counsellor, The Mighty God, The Everlasting Father, The Prince of Peace" (Isaiah 9:6).

Salvation in the New Testament

In Luke 2:11, as the shepherds were keeping watch over their flock, the angel of the Lord proclaimed a divine message to them: "[f]or unto you is born this day in the city of David a Savior, which is Christ the Lord." In Acts 5:31, Peter declares to the Sanhedrin it was Christ they murdered, but "Him [Jesus] hath God exalted with his right hand to be a Prince and Saviour, for to give repentance to Israel, and forgiveness of sin" (emphasis added; see John 4:22).

Salvation: Granted as a Gift from God

There is nothing that we can do to save ourselves, because of our sinful nature. We all need to be saved from the wages of sin, which leads to death. How many times have you heard the excuse, "I need to get right before I become a Christian?" Gently and in love, it is important to inform the misguided person, they are already dead in sin. If he has to wait for himself to get right with God, there will always be an excuse to wait. The truth is there is nothing "he" or "she" can do in their own "strength" to change their disposition. It is impossible to overcome a life of sin without Christ. He said "…for without me ye can do nothing" (John 15:5). Why? The Apostle Paul explains:
"For they that are after the flesh do mind the things of the flesh; but they that are after the Spirit, the things of the Spirit. For to be carnally minded is death; but to be spiritually minded is life and peace. Because the carnal mind is enmity against God: for it is not subject to the law of God, neither indeed it can be. So then they that are in the flesh cannot please God" (Rom. 8:5-8).
Everyone on this side of Heaven needs the risen Savior, Jesus Christ. Salvation is not about how well you can sing, feed the homeless, preach, usher, or maintain an impeccable thirty-year church attendance. Doing

these things even for righteousness' sake doesn't make a person saved. Anyone can look all spiritual while carrying a big Bible or quoting Scripture whenever they exhale. None of these works can guarantee a person is saved. Even the demons know Scripture and fear Jesus. Satan will even allow for his minions to take up seats in the pews, and we know from Scripture that salvation is impossible for them. Saint Augustine once declared: "It was pride that changed angels into devils; it is humility that makes men angels."

Here is what it means to be saved – realizing that we are saved by grace through faith in Jesus Christ. "For by grace are ye saved through faith; and that *not of yourselves:* it is a gift of God" (Ephesians 2:8, emphasis added). It is not our own deeds that will save a person, it is only through Jesus. The New Birth is not a collective effort between man and God. It is God's duty. In John 3:3, Jesus told Nicodemus, "except a man is born again, he *cannot* see the kingdom of God" (emphasis added). It is important to note the New Birth generates saving faith, and to believe in Jesus Christ as Lord, one must be born again. Nobody will see the Kingdom of God if one has not experienced the New Birth. Through the New Birth, the person regenerates into the new believer. Hence, Christ is our atonement, the reconciliation from a severed relationship caused by sin. The paying of our sin-debt came by Christ's work on the Cross that qualified Him as our atonement, and He allows us to be "at one with God, the Father (notice, to "atone" allows us to be "at one"). He forges believers with His grace as a divine blacksmith, joining mankind to God.

We are to rejoice and praise our Lord "for God so loved the world, that he gave his only begotten Son, that whosoever believeth in him should not perish, but have everlasting life. For God sent not his Son into the world to condemn the world; but that the world through Him might be saved" (John 3:16-17). When we received Christ as Lord, we are granted access to believe in Him. Do you think all people can come to Jesus on demand? Look what Jesus says in John 15:16: "Ye *have not* chosen me, but *I have chosen* you, and *ordained* you, that ye should go and bring forth fruit, and that your fruit should remain" (emphasis added). First, ponder these words of Christ specifically telling "you" how important you are to Him. How does that make you feel to know that you did not find Jesus, as people are accustomed to believing, but that Jesus chose you? Amen!

The Bible says, "for it has been given in the behalf of Christ, not only to *believe on Him,* but also to *suffer* for his sake" (Philippians 1:29, emphasis added). A lot of believers don't realize suffering is part of the job description of a believing Christian. Believing comes before our suffering in Christ. In this passage, the Greek verb, *charizomai*, simply means "to grant the deliverance of a person in favor to the desire of others."[34] Jesus granted us the deliverance (salvation) and suffering to the desire of God, the Father.

Further, Jesus communicated with the Father and prayed, "I have manifested thy name unto the men which thou gavest me out of the world: thine they were, and thou gavest them me…" (John 17:6). He basically states to God these are the men You handed over to me, that You supernaturally rescued from the world, and You gave them to me. He goes on to confirm this by asserting, "All that the Father giveth me shall come to me; and that cometh to me I will no wise cast out" (John 6:36). Even the Apostle Paul alludes to Christ granting us mercy: "as he hath *chosen* us in him before the foundation of the world, that we should be holy and without blame before him" (Ephesians 1:3b, emphasis added).

We serve a sovereign God who has the authority to show mercy as He desires. Indeed, salvation is the evidence of His love and mercy that is granted to whomever He desires to show mercy. However, He also hardens the hearts of those whom he chooses. Bottom-line, He is God! As Paul wrote,

> "For he saith to Moses, I will have mercy, and I will have compassion on whom I will have compassion. So then it is not of him that willeth, nor of him that runneth, but of God that sheweth mercy…Therefore, hath he mercy on whom he will have mercy, and whom he will he hardeneth." (Romans 9:15-16, 18)

The hardened heart means that the "natural man receiveth not the things of the Spirit of God: for they are foolishness unto him: neither can he know them, because they are spiritually discerned" (1 Corinthians 2:14). This all points to the Jewish nation's rejection of Christ. Of course, those who have heard the Gospel message, but made a decision to reject the gift of salvation, also fall within this category. It comes down to "He had blinded their eyes, and hardened their heart; that they should not see with their eyes, nor understand with their heart, and *be converted*, and I should heal them" (John 12:40; Romans 11:7-10, emphasis added). I'm a true believer that no man can do anything that his character will not allow him. As a well-known pastor once said, "You can do nothing wrong and still do nothing right." Huh, imagine that?

Replacement Theology is a False Doctrine

The Apostle Paul expressed to the saints, "[b]rethren, my heart's desire and prayer to God for Israel is, that they might be saved" (Romans 10:1). This will change during the Tribulation, and the Nation of Israel will be saved. Until then, the Church never has, and never will, replace Israel. I have noticed an increase in a false teaching called replacement theology. Its primary belief states that because of Israel's repeated failures and rejection of Christ, their covenantal blessings are void. It is believed these blessings have been shifted over to the Church, thus designating the Church as a "spiritual Israel." Nowhere in the New Testament is the Church called the "new Israel" or a "spiritual Israel." Absolutely not! Replacement theology is a lie from Satan himself to strip Israel from her place in God's divine plan. In doing so, this action would blatantly nullify the Old Testament promises, as well as enormous chunks of the New Testament. This would mean we all are in trouble; salvation would no longer be unconditional.

Let's take a moment to explore the truth that the Church did not replace Israel. Clear as a cloudless day, the Apostle Paul states this very case in Romans 11: "I say then, Hath God cast away his people? *God forbid.* For I also am an Israelite, of the seed of Abraham, of the tribe of Benjamin" (v.1, emphasis added). I emphasize "God forbid" to illustrate Israel is sitting in "time-out" for a season, and that God will never remove Israel from her proper place as His people. To claim Israel was replaced is a lie. Paul continues, "God hath *not cast away his people* which he foreknew" (Romans 11:2, emphasis added).

In the next verse, I believe Paul seals the deal. He explains: "I say then, have they stumbled that they should fall? God forbid: but rather through their fall salvation is come unto the Gentiles, for to provoke them to jealousy" (Romans 11:11). The Church was granted access to experience the covenantal blessings to make the nation of Israel jealous. It is through this jealousy they will remember and eventually believe. In time, after the Rapture and during the Tribulation events, a great revival will happen and Israel, as a nation, will believe and confess with her mouth: Jesus is the Messiah, that He died on the Cross for the remissions of our sins, and risen on the third day. The Bible says, "[i]f thou shalt confess with thy mouth the Lord Jesus, and shalt believe in thine heart that God hath raised him from the dead, thou shalt be saved. For with the heart man believeth unto righteousness; and with the mouth confession is made unto salvation" (Romans 10:9-10). "Salvation is of the Jew;" "...does their faithlessness nullify the faithfulness of God? By no means!" (John 4:22; Romans 3:1-4).

Israel will soon believe Jesus is at the right hand of the Father, coming back to establish His Kingdom physically on Earth, to fulfill the Abrahamic, Davidic, and Palestinian (land) covenants. Instantaneously, the nation will experience the indwelling of the Holy Spirit; He will guide them to the truth. "But the Comforter, which is the Holy Ghost, whom the Father will send in my name, he shall teach you all things, and bring all things to your remembrance, whatsoever I have said unto you" (John 14:26). He will guide us to the truth; He will not glorify Himself, but will glorify Christ. It is important to note how essential repentance is to the new birth and our sanctification process as we are set apart from wickedness for the purpose of God.

A Call to Repentance

Peter proclaimed, "[r]epent ye therefore, and be converted, that your sins may be blotted out, when the times of refreshing shall come from the presence of God" (Acts 3:19). Repentance comes from the Greek word, *metanoia*, which means a change of one's mind and direction from past moral injuries. It signifies the turning from casual shopping at the marketplace of sin to marching in the direction of holiness in Christ, our Lord. God is in the business to save as He is "not willing that any should perish, but that all should come to repentance" (2 Peter 3:9).

In the message to the seven churches in Revelations, Jesus conveys a message of repentance that is overshadowed by the consequences of His judgement. John points out that the church in Thyatira was engulfed in wickedness, and there was this so-called woman prophetess, Jezebel who would "teach and...seduce my servants to commit fornication, and eat things sacrificed unto idols" (Revelation 2:20). This woman was indeed a false prophetess who led many astray. Many in this fellowship were recognized by Christ for their "charity and service and faith" but there was those whom were accustomed to sharing their wives (Revelation 2:19).

Jezebel's false doctrine of hyper-grace led many to commit sin, while downplaying the carousing and orgies that showcased the corrupt nature of sin itself. For instance, she most likely encouraged members to partake in cultic worship of gods, while stamping their passports with an excuse: "these so-called patron gods are not real. Therefore, you can eat the meat at the temple, to honor the patron gods." Look at Jesus' response in Revelation 2:22: "Behold, I will cast her into a bed, and them that commit adultery with her into great tribulation, except they repent of their deeds." For the rest of the churches, the call to repent has echoed throughout the Church Age with the words of John the Baptist: "Bring forth therefore fruits worthy of repentance..." (Luke 3:8).

Doctrine of Eternal Security

One time, I heard a joke. It goes: one day, little Dennis was climbing a tree, as he often does in his family's yard, when all of a sudden, Dennis begins falling out of the tree and cries out, "Lord, save me! Save me!" Dennis struggled for a second, and then realized he wasn't actually falling. Then, he said, "Never mind, Lord. My pants just caught on a branch." Sometimes, we are like a little Dennis, not realizing our Father has us in the palm of His hand the entire time.

Do you believe a person who is saved can lose their salvation? The first thing that must be established is that those who have received Christ as Lord, and believe in Him, are saved. Once you are save, salvation cannot be lost. The assurance of eternal security is witnessed throughout the Bible with substantive evidence affirming that those who believe and trust in Christ are granted this promise. Indeed, eternal security occupies the understanding that the subject belongs to the Father, who transmits this gift to all genuine believers in Christ Jesus.

Aiōn is the Greek word that means "eternity" and "forever." In Latin, "security" comes from the word, *securitas,* meaning "something given as a pledge fulfillment of a promise, a guarantee; or any evidence of ownership."[35] Just the indication of eternal security simply points to "eternal life" (Gk. *zōē:* "life") that is crafted within a relationship secure in the future. "Eternal life does not therefore just begin in the future; it is already the possession of those who have entered fellowship with Christ."[36] Rejoice! Christ has prepared a place for us in Heavenly places, all because of His love for us.

Security in the Old Testament

In the Old Testament, eternal security was based on a covenantal blessing with an eschatological formula. In this fashion, we can begin to understand this divine formula as it takes shape during the process of God's renewal of His covenant with Abraham. God said to him, "all the land which thou seest, to thee I give it, and to thy seed forever" (Genesis 13:15). Further on in Genesis 17, God said to Abraham, "I will establish my covenant between me and thee and thy seed after thee in their generations for an everlasting covenant, to be a God unto thee, and to thy seed after thee" (v.7). These promises are sealed not just for Abraham, but also for his generations after him, to include the Church.

We will return with Christ in our glorified bodies to witness the fulfillment of the Abrahamic covenant, which is unconditional. Similarly, King David in Psalms 23:6 testifies: "...we shall ultimately dwell in the house of the Lord forever." We, too, will witness the fulfillment when Christ establishes His Kingdom here on earth, satisfying the Davidic covenant. Details of eternal security are present within the Old Testament record and confirmed in the New Testament.

Eternal Security in the New Testament

In the beginning of this section, I raised a question as to whether or not believers can lose their salvation. It is through God's grace that no one can ever "confiscate" nor "pluck" a genuine believer from His hands. In the Good Shepherd discourse in John 10, Jesus delivers an admonishment to the Jewish leaders for dereliction of duty, for having an attitude non-conducive to the proper handling of their flock. This stingy parable was a depiction of a "robber" (Jewish leaders) and the "sheepfold" (body of believers).

First, I like to point out in John 10:16, Jesus alludes to the "**other sheep** I have, which are **not of this fold**: them also I **must bring**, and they shall hear my voice; and there shall be one fold, and one shepherd" (emphasis added). The *other sheep* signifies the Gentile Christians (us) who will be gathered in His future; they will listen to Him. Look what follows after this statement: "My sheep will hear my voice, and I know them, and they follow me: And I give unto them **eternal life;** and they shall **never perish, neither** shall any man **pluck them out of my hands**" (John

10:27-28, emphasis added). The verb "pluck" comes from the same Greek word, *harpazō*, meaning to snatch up by a degree of force.[37] Basically, Jesus is reaffirming the unilateral covenant made with Abraham, Isaac, and Jacob, but indicating the impossibility of being taken from His hands. Now, if you have doubts, Jesus asserts: "My father, which gave them me, is greater than all; and **no man is able** to pluck them out of my Father's hand. I and my Father are one" (John 10:29-30, emphasis added). Amen! There are three factors identified within these affirmations:

Commitment is protection. "In hope of eternal life, which God, who cannot lie, promised before the world began." (Titus 1:2)

Future relationship as a gift. "For the wages of sin is death; but the gift of God is eternal life through Jesus Christ our Lord." (Romans 6:23)

Fire insurance policy. "In whom ye also trusted, after that ye heard the word of truth, the gospel of your salvation: in whom also after that ye believed, ye were sealed with that Holy Spirit of promise." (Ephesians 1:13)

An evangelist once said: "the witness of God must be bigger than more reliable than the witness of men, and the complete witness of God in relations to His Son."[38] I want to encourage you, it is not necessary to continue "trying" to be saved, because there is nothing you can do, but to believe in Christ as your Lord and Savior. It doesn't matter if you feel saved on Sunday, and then on Wednesday panic, because you do not feel saved. A feeling has nothing to do with your salvation. Did you genuinely accept Christ as Lord and Savior? If so, you have nothing to worry about for your sin-debt has been paid forever. Right here is a good place to praise the Lord for His goodness and mercy and for exhibiting His unconditional love to you.

Doctrine of Sanctification

"Effort is one of the things that gives life meaning. Effort means you care about something that something is important to you and you are willing to work for it. It would be an impoverished existence if you were not willing to value things and commit yourself to working towards them."

-Carol Dweck

If you have ever heard me preach, I often point out how all Christians have two stories. One story pertains to who we once were – our past – and the other story is who we are now. If we are still engaged in the first story, how much have we really grown? Whenever I would engage in soul-winning, it was my duty to educate the new believer that spiritual growth takes time, in a process called *sanctification.* The Greek word, *hagia,* means "holy" or "saint," and the word, *hagiasmos,* means "sanctification" or "moral purity," which translated to being set apart for the use of the sanctuary. When new converts hear the phrase, "be holy," the Enemy saturates them with feelings of shame, then guilt begins to coach them into believing a lie, that their past stumbling's and struggles has disqualified them. All of this can occur because of a misunderstanding on the sanctification process. I have heard people believe they had to behave in a certain manner within a few days, weeks, or months after conversion. When their unrealistic expectations are unmet, discouragement seeps in and they fall away. From the beginning, what must be explained to the new believer after conversion is that it is uncommon to witness changes within days or months. For most of us, the process will take time, in some cases, years, to break stronghold with God's grace lynch-pinned to our personal effort and watered with much prayer to overcome our imperfections.

I remember my journey was not easy. I can recall my struggle to break out of those old habits which had a tendency to sneak back up to frustrate my purpose, even as I grew closer to Jesus Christ. My daily Christian walk consisted of church on Wednesday, Saturday, and Sunday; at home, I would listen to the messages from my pastor, at the time, Bishop T.D. Jakes. I would memorize his sermons along with the Scripture references. I was really determined to find help through the Word of God to nurture my spiritual walk as a young Christian, through the power of the Holy Spirit within me. I wanted a new walk, a new talk, and a new way of thinking. Thus, I strove to find opportunities of being a better servant, father, son, friend, and potentially a husband to a good woman of God, because I knew anything opposite of good is definitely bad.

You will Stumble

"Wash you, make you clean; put away the evil of your doings from before mine eyes; cease to do evil; Learn to do well; seek judgment, relieve the oppressed, judge the fatherless; plead for the widow" (Isaiah 1:16-17). On this side of Heaven, God expects us to fall short and sin. However, believers are expected to not rest in a depraved state. Christ died; His blood cleansed us from the sting of death, and He's risen. "If we confess our sins, he is faithful and just to forgive us our sins, and to cleanse us from all unrighteousness" (1 John 1:9). No one can perfect a life without sin until the day of glory. The only way to be immune from sin will happen in Heaven with Christ, sporting our glorified bodies. It is God who consecrated believers, because He is sovereign. The Bible tells us, "there is none holy as the Lord: for there is none beside thee: neither is there any rock like our God" (1 Samuel 2:2). Look, there is no one who has the moral adroitness to be set apart from His creation and the stench of evil. It is through God's moral perfection that, we too, can be holy. "But as he which hath called you is holy, so be ye holy in all manner of conversion; Because it is written, Be ye holy; for I am holy" (1 Peter 1:15-16). We have the free choice to decide to do right. Most certainly, all believers have the free choice to do wrong. What designates Christians as a "holy people" has nothing to do with one's moral accomplishment gained by oneself, rather God had elected, chosen, and ordained you to be peculiar. "But ye are a chosen generation, a royal priesthood, a holy nation, a peculiar people..." (1 Peter 2:9). We were created in the image of God; therefore, His image requires us to be holy, and through this process, God grant believers the ability to be set apart for the good of His glory, not your own glory. The apostle Paul once said, "now being made free from sin, and because servants of God, ye have your fruit unto holiness and the end everlasting life" (Romans 6:22).

Sanctification Requires Some Fruit

All believers are encouraged to "keep thy heart with all diligence; for out of it are the issues of life" (Proverbs 4:23). Struggle will seek you and I as long as you live for Christ. In fact, out of Christ's mouth are encouraging words for "in the world ye shall have tribulation: but be of good cheer; I have overcome the world" (John 16:33). We will have hardships (tribulations) in this evil world; but Jesus is saying, regardless of the hatred towards you or your past, be of good cheer. Why? He has overcome the world. What all this comes down to is the need to change the way we see ourselves in difficult times.

Sanctification calls us to a changed heart; it is the change of heart that renews the attitude of a believer. I'm a true believer that a man cannot do anything that his character will not allow him. The Apostle Paul described to believers "that ye put off concerning the former conversation the old man, which is corrupt according to the deceitful lusts; and be renewed in the spirit of your mind; and that ye put on the new man, which after God is created in righteousness and true holiness" (Ephesians 4:22-24). We are called to bear fruit; therefore, sanctification requires a human response. The fruit is your actions, results in ministry, and evidence of one's Christian walk. You can tell if a tree is healthy by the richness of the fruit. Bad trees do not have good fruit, nor does a good tree bear bad fruit. A tree that is supposed to bear fruit in season and has none is rendered worthless. Jesus said unto His disciples, "If a man abide not in me, he is cast forth as a branch, and is withered; and men gather them, and cast them into the fire, and they are burned" (John 15:6). When an olive tree is planted, it takes at least seven years for it to bear fruit. Once the tree has reached maturity to develop fruit, then it is good. Likewise, once saved, the believer will experience growth for a time. When the level maturity advances from spiritual infant to babe to spiritual adolescent, fruit must be evident. Some will disagree with this, assuming this is judgmental, when, in fact, it is Scriptural. We are called to be fruit inspectors as Jesus and the Apostles were (Romans 16:17; 2 Timothy 3:1-5).

When people look at us, our actions should march-in-step with Scripture. In fact, you may be the only Bible someone will ever read. Amen! Jesus goes on to say, "If ye abide in me, and my word abide in you, ye shall ask what ye will, and it shall be done unto you. Herein is my Father glorified, that ye bear much fruit; so shall ye be my disciples" (John 15:7-9). Here are seven fundamentals of sanctification:

1. "Study to shew thyself approved unto God, a workman that needeth not to be ashamed, rightly dividing the word of truth" (2 Timothy 2:15).

2. Remember who you are in Christ, "who gave himself for us, that he might redeem us from all iniquity, and purify unto himself a peculiar people, zealous of good works" (Titus 2:14).

3. The sanctification process takes work, as we are to "refuse profane and old wives' fables, and exercise (train) thyself rather unto godliness" (1 Timothy 4:7).

4. "Speak not evil one of another, brethren. He that speaketh evil of his brother, and judgeth his brother, speaketh evil of the law, and judgeth the law" (James 4:11).

5. We must seek peace in our dealings, as "[i]t is an honour for a man to cease from strife, but every fool will be meddling" (Proverbs 20:3).

6. "And he (Jesus) spake a parable unto them… that men ought always to pray, and not to faint" (Luke 18:1).

7. "And that ye study to be quiet, and to do your own business, and to work with your own hands, as we commanded you" (1 Thessalonians 4:11).

Doctrine of Heaven and Hell

And immediately I was in the spirit; and, behold, a throne was set in heaven, and one sat on the throne. And he that sat was to look upon like a jasper and sardine stone: and there was a rainbow round about the throne, in sight like unto an emerald. And round about the throne were four and twenty seats: and upon the seats I saw four and twenty elders sitting, clothed in white raiment; and they had on their heads crowns of gold. And out of the throne proceeded lightnings and thunderings and voices: and there were seven lamps of fire burning before the throne, which are the seven Spirits of God.

- Revelation 4:2-5

When attempting to find a description of Heaven, I recommend Revelations 4 and 5. Theologians have been uncertain as to the mode of experience John had, questioning whether John was taken from the isle of Patmos and given a tour of Heaven, or John was supernaturally transformed to witness these events. Either way, the experience was provided by the Lord, and has become perhaps some of the most detailed description of Heaven that blends together with other Biblical accounts within the Old Testament.

What is the most common description people have of Heaven? The answers vary, the most common being "the place where God abides." Heaven is more than just an abode where we can find Him. Everything that your eyes can see from the sounds you hear came by the precision of God's work. All things were created thus, drawn up by divine blueprints within the mansion. Here, God observes the actions of His people, and their prayers are heard from. It is a holy place designated for holy people, a forgiven people. Everyone wants to go to Heaven, but not everyone is willing to die.

During the Israelites' 40-year-journey God instructed Moses, "I will rain bread from Heaven for you" (Exodus 16:4). Bread was not the only thing that was launched down from Heaven; the fire of judgment was unleashed upon those who were swimming deep within the sea of iniquity. Jesus reminisced and said to the seventy in Luke, "I beheld Satan as lightning fall from Heaven" (Luke 10:18). It was the place where Satan's attempted coup convened, and the choir director took a third of the Heavenly host to their new destination – Earth. "And the great dragon was cast out, that old serpent, called the Devil, and Satan, which was cast out in the earth, and his angels were cast out with him" (Revelation 12:9).

Satan accuses the brethren today as he did with Job, "Now there was a day when the sons of God (angels) came to present themselves before the Lord, and Satan came also among them... And the Lord said unto Satan, Hast thou considered my servant Job, that there is none like him in the earth... Then Satan answered the Lord, and said, Doth Job fear God for nought? ... But put forth thine hand now, and touch all that he hath, and he will curse thee to thy face" (Job 1:6, 8-9, 11). This is but an example of what Satan does to each believer, even today.

The Throne Room

One day, right before it rained, there was a rainbow cascading across the sky. The first thought that came to mind was the throne of God. For much of the morning, the rainbow was the conversation on people's lips. I asked if they knew God's throne in Heaven was encircled with a rainbow. Of course, I got the various responses, but my intention was for them to know what to expect if they got to Heaven. See, the rainbow is a sign of the covenant after the Great Flood; it signifies how God will refrain from destroying the Earth with water. As evidence to this illustrious covenant, all of mankind can witness this 5,000-year-old agreement in the twenty-first century. I don't know about you, but that is pretty cool. However, God will not use a great flood to judge the world. The next time, it will be by fire, as described in Eschatology.

It is important to note, however, the Prophet Ezekiel provides a detailed description of the throne, stating: "Then I looked, and, behold, in the firmament that was above the head of the cherubim there appeared over them as it were a sapphire stone, as the appearance of the likeness of a throne" (Ezekiel 10:1). John further describes the seating around the throne has 24 seats, and seated in each of those seats are elders. I believe the elders represent the twelve tribes of Israel and the twelve apostles of the first century, as they are dressed in their uniform of victory, white raiment with their heads adorned with a gold crown (Revelation 4:4). One of the interesting depictions of the Holy Spirit's perfection is in verse 5; John wrote: "and out of the throne proceeded lightnings and thunders and voices: and there were seven lamps of fire burning before the throne, which are the seven Spirits of God." Notably the seven Spirits are also referred to in Isaiah 11:2 as the Sevenfold Spirit. Throughout the entire Bible, numbers have significant meaning; for instance, the number seven represents the number of completeness as the supreme glory of the Lord. The functions of the seven Spirits are:

1. Spirit of the Lord (Isaiah 11:2)

2. Spirit of Wisdom

3. Spirit of Understanding

4. Spirit of Counsel

5. Spirit of Might

6. Spirit of Knowledge

7. Spirit of Grace (Zechariah 12:10)

The spirits here, represented by these seven lamps before the throne, are another manifestation of Himself, namely the physical manifestation of the Holy Spirit, which is fully embodied in Jesus Christ Himself. This physical manifestation is important, as God Himself is still covered.

The surroundings, maybe referencing the floor, was a sea of glass that resembled crystal. Guarding the throne were four living creatures, and are said to be "full of eyes" where nothing can escape their view. These beasts repeat all day long: "Holy, holy, holy, Lord God Almighty, which was, and is, and is to come" (Revelation 4:8). Revelation 4:9-11 is essential for believers to practice in anticipation for the Rapture or death (whichever is first). This side of Heaven is our rehearsal phase before actually giving up the ghost and being with the Lord. Once we are in Heaven, all believers will worship the Lord in the following fashion. I'm excited to share this, for many pastors are derelict in their duty to educate their members on Revelation 4 and 5. Did you know our Sunday worship is just a rehearsal for the *Bema Seat* (Judgment Seat of Jesus Christ) in verse 9-11? The *Bema* is the time believers will be judged for their works while on Earth (1 Corinthians 15:51-55). We will not be judged for the sake of salvation. Amen!

You probably have heard church folk say, "We will receive our crowns and cast them at the feet of Jesus." Assuming you had, the Bema Seat is exactly where this statement derives. When the creatures gave glory, honor and thanks to the Lord, the twenty-four elders will "fall down before him (Jesus) that sat on the throne, and worship him that liveth for ever and ever, and vast their crowns before the throne" (v. 10). The elders' worship consisted of them falling prostrate (Gk. pipto) and casting their crowns before the throne. The relevance of this verse invites each of us during the Bema to collectively "pipto" beside the 24 elders. Then we will cast our crowns, while in concert, singing, "Thou art worthy, O Lord, to receive glory and honour and power: for thou hast created all things, and for thy pleasure they are and were created" (v. 11). I believe this verse should be recited on every Sunday for the Church's edification. In doing so, they will become a high voltage church, on fire with the expectation for these events.

Beloved, before you go any further, I want to encourage you to pretend you are in Heaven. Find yourself some headgear wherever you are.

Fall prostrate on the ground, then quote the song that the twenty-four elders sung. Try it at least 3 times – you would be surprised how intimate of an act of worship this is. If possible, you could invite your friends, roommates, children, or spouse to practice this with you.

Hell is Real

Pew Research identifies that 62% of Americans believe hell is an actual place of suffering.[40] A shocking 38% of Christians do not believe in an actual place of torment and misery. What stands out to me, when so many proclaiming Christians do not believe in Hell, this is hard to believe. You have to wonder how many do not believe Satan exists? It breaks my heart to see how people are being deceived and placed on a collision course with the very place they believe does not exist. Have these people really been saved? It also may suggest the Bible has been spiritualized or they don't believe it. These people are walking in dangerous territory! It will only get worse before the Rapture of the Church and Christ's return. There will be a great revival during the Tribulation where millions of people will turn to Jesus. Until then, we are witnessing the beginning of the Great Apostasy. "One-third of adults (33%) believe they will go to Heaven solely because of confession of their sins and embracing Jesus as their Savior, yet 15% said they do not know what will happen after they die."[41] However, 30% of Americans believe Purgatory is a real place.[42] All you have to do is look around you and see the people going their own way. Imagine them without the One True Living God; to me, it is like digging your hand into a giant bowl of Skittles where 20% are laced with poison, then chomping away like the Cookie Monster. Many of them are just diving into the cesspool mouth first, having no care whatsoever. It's no wonder we are seeing more and more young pop artists spreading faddish, New Age, and demonic messages to children and young adults, such as Billie Eilish. I saw this young lady on an award show once, and I was not too interested in her performance, due to the dark, mystic nature. However, in my opinion, her performance matches her music style. A Biblical Researcher and author, Ryan Pitterson, affirms Eilish sings praise to Satan, in a song titled "All Good Girls Go to Hell," in it, she sings: "All the good girls go to hell/ 'Cause even God herself has enemies."[43] All you can do is shake your head and pray the Lord will bring her to Himself before it is too late. Eilish is totally misguided and lost; somebody needs to pray an emergency 911 for her to seek the risen Savior. She is evil for spreading blasphemous New Age garbage about our Heavenly Father with no shame (Zephaniah 3:5). Look, Hell is a real place. There are people skydiving into Hell as you read this sentence. Did you know there are good girls in Hell? Oh yes, there are good people who lived morally good lives, yet failed because they rejected Christ as Lord and Savior. The problem is they were not truly converted, thus were like goats who love to go their own way. God never intended for His creation to experience this place of torment and pain that was specifically made for Satan and his fallen choir. In fact, Jesus spoke in Matthew 25:41 of a time when there will be a separation of sheep and goats and "[t]hen shall he say also unto them on the left hand, Depart from me, ye cursed, into everlasting fire, prepared for the devil and his angels." In addition, "if God spared not the angels than sinned, but cast them down to hell, and delivered them into chains of darkness, to be reserved unto judgment," what do you think He'll do to us (2 Peter 2:4)?

What motivated Billie Eilish, or anyone, to think they will attain a holy pass to Heaven in this current state? I'm reminded of the rich man and the beggar named Lazarus (do not confuse with the one Jesus raised from the dead) in the book of Luke. The story has in it the rich man died and was buried while "in hell he lifted up his eyes, being in torments, and seeth Abraham afar off, and Lazarus in his bosom. And he cried and said, Father Abraham, have mercy on me, and send Lazarus, that he may dip the tip of his finger in water, and cool my tongue; for I am tormented in this flame" (Luke 16:23-24). Beloved, Hell is real! The rich man was subjected to the flames of Hell, needing some water to cure his dehydration. He wanted a drip of water from the finger of the beggar who had sores and laid outside in the nasty streets. You know one thing, the rich man is still in the same predicament asking for mercy, for someone to dip the tip of his finger in water, and cool just his tongue because of the flames. In Hell, there is only perpetual torment, for "There shall be weeping and gnashing of teeth" (Matthew 8:12). Equally important, in hell remembering the past is part of the torment. For instance, what did Abraham assert to the rich man? He said, "son, remember that thou in thy lifetime..." (Luke 16:25). People in hell will remember all the times of being told to turn from sin and repent.

Doctrine of Satan

In June 2020, William Falk wrote a short piece in the *Weekly* about Will Carroll, the drummer for a heavy-metal band called, "Death Angels."[44] Carroll, like many others around the world, unfortunately had spent twelve days in a coma, due to complications from COVID-19. Carroll's experience had frightened him to the point of altering his religious view. During the interview, he claimed to have had an encounter with Satan in Hell. Some of us may suggest this story is fictitious. For someone like Mr. Carroll, whom routinely paid homage to Satan, to profess: "I don't think Satan's quite as cool as I use to," this is impactful. In my opinion, his experience was real.

A Gallup poll suggests that 27% of Americans believe Satan is actually real.[45] In contrast, 40% of Christians believe the same.[46] Then, what is the case with Satan? Is it fact, there is some archenemy of the Creator who is attempting to destroy mankind and secure for himself a dictatorship of all universe? How should believers take the historical narratives about Satan? The answer to all these questions will be explored. First, I must state a fact that the reason why society has gone off the scales of truth is because the pulpits are no longer on fire – they are soaking wet. Obviously, it is the neglect of the full counsel of God being preached about holiness, sin, Hell, or Satan, but substituted for watered-down, unsound Biblical teaching and preaching that focuses on inclusivity, including: transgender identity, critical race theory, social (justice) gospel, Easter religious rites, and neo-Marxist doctrine within the household of faith.

Who is Satan

Satan is a Hebrew word meaning *adversary*, one who is an "opponent" or "enemy."[47] He is also known as the devil, which describes him as a "false accuser" and "slanderer." In Isaiah, the name, Lucifer, is given to mean the "bright one." Other names that are frequently referenced in Scriptures are:

- Beelzebub   Matthew 12:24

- The Wicked One   Matthew 13:19, 38

- The Enemy   Matthew 13:25, 28, 39

- The Ruler of This World   John 12:31

- The "god" of This World   2 Corinthians 4:4

- Belial   2 Corinthians 6:15

- The Prince of the Power of the Air   Ephesians 2:2

- The Tempter   1 Thessalonians 3:5

- The Accuser of Our Brethren   Revelation 12:10

We can find passages furnished in Isaiah 14:12-15 and Ezekiel 28:11-19 containing details of God's archenemy. The Ezekiel 28:11-19 account provides explicit description, that God had created Satan as the guard of cherubs; thus an angel of light – perfect in beauty and pregnant with wisdom. He was perfect (without sin) "until iniquity was found" in him. It was because of his pride that ambition pervaded his person with his consequently becoming aroused by the infatuation of his own beauty, which led to the corrupt nature of lust. In Ezekiel 28:13-14, the Bible described him as being the music minister in Heaven. God created Satan like a musical instrument, something meant for worship. He was important for worship, as our own music is today. In fact, music is a tool still used by Satan to corrupt people, especially those within the Church, for it is through music that the people of God are ushered into the Spirit of the Lord. Hence, if you pay close attention, you can discern the correlation between Christian music as evidence to the Church's spiritual condition. How? Simple. If you cannot tell the difference between what is Christian music versus secular music, this is a serious problem. I have experienced music that took my mind to a place it should not have been. Don't get me wrong. I'm not knocking people who enjoy certain secular music (i.e. Jazz). However, I'm specifically referring to Christ-centered music. Take, for instance, there are many new praise and worship songs where Jesus is not mentioned or in the title. This is the device Satan uses to slowly peel away the sensitivity of holiness. Godly music ushers worshippers into the Spirit of the Lord. Lucifer was originally created without sin, but sometimes after witnessing God receiving praise and being worshipped every minute of the day, something changed within him. He said in his heart, "**I** will ascend into Heaven, **I** will exalt **my** throne above the stars of God: **I** will sit also upon the mount of the congregation…**I** will be like the Most High" (Isaiah 14:13-14, emphasis added). It is probable that Lucifer was tolerant for a while until he witnessed God's zeal towards man, making man above angels. When man became the apple of His eye, this frustrated him. At first, man was obedient and was granted dominion over all living creatures. Man was even given, by the love and grace of God, the right to name the animals, just as God named Creation during the first two chapters of Genesis.

The enemy could not handle this authority being disseminated to man. Just think, jealousy became his appetite. According to Scripture, Lucifer did not even confront God but God, being omniscient (knowing all things), saw what was building in the Enemy's heart. God evicted him, and a third of the choir, from the holiness of Heaven (Revelation 12:9). Our Lord's word stung him forever: "[d]epart from me, ye cursed, into everlasting fire, prepared for the devil and his angels" (Matthew 25:41). Jesus had a front row seat to this blockbuster eviction (Luke 10:18). Since then, Lucifer made his debut in the garden and has caused:

- David's numbering of Israel by census,

- Job's calamity,

- Joshua to be accused,

- Peter's denial of Christ,

- Christ's temptation in the wilderness and His death on the Cross, and

- The persecution of the believers.

The Enemy's Capabilities

Satan has power over the world and below, as mentioned in John 12:31 and 1 John 5:19. In Job 1:7, God asked Satan, "whence comest thou?" Satan answered and said, "From going to and fro in the earth, and from walking up and down it." He still has limited access to Heaven to accuse the brethren. In Jude 9, the archangel Michael contended with Satan over the body of Moses. Satan has inflicted sickness upon God's creation, among other things. Also, there is a surmount of pleasure for him in tempting believers to divorce holiness to quench one's sinful lust. He is a liar and will deceive everyone to persecute every human being on this Earth.

The Enemy's Limitations

Satan **cannot** control your thoughts, **cannot** read your mind, and **cannot** see into your future. He doesn't know anything that will take place in the future, other than what has been revealed in the Scriptures. God alone is omniscient, for there is none like Him. Remember, Satan's desire is to be like God (Isaiah 6:9-11)!

Questions pertaining to demonic possession and oppression have so many believers and non-believers in a state of curiosity. Recently, Hollywood has produced movies, such as *The Unholy,* which came out during a holy day that highlights demon possession. Demons are real, as are demonic possessions! I have seen people who were oppressed; though perhaps unaware. You may have been exposed to someone who is or was overtaken by a demon. Nowhere in Scripture does it state that believers are to fear Satan or his demons. In fact, demons fear anyone who professes Christ as Lord. The Bible teaches us that demons tremble at the name of Jesus, and they are subject to the authority of God and His people (Mark 3:15; 5:7; 9:38-50; Luke 10:17-19).

Christians cannot be possessed, because the Spirit of God cannot occupy the same space as a demonic spirit. One has to go and the demonic always loses. Previously in this chapter, I mentioned once a believer is saved, the Holy Spirit instantly indwells. However, if you hear that some Charismatic believer was possessed by a devil, it is likely they were never born again.

A Thought on Fortunetelling

People under demonic authority cannot read minds nor the future. It is possible for someone to get names, dates, or details of a person's life that no one could know. The reason for this is that demons are all around us. We cannot see them. There are some people who I believe have the ability to sense them. If people could see demons, the sight or smell of them would drive many insane. Nevertheless, the demonic has observed everything about you – and there may be one near you right this minute. Have you ever felt like something was right next to you, as if someone was present, but no one was physically there? Satan's demons have observed relationships and conversations, the things you say and do in secret.

I will never forget this hot day in college when I was walking back to my campus apartment. All of the sudden, I walked into this great swarm of gnats. Normally, you can see them as you approach, but somehow, I missed the early warning. After passing through the swarm, some clung to my clothes. Then, a thought hit me: this is exactly what spirits do – they congregate to "seek who they may devour." Once a host meets their specifications, it is too late to respond, because of the lack of vigilance. Ever since then, I have made it my purpose to warn people to be prayed up. Word up, so the devil don't mess you up!

In the early 1990s, while serving at Ft. Hood, Texas, hours were spent training for Nuclear, Biological and Chemical attacks to survive and defeat our enemy. Likewise, we must learn Satan's tactics by studying the Word of God to overcome daily battles, to win the fight.

A Biblical Example of Demonic Possession or Oppression

In 1 Samuel 16:23, King Saul was a victim of a demonic spirit, which included signs of depression, and it was possibly the spirit of suicide. The Bible demonstrates that as the evil spirit oppressed him, David would play the harp, through which Saul was refreshed. In Acts 16:16, a spirit of divination possessed a young woman and granted her with unusual knowledge. She grieved Paul for many days until he finally cast out the spirit. Finally, in John 13:27, Satan entered into Judas and became the "son of perdition" to betray Jesus (John 17:12).

Doctrine of the Second Coming of Christ

In Matthew 24, Jesus departed from the Temple with His disciples. Being eager for divine knowledge, the disciples asked Jesus, "What shall be the sign of thy **coming,** and of the end of the world" (emphasis added)? For centuries, the Second Coming, also known as the Second Advent, has been preached with the anticipation of Christ's return. Advent means "coming." The first advent, was the virgin birth of Jesus Christ. Notably in this passage, Jesus cited a two-part list of events to take place prior to His Coming, such as the Great Tribulation (Matthew 24:21), the rise of the Antichrist and false prophets, and some atmospheric changes. In a clear examination, Jesus warned the people to also be ready, because the Son of Man is coming. Jesus did not make a casual assertion, such as "take your time." No! He emphasized that He is coming **quickly**. "And behold, I come quickly; and my reward is with me, to give every man according as his work shall be" (Revelation 22:12).

The Purpose

There was, and still is, a sense of urgency for the Church to take notice of Christ's imminent return. Apostle Paul emphatically reaffirmed to the Church at Colossae that God's wrath will fall upon the disobedient. Even today, there is a lack of apprehension among Christians who are enmeshed in their six-figure jobs, homes, and little Johnny's college fund, while neglecting to place Christ at the head of their priorities. This assertion is not in any way implying that people should repudiate long-range planning for their lives, but to prioritize the essential nuts and bolts needed for eternal life.

Christ was born to bear our sins. Therefore, in the Second Coming, Christ will come to fulfill the covenants the Father had promised Abraham, Isaac, and Jacob. Israel will be saved and brought back into their rightful place, receiving the blessings from the promises of God. The Church will not enjoy certain promises that were only made for the nation of Israel, such as the land of Palestine (Numbers 34:1-12; Deuteronomy 30:1-10). Regardless, all who believe in Christ as Lord will see His face and will dwell with Him in New Jerusalem, the eternal Kingdom (Revelation 21).

Implication Surrounding Christ's Return

I thought about the manner in which Jesus will return to this world. Will it be as a great trumpet blast, where the sound will break windows?

I remember an event that happened in Russia on February 5, 2013. People were going about their day like any other, when, without warning, a ten-ton meteorite streaked across the sky. First, there was a blinding light, then a massive explosion. Fearful people, interviewed by the media, thought the world was coming to an end. The aftermath of this rare celestial event left an estimated one thousand people injured with extensive property damage.

Amazingly, Matthew 24:27 came to mind with a narration pointing upward: "[f]or as the lightning cometh out of the east, and shineth even unto the west; so shall the coming of the Son of man be." Although the Russia event was not Jesus, I can only imagine His return being comparable to this event. How do you imagine Christ's return to Earth? When He returns, the Bible teaches us our Savior will come like a thief in the night with great power, for no man knows neither the day nor hour, including the angels in Heaven. Just like that Friday morning in Russia, Christ's return shall be with great power, like a sonic boom heard globally, coupled with the blinding light of His glory filling the atmosphere.

CHAPTER 3

MATTHEW 24: A NEAR PROPHETIC VIEW

It was a Tuesday, days before His Crucifixion. Jesus departed the Temple after preaching scathing woes to the Scribes and Pharisees (Matthew 23:1-29). Desiring some relaxation, Jesus decided to rest on the western slope of a place called the Mount of Olives. Just 300 feet above ground, the altitude provided our Lord a breathtaking view of the entire Kidron Valley, Hinnom Valley, and Herod's Temple. As the warm breeze swept across His feet, I imagine Him just looking into that valley, at a place which will testify to His glory. There is more to this story. His disciples – Peter, James, John, and Andrew – privately pulled the Lord aside, as a student would his professor. Bound and entangled in chains of curiosity for the key to unlock the end of days, they asked, "tell us, when shall these things be? And what shall be the sign of thy coming, and of the end of the world?" (Matthew 24:3). Their curiosity, and Jesus' answer, became known as the corpus of prophecy, the Olivet discourse. In this very private moment, the world received its first prophecy account of Christ's Second Coming and the end of the age.

The Temple Show-and-Tell

Verse one describes Jesus departing the temple and while walking away, His disciples decided to follow after Him, to call His attention to "the buildings of the temple." Joachim Jerimiah suggests the Herodian legacy had a reputation for their architecture and engineering adroitness. First, this particular temple had been under construction during the eighteenth year of Herod the Great's reign in 20 or 19 BC.[1] The completion of the temple in 64 AD was during the leadership of Governor Albinus, although Herod was known for his beautiful architectural innovation, according to Josephus' account. Thus, all ancient accounts describe the Temple exterior as "gleaming all over with gold," silver, and bronze.[2] The Temple was built upon a thirty-six acre site, which is roughly equivalent to twenty-seven football fields. There were nine gates, coupled with the "threshold and lintels, [that] were overlaid with gold and silver, but... one was made of Corinthian bronze and far exceeded the others in value."[3] Inside the Temple, it was nearly impossible for visitors to not pass through gold-covered entrances, for all the panels were made from white limestone or marble, and "colonnades which encircled the Temple court was roofed with cedar paneling" imported from other countries.[4]

Now, we have an idea as to why the disciples were in awe over the manner of stones, and "how [the temple] was adorned with goodly stones and gifts," which is supported by Josephus' account of this uncommon internal and external beauty (Mark 13:1, Luke 21:5). However, we should take Jesus' response as a type of watchman warning for believers to prepare for Christ's advent.

"And Jesus said to them, See ye not all these things? Verily I say unto you, there shall not be left here one stone upon another, that shall not be thrown down" (Matthew 24:2). It appears Jesus was stating: take a look at all this magnificence and recognize that in short order, none of what you are seeing will exist, not a stone. At the same time, these excited men were nodding their heads in fascination, because Jesus had acknowledged their eagerness to consume the Word of God. In reality, these men were clueless to what was happening at that very moment, that everything Jesus was telling them was of the future. I believe this verse alone is pregnant with meaning with four significant interpretations:

1. The Passion of Christ (John 2:18-20)

2. The Destruction of the Temple in 70 AD during Titus Flavius Vaspasinus' invasion

3. Events throughout the Church Age (verses 4-13)

4. Jacob's Trouble, also known as the Tribulation (Daniel 9, Ezekiel 38-30 & Revelation 4-22)

I mentioned something about the Tribulation in the previous chapter, and will touch more on the events throughout the church Age, but here, I will explain the historical significance of the Temple's destruction.

The Destruction of the Temple in 70 AD

Gessius Florus was a Roman governor who was disdainful towards the Jews to the point of being antagonistic. Burge and Green's book, *The New Testament In Antiquity*, mentions the governor struggled to maintain order, as the people began to test Florus' authority and exposed his weaknesses. He disrespected the Jewish customs and traditions, which aggravated the people to the point of no return. A riot eventually erupted, spreading into Jerusalem and resulting in nearly 4,000 residents crucified for their participation.[5] Unsurprisingly, Emperor Nero ordered Florus to inflict harsher punishments to intimidate the people into submission. Despite those decisive actions, this only emboldened the Zealot fighters to attack the Temple Complex and caused its destruction. The fighters' morale was high, due to their victories, but consequences and repercussions began to effect the community. The Emperor's next actions appears to be ill-advised, as he ordered a "cease and desist" on all Temple sacrifices in preparation for war.[6]

Cestius Gallus, a Syrian delegate, along with over 6,000 soldiers, was summoned to Caesarea for his final combat brief, just prior to engaging the Zealots.[7] Gallus and his troops were equivalent to deploying Seal Team 6 for a combat mission today. However, once they arrived at Jerusalem and witnessed the rioting and the fervor of the Zealots, their morale melted away. Like every coward, Gallus abandoned the mission, and while unfamiliar with the terrain, decided to take an alternate route to escape. This fear took a toll on Gallus and his troops, causing them to lose military discipline and became complacent. This lack of military bearing left the 12th Legion open to a surprise attack, and it happened. The Zealot fighters maintained stealth enough to intercept Gallus and his 6,000 men, which resulted in an annihilation of the unit. However, Gallus and some of his leaders were fortunate enough to evade being captured alive.

Now, Titus and his father, Vespasian, a renowned general, received word of Gallus' failure. The situation on ground had changed significantly, requiring the guidon to be passed on to Titus, as he was the best choice to quench this insurrection once and for all. Equally important, Vespasian's high-octane leadership acumen carved out a fighting force of "60,000 soldiers" that were proven and battle-ready.[8] It was soon obvious that Titus was a polar opposite to Gallus, as within several months of intense fighting, Titus' task force successfully controlled major access points into several cities like Jericho, and all passages within a 40-mile-radius around Jerusalem were choked off, thwarting any potential for an evacuation.

In the end, Jerusalem was destroyed. The majority of the population died from the battle. Apparently, history has it that Titus was so overwhelmed by the beauty of the Temple Complex that he made a desperate attempt to save the structure from burning.[9] Unfortunately, he failed.

Do you think each disciple understood the enormous volume of events resting in the queue of the future? Of course not, but our Lord did. Notably, Jesus' response to the disciples was one of over 200 prophecies that must occurs before returning and establishing His earthly kingdom. Nevertheless, we will explore a culmination of events with elevating levels of concern within the last five years. The author of Revelation fore-tells of the rebuilding of the Temple "during the Tribulation." I must add: no one truly knows how much construction of the Third Temple will happen before the Rapture of the Church. There are "great signs" of the reddish-dark cloud that covers the 21st century. Indeed, the Apostle John was provided an eschatological preview and writes:

And there was given me a reed like unto a rod: and the angel stood, saying, Rise, and measure the **temple** of God, and the **altar,** and them that worship therein. But the court which is without the temple **leave out,** and **measure it not;** for it is given unto the **Gentiles:** and the holy city shall they tread under foot **forty and two months.**

-Revelation 11:1-2, emphasis added

The angel tells him to measure the dimension of the temple and the altar, but to refrain from measuring *the court outside the temple.* The Greek word, *ekballō* means "to cast out," which generates the question: Why is it so important to not measure the outside court, with an emphatic "leave it out" following this command? Simply, this reservation for the outer court has been granted to the **Gentiles** (Gk. ethnesin: nations or certain ethnic group of people).[10] These people, by their actions, will trample or tread on the grounds of the temple for 3 ½ years, giving inference to the Great Tribulation. "Tread" is defined as: to set down one's foot with the ability to walk or step upon.[11] However, "trample" is more descriptive in meaning, as it means to put out, destroy, extinguish, or defeat.[12] The Greek word, *pateō,* is used five times in the New Testament to describe:

1. The "treading on serpents" (Luke 10:19),

2. "Jerusalem is said to be trodden down by Gentiles" (Luke 21:24),

3. "Jerusalem is said to be trodden by the Gentiles" (Revelation 11:2),

4. "The treading of the winepress" (Revelation 14:20), and

5. God's wrath judgement of the Tribulation (Revelation 19:15).[13]

When people hear "Gentiles," what usually comes to mind is the Church, which is a false identification. There is strong indication those being referred to are non-believers whom utterly reject the Gospel message. For instance, in the Bible, "Gentile" often refers to any ethnic or religion outside of Judaism. Many prophecy watchers believe the instructions to "leave out" the measurement of the outer court is a sign of abandonment, because of the so-called Gentiles. By leaving an empty plot, it could indicate a probable joint-domicile with the Muslim occupiers of the Temple Mount. The Jewish temple was built on Mount Moriah, the same location Abraham was to sacrifice Isaac, according to Genesis 22, which is also the same location the Muslims claim as their sacred site, because they claim they are a part of the Abrahamic covenant through Ishmael.

According to an article regarding the funding of the Third Temple from *JewishVoice.org*:

> Muslims consider the Temple Mount holy because they believe the prophet Mohammed ascended to Heaven from there in his alleged *Night Journey*. They consider the entire Mount to be the Sanctuary and claim sovereignty to the area, denying that Solomon's Temple or Herod's Temple ever stood there. In doing so, they suppress and reject the overwhelming weight of historical and archaeological evidence.[14]

What does this mean? In his book, *The Last Hour: An Israeli Insider Looks at the End Time,* Amir Tsarfati, a phenomenal Israeli preacher, described the attitude of many Israelis whom believe a new Jewish temple is out of the question. Brother Tsarfati explains: "The Temple Mount is already the home of the Dome of the Rock, the Al-Aqsa Mosque and the Dome of the Chain, it is inconceivable that the Muslims would allow [the building of the Third Temple]."[15] What Brother Tsarfati is alluding to has gone unreported in American media. Since 1967, Israel has relinquished "administrative privileges" of the Temple Complex to the Jordanian waqf, while Israel still maintains legal control over the complex itself.[16] The Jordanian waqf has used passive-aggressive antagonistic tactics to prevent Jews from exercising their right to pray on site. Unbelievably, this organization even goes as far as arresting those whom are discovered praying. Again, American media refuses to cover such foolishness, while "Arab children are being paid monthly salaries by Hamas to harass Jewish pilgrims on the Mount, and riots often erupt against Jewish visitors, causing the wooden bridge that Jews are allowed to use to enter the Mount to be closed."[17] Even the Israeli Parliament, known as the Knesset, has diligently sought after solutions to maintain peace by having different days or segregated areas where Jews and Muslims can access. The Palestinian Authority has done their best to make any effort to maintain peace as painful as possible. It was proposed to have a "100-meter buffer zone" as part of the separation method, but this was rejected by the Palestinians.[18] Therefore, you can imagine the kicking and screaming from the Muslims, if the rebuild was forced upon them. However, I agree with Brother Tsarfati that no one has a clue how it will happen, but make no mistake, the Temple will be rebuilt in the near future.

In February 2019, *The Guardian* reported that Pope Francis and Sheikh Ahmed al-Tayeb, the head of the Sunni Islam's most prestigious seat of learning, both arrived "hand-in-hand as a symbol of interfaith brother-hood," along with the grand imam of al-Azhar during a three-day summit in Abu Dhabi, United Arab Emirates.[19] The whole premise behind the meeting was to sign a "historical declaration of fraternity" in the presence of global religious leaders that hailed from Christianity, Judaism and other faiths.[20] Each attendee signed the agreement, assuring: "we resolutely declare that religion must never incite war, hateful attitudes, hostility and extremism, nor must they incite violence or shedding of blood."[21] At the end of the meeting, Sheikh Tayeb had addressed the Pope as being "my dear brother."[22]

On May 14, 2020, an agreement of unity with Islam codified the interfaith formation of "Chrislam," which is an end-time sign that the outer court could possibly accomodate for joint-worship. It will likely be a building constructed in the outer court which is large enough for a mosque that would replace the three current Muslim structures. Further, these future structures may resemble the interfaith church and mosques in the UAE. The planning has gone into high-gear with the Temple Institute Rebuild Initiative in Jerusalem. According to the Jewish Voice, currently, the Temple blueprints are completed, along with the land survey in 2018 and 2019, and a 3-D scale of the Temple design and are simply waiting for the approval to break ground.[23] The Temple Institute's International Director, Rabbi Chaim Richman, mentioned: "The architects will fuse Jewish law with modern technology to prepare for a fully modern third Temple, Kosher to the letter of the law."[24] The Temple Institute disseminated a press release, citing more details to support Rabbi Richman's account. Within the design are several comfort amenities to facilitate a seamless worship experience with underground parking, heating and computerized washing stations that minimize water waste.[25] There is a database with names of the living descendants of Aaron being confirmed through a DNA registry. Every male verified and affirmed by DNA can be assigned to priestly duties within the Temple.

In December 2018, the ancient Sanhedrin was reconstituted and will again become the highest authority, both administratively and judicially, in the land. In fact, in the Gospel of Mark, it is with the Sanhedrin that Judas agreed to betray Jesus for 30 pieces of silver and Peter denied Christ three times. Now, we have to shift focus from the measurements of the court to the sacrificial system. Since 1948, several essential Temple items are in the custody of the Vatican (because the Vatican confiscated them), which Israel has never regained since. Israel has petitioned the Vatican for the release of these essential items, but we will see how long the Vatican will procrastinate before releasing the items. Currently, Israel has the following items stored until the activation of the worship services: the Temple altar, the priest's breastplate, the show bread, the vestments, the candles, and the incense.

Numbers 19:1-10 outlines the "red heifer" sacrificial ritual conducted by the priest, Eleazar. God had spoken the *ordinance of the law,* indicating for Moses and Aaron to bring Him "a red heifer without spot, wherein is no blemish," and had never been harnesses (v.2). Once the heifer was secured, they were to provide the animal to the priest, who then would escort the animal outside the camp and slaughter it himself. Once the throat is cut, the priest is to take the blood with his fingers and sprinkle the blood seven times directly onto the tabernacle of congregation. The entire animal is to be burned, including the blood and offal, and while the sacrifice is burning, the priest is to toss in some cedar wood, hyssop, and scarlet. Verse 7 is where things get a little technical, but the bottom-line is the priest must clean his clothes and himself. Then, another priest is to gather the ashes, and "lay them up without the camp in a clean place, and it shall be kept for the congregation of the children of Israel for a **water of separation**: it is a purification for sin" (v.9, emphasis added). Israel has negotiated contracts with local farmers to raise red heifers suitable for temple sacrifices. Currently, there are several red heifers currently available for service.

Finally, on Israel's 70th birthday, former President Donald J. Trump moved the American embassy to Jerusalem with the world watching, fulfilling ancient prophecies. Many nations still, to this date, have refused to move their embassies to Jerusalem, for fear of angering the fatuous Palestinians. The last significant piece to the rebuilding of the temple is the temple coin. The coin was minted with the following inscription on the front, "Like doves to their nest, Isaiah 60:8" written in Hebrew, English, and Arabic, framed by a picture of the Temple and a dove with an olive branch in its mouth. The other side of the coin has the inscriptions, "To fulfill 70 years" and "And He charged me to build Him a house in Jerusalem." It also includes a picture of former President Trump and Cyrus the Great (the Persian king who allowed the Jews to return to Jerusalem after the Exile), flanked with the two seals of the American President and the Persian Empire. What a blessing to have a legacy recognized by God in such a great magnitude.

Right now, you may be wondering why these things haven't been covered in the mainstream news? Considering the historical events described in this chapter, one would think these events have some significant value worth discussing. The problem is the media has lost the trust of the people since the 2016 election. Joshua Peace wrote in *Popular Mechanics* that a 2019 poll found only 48% of Americans trusted the media, and in 2021, those numbers have dwindled.[26] It all comes down to this understanding: America has crossed the threshold into an era of Great Deception.

CHAPTER 4

DECEIVED PEOPLE DECEIVE PEOPLE

Let no man deceive you by any means: for that day shall not come, except there come a **falling away first,** and that man of sin be revealed, the son of perdition.

-2 Thessalonians 2:3, emphasis added

The Mount of Olives was not an unfrequented place during Jesus' ministry. The disciples has accompanied Him up that hill many times, yet there was something different about this particular moment. Their lives, whether they knew it or not, had changed after hearing the stark seven word warning that was as potent then as it is now: "take heed that no man deceive you" (Matthew 24:4). I imagine these words were the authentication code of relevance for believers past, present, and future. He was preparing the world for an outpouring of lawlessness and deception, as people and communities become submerged in the confusion which flows destruction.

In Ephesians, the Apostle Paul wrote, "[f]or we wrestle not against flesh and blood, but against principalities, against powers, against rulers of darkness of this world, against spiritual wickedness in high places" (Ephesians 6:12). Indeed, we are wrestling against the Spirit of the Antichrist which has pervaded the media, politics, and global affairs in full force. I have never seen anything as sudden and deliberate that endorsed the levels of confusion, violence, and deception leading to the 2020 election. It is my understanding that all the lawlessness that became propaganda through the media is just a foreshadowing of the Beast's system. Nevertheless, this will only manifest once the Tribulation begins, right after the Rapture of the Church. The World Economic Forum (WEF) has devised a diabolical plan that is designed to be a building block within a movement called the "Great Reset" or "The Fourth Industrial Revolution." This is a socialist-Marxist agenda, insidious like a parasite borrowing a hole into the heart of America (I will discuss this in great detail later). There must be a crisis before the Antichrist can make his appearance. He will appear to have all the answers, as efforts are taken to join the world in perfect harmony due to the departure of the Church, but until then, "And many shall follow their pernicious ways; by reason of whom the way of truth shall be evil spoken of. And through covetousness shall they with feigned words make **merchandise of you:** whose judgment now of a long time lingereth not, and their damnation slumbereth not (2 Peter 2:2-3, emphasis added)."

We have entered a season of the Great Apostasy, where the Church will become complacent and complicit by not speaking against whoever abuses holiness. Equally important, Christian leaders who speak Biblical Truth against a secular worldview will be demonized and called racist, ethnocentric, or a homophobe.

You might find yourself asking a few questions concerning the end-time. What is behind this derisive and divisive spirit? Why is it important to eliminate America's resource independence, but exempt China from the same regulations which have destroyed American businesses and crippled America's economy? Why is there an urgency to have a dominant "one party system" similar to Hitler's Germany? Why is it important now to expand the Supreme Court, which has had only nine seats for 152 years, and allow liberal-minded justices to fill the new seats, much like Venezuela has recently done? Is it the same ambition that drives the push to add two more liberally-leaning states to the Union? Why discard the

184-year-old Senate Filibuster tradition, meant as a tool to prevent tyranny? Why is there an urgency to indoctrinate our children in their tender years about a variety of liberal worldviews on sex, abortion, homosexuality, gender identity, and so many more? Why has it become popular to hate our own country? We must remember that none of this is new. In fact, as you travel back through history, lawlessness is a symptom of a spirit and an ideology that has been around for some time.

Marxism: Wolves Out to Destroy the Sheep

Ever since the Biden Administration has assumed responsibility over Former President Trump's *Operation: Warp Speed,* America has emerged victorious over the Chinese Communist Party's "plan-demic," although many believe America will never be the same again because of the birth of a "new normal" guided by a new interpretation of living. While pondering this thought, here are three "yes/no" questions which may help you to process this "new normal:"

1. Do you agree "private property encourages greed and envy"?[1]

2. Do you agree "the government, rather than individuals, should control as much of the resources as necessary to ensure that everyone gets their fair share?"[2]

3. Do you believe "significant government regulation is necessary for the good of society?"[3]

These questions were generated from a Barna Group poll that state "36% of practicing Christians embrace at least one of these three Marxist statements."[4] If you selected "yes" to any one of these questions, ask yourself "why?" Here are some facts from the study – roughly 11% of practicing Christians agree that private property influences greed and envy; whereas 20% of Millennials, 22% of Gen-Xers, and only 4% of Baby Boomers agreed.[5] 45% of Christians believe that "the government, rather than individuals" should control resources.[6] Lastly, 36% of Christians agreed that government regulations is necessary for the betterment of society.[7] Many people are unaware of the destructive ideologies seated within Marxism.

The Marxist worldview is an antithesis to Capitalism.[8] The Marxist model of oppression is absolutely irreligious and practice violence towards all religions, particularly Christianity. Pay attention to the conversation about religious freedom within the next three years. You will begin to hear language that echoes the voice of Karl Marx and his contemporaries.

Consider this: many Christians accept socialism because we have a responsibility to take care of widows, orphans, and the impoverished. However, what many fail to understand is the **root** of ungodliness that rests within Marxism. On the surface, Socialism appears to align with Christian values, but in reality, it is an antithesis to the Message of the Cross. When set in motion, socialism strips the people of their voice and constitutional powers. Someone once said, "You cannot vote your way out of socialism, you have to shoot your way out of socialism." This is true. A good example, if you want to witness the horror of a once prosperous, oil-rich nation falling victim to Socialism-Communism is modern-day Venezuela. People are eating rats and pets. The rationing of food, water, and energy is the succulent fruit of Communism. Look within our own borders: California and other Democrat-led states are now imposing similar restrictions, just as Venezuela did, and using climate change as a cause for exhausting their resources.

As a watchman, it is necessary to diligently dissect this doctrine to identify key Marxist vernacular. When you hear Klaus Schwab, Bill Gates, or politicians share their big ideas, you can protect yourself from any deception. Jesus instructed the disciples to protect themselves from those seeking to do them harm. He said: "Behold, I send you forth as sheep in the midst of wolves: be ye therefore wise as serpents, and harmless as doves" (Matthew 10:16). I once heard a preacher suggest, "No sheep ever harmed a wolf; no wolf ever was destroyed by a sheep." Indeed, it is important for us to remain vigilant of these dangers as a watchman. Stay prayed up. Word up, so the devil doesn't mess you up!

The Historical Context of Marxism

Karl Heinrich Marx (1818-1883) was a social scientist, historian, and revolutionist; David McClellan, author of Marx, Karl Heinrich, mentions Marx was born in Germany to Jewish parents who were descendants of rabbis.[9] He was married with six children, though only three survived into the late 1850s. In Paris, Marx was influenced by the French Socialist Movement that ultimately fed his ideas on Communism. Marx became intrigued with history and began to study the "various modes of production and predicted the collapse of the present one – capitalism – and its replacement by communism."[10] He developed a deep friendship with another philosopher from Manchester, England, Friedrich Engels, and in 1848, the two collaborated on the now-infamous *Communist Manifesto*. Israel Wayne describes in the book, *Deceivers: Exposing Evil Seducers & Their Last Days Deception*, said the *Manifesto* was designed "to destroy the family and break the allegiance of children to their parents."[11] Marxism is antagonistic, as it portrays, and perpetuates, a conflict between two classes of people: the *bourgeoisie* (meaning "with capital"), who are wealthy business owners, and the *proletariat* (meaning "peasantry"), who remain poor through the abuse of the bourgeoisie.[12] Marxist doctrine then sails deeper into the abyss of darkness. The concept of "economic forces production" actually determines a person's "social class, religion and intellectual superstructure of society."[13] The easiest way to explain this concept is that you determine your "revolution." One's economic circumstances can be influenced through commerce (entrepreneurship) in the form of manufacturing, or the buying and selling of goods; whereas property ownership is labeled as "relation of production," which is greatly opposed within Marxist doctrine.[14] In fact, in recent news, there have been discussions of states wanting to eliminate single-family homes and land ownership in compliance with the United Nations: Vancouver Declaration. The Marxist-left believe it is unfair for a certain class of people to own single-family homes and property. Since there is a housing shortage with a growing homeless population, the Marxist-left believe those homeless are exploited, because of their homelessness (I'm not making this stuff up). If they get their way, the local municipalities could seize your home and demolish it, then build a high-rise building on your one-acre lot to house 100 people. In their minds, such an aggressive move would quash the housing shortage and eliminate the line of opportunity between low-income people and allow these people to experience living among wealthier citizens. In George Orwell's novel, *1984*, he mentions "the so-called abolition of private property which took place... the concentration of property [is] in far fewer hands than before; but with this difference, that the new owners were a group instead of a mass of individuals."[15] Right now, the states that are currently flirting with this

Marxist "relations of production" is Oregon and Washington. The way things are developing around the country, one could expect to see some results in the next year or so. I have suggested to family and friends to leave the suburbs and purchase some land several miles away from the city to insulate their livelihood. You have Bill Gates, a die-hard Marxist, and other billionaires purchasing over 242,000 acres of farmland throughout America. Once the land is all purchased, those who own it will not sell it again. Either way, the progressives have the ability to make land ownership less appealing through taxation, new legislation, or new regulations. If the current political system remains, they will likely find a creative method to circumvent the Constitution.

Karl Marx identifies a "superstructure" as the model of a system or institution where people are likely to congregate. For instance, your church is a superstructure, as are the courts, police, and military. Thus is Karl Marx indicating the "economical force of production" and "relations of production" divides society into two classes. In order for this method to work, there must be an antagonist willing to throw straw upon the flame, pointing out the less obvious issues to evade direct confrontation with their own issues. Deceived people deceive people.

In Marxism, there is no middle class; either you are wealthy or poor. There is no in-between. Marxists believe:

> That society has been dominated by a ruling class of 'property owners' who exploit the lower class, and that according to the laws of the 'dialectic,' each social system generates the forces that will destroy it and create a new system, with political revolution and the emergence of a new ruling class marking each transition.[16]

Marxism is "materialist," which is a term to describe its process of social change. It appears Karl Marx was a staunch supporter of retribution towards his opponents. The delivery had to be "spontaneous" and "violent" against any contender, with the "revolution" becoming the "norm."[17] Overall, Marx's idea did not clearly establish a blueprint for a specified basis of the revolution; he only made a range of predictions about a concept that hinged upon the idea of a revolution. Any ounce of success among the working class would depend upon the proletariat's hand-and-feet movement to replace a "bureaucratic government." This part is interesting, considering the removal of a republic would be replaced with a "dictatorship of the proletariat."[18] In other words, the first phase of this doctrine is the abolition of the class differences that victimizes and exploits the property-less class. Even in this state, Marxists believe through the "first phase of Communism" that everyone can receive compensation for their work until the "final phase of Communism, in which the State would disappear, national differences would subside, and the entire system of monetary rewards and inequalities would vanish."[19] For the next two decades, Marx spent time with the "Social Democratic" movement. Interestingly, Bernie Sanders, a 2020 presidential candidate, ran as a Democratic Socialist and nearly won the Democratic nomination.

Later in history, an acolyte to the demonic Marxist scheme, Vladimir Llyich Ulianov, also known as Vladimir Lenin, rose to power. Historians, such as Lawrence W. Reed, suggest that Lenin's toxic fight against the Russian Tsarists elevated him to being the first Communist dictator, who oppressed millions.[20] He was the muscle behind a movement which began with Marxism as a philosophical dogma, but Lenin, a *Bolshevik* (meaning "man of the majority"), turned it into a tool of terror. The idea for labor unions first gained momentum during the three-year "strike movement," which demanded better economic stimulus in the form of better wages and hours. The spirit of these movements spread to America, and were instrumental in the formation of the American Clayton Antitrust Act of 1914 and the Warner National Labor Relations Act of 1935.

Later, in 1898, Lenin wanted to emulate the same spirit through the incorporation of the Social Democratic Workers (SBW) party. Donald W. Treadgold wrote in "Bolshevik" that one advantage to the SBW was its ability to organize, then absorb, protesters to promote demonstrations and strikes as "new revolutionary opportunities."[21]

Lenin knew that in order to reach the Marxist goal of a proletariat dictatorship for his revolution, this could only be achieved through the might of the "peasants." It was not that easy, for there was so much internal conflict between the different factions of the party, it was almost impossible for Lenin to accomplish anything. After World War I, an agreement for a coalition government had promised to be a voice for the workers and the poor.

The land became more of an issue as the process of nationalizing socialism continued. Lenin's following actions were "spontaneous" and "violent," exactly as Karl Marx had prescribed: he instigated strife, and pit the "poor peasantry" against the *kulaks*, the rich peasantry who were the land owners to meet the revolutionary objective. Lenin instructed "We must be ready to employ trickery, deceit, law-breaking, withholding, and concealing the truth... We can and must write in a language which sow among the masses hate, revulsion, scorn toward those who disagree with us."[22] The people Lenin was referring to perhaps suspected they were on the receiving end of terror, while they vainly hoped for peace. These so-called rich peasants were hardworking people wanting to make a living too, and someday pass their legacy down to their children's children. Deception is a prerequisite Marxists use to gain advantage over their opponents by any means necessary to gain dominance over the collective body. Be advised; this is the same requirements the progressives are employing in order to gain the upper-hand on the nation. All you have to do is watch and gather facts to measure the validity of any policy or plans.

One day in the Penza region, the local Bolsheviks received a telegram encouraging them to begin an insurrection against local *kulak* (farmers), because they would not relinquish their land, thus hindering the final process of the Nationalization of Russia. Lenin's telegram was the *Hanging Order* that began the infamous "Red Terror" during the summer of August 1918. Pay close attention to the tactics used against the victims:

Comrades! The insurrection of five Kulak districts should be pitilessly suppressed. The interests of the whole revolution require this, because the last decisive battle with the kulaks is now underway everywhere. An example must be made.

Hang no fewer than one hundred known kulaks, fatcats, and bloodsuckers

Publish their names

Seize all grain from them

Designate hostages, in accordance with yesterday's telegram. Do it in such a fashion, that for hundreds of miles around the people see, tremble, know, shout: 'The bloodsucking kulaks are being strangled and will be strangled.'

Telegram receipt and implementation.

Yours,

Lenin

P.S. Use your toughest people for this.[23]

How long will it be before we find out that our modern-day "protesters" are sending each other similarly worded e-mails?

Marxism is Alive Today in the BLM and Antifa

In America, the Marxist revolution could not happen in this manner because of the middle-class. However, it appears the revolutionary objective today has been changed to use race – the African-Americans against White-Americans, and Asian-Americans against African-Americans – instead of class to overthrow our current republic and its capitalist economy for a new system of communism. In order to reach global communism, there must be a complete rupture of the constitutional framework of America. According to a filmmaker quoted in *The Epoch Times*, the "United States socialist model is a cross between China's and Brazil's."[24] Likewise, the United States' diversity is similar to Brazil's population with a robust Black population. Communism is not new to Brazil, as their former President Luiz Inacia Lula de Silva, was a communist who "played those ethnic minorities off against each other, and he elevated some at the expense of others to bring about his revolution... But the ultimate model is the Chinese model."[25] One could ask who would desire to bring such horror to a people and why? The American elites and globalists are infatuated by the Chinese model that establishes an "authoritarian state" to maintain total control, resembling a slave-master relationship over its workers, while the wealthy can still sustain their wealth.[26]

These tactics and applications are recognizable in the spirit of the Black Lives Matter (BLM) movement. In 2015, *The Real News* had interviewed the co-founder, Patrisse Cullors, who by her own admission stated: "We actually do not have an ideological frame. Myself and Alicia, in particular, are trained organizers. We are trained Marxists."[27] The "Alicia" she is referring to is one of the other founders of BLM. Apparently, in May 2021, Ms. Cullors resigned from the BLM Global Network Foundation over a scandal, after being exposed for personally spending $3.2 million on four homes in several states.[28] As the Word of God proclaims, "evil men and seducers shall wax worse and worse, deceiving, and being deceived" (2 Timothy 3:13).

Today, we are exposed to the same mind-bending methods of wealth redistribution through raising taxes on the wealthy, while taking less from the lower-income class. The first signs of this movement began in 2011 with the Occupy Wall Street movement, which was an indictment against America for the unfair economic practices and social injustice. Now, we hear politicians agreeing to give money for more welfare programs, while raising corporate taxes and reducing the military budget. When this happens, corporations depart America, causing middle-class to shrink, creating more lower-income earners. The middle-class will carry the burden for lost wages and higher taxes, because there still remains deep wells of exemptions for the rich to hide their wealth. It is a continuous cycle of lies and more promises which lead to more job losses and higher unemployment, which leads to more homelessness, drug addictions, and incarcerations. The deception is that the adherents of such a doctrine instigate a conflict by repeating the mantra: "the rich need to pay more in taxes." The goal of this Marxist tactic is to squeeze the life out of the middle-class with higher taxes. Look at it from this perspective: there are more Americans within the middle-class than there are millionaires or wealthier. Do you really think those in Congress promoting such rhetoric really want to pay more in taxes? Many of them are millionaires, which would seem to indicate most rich politicians prefer to tax themselves. Are these not the same people who voted a for themselves pay raise during the "plan-demic?" Think about it. Who would seek a pay raise, then turn around to say, "I want to pay more taxes?" No one would.

Be mindful: these are the same methods being used today by the Marxist/anarchist organization, Antifa (Anti-fascist). This organization was incorporated out of Germany during the 1930s by the Communist Party of Germany (KPD). Communist in nature, the members described the entity as a "red united front under the leadership of the only anti-fascist party, the KPD."[29] What the leftists Democrats won't tell you is how Antifa has a panting thirst to destroy illustrious American values and heritage. You might have witnessed the Communist fist emblem being used by members of both BLM and Antifa, beating against the sky during protests, symbolizing their tireless efforts to crush "fascism," which translates to crushing America, Capitalism, Christianity, Black people, and wealthy citizens. It is only a matter of time before the muscle will be unleashed on the African-American community after the "race baiting" has dissipated, and the racism has wedged a deep divide between Blacks and Whites. Unfortunately, the support that Black people have grown accustomed will be pulled from underneath them like a rug. Therefore, a day is rushing towards us, like a hungry tidal wave, when racial discord in this country reaches the levels last seen during the 1950s and 1960s.

America was introduced to these left-wing anarchists after they hijacked the peaceful protest over George Floyd's death as an ember to ignite their Communist revolution. Seen in videos, marching alongside African-American protesters, were mostly young whites, proudly wearing military-style black outfits. According to Jean Chen, a writer for *The Epoch Times*, "numerous social media posts and videos also depict African-American protesters objecting to rioting perpetrated by groups of white men clad in full black outfits- the black costume has long been associated with Antifa."[30] What is most disrespectful about their actions is the destruction that was unleashed by their actions, leaving Blacks blamed for the destruction. In Atlanta, several Antifa members set fire to fast-food restaurants which subsequently burned down. The media accused Black people for the destruction, because the Antifa hoodlums would blend in with the crowd, and then scatter to avoid the consequences. A group of Black men, armed with rifles, were interviewed and expressed their intentions to stand as a deterrent against Antifa's tactics. For over a year, these extremists have destroyed cities like Portland and Seattle, whose government's inability was exposed by the destruction of businesses and the hostile takeover of a district, creating an "autonomous zone."

Antifa is no joke. They are a Marxist tool for the left-wing Democrats to flex as their muscle and have already assaulted over five hundred cities. Indeed, it has become a sport to them to restrict citizens' ability to function, while they remain insulated within localized violence. Sadly, Democratic leader Nancy Pelosi had labeled their actions as being a "peaceful" protest. Antifa has destroyed cities, attempted to murder police officers by torching police departments and Federal court buildings, and assaulted the homes of conservative journalists. During the chaotic year of 2020, people's lives were put on hold, not just for COVID-19, but for fear of being harmed by these terrorists. It is a reminder of the lawlessness that occurred during the terror of the Ukrainian Communist Party (UCP), which was guilty of the mass starvation of more than 5 million Ukrainian citizens within two years. Dennis Prager, a political commentator, explains over 15 million Soviet citizens were rounded up and murdered for "the systematic stripping of people of their rights to speak freely, to worship, to start a business, or even travel without party permission," which creates the "near-poverty of nearly all communist countries; the imprisonment and torture of vast numbers of people."[31] Those starving people took matters in their own hands and desperately "ate the flesh of people, often children, sometimes including their own."[32] Believe it or not, our Lord and Savior, Jesus Christ, has afforded us the spiritual tools to discern the bench marks of deception, stained within the sinister playbook of Satan. America is on a collision course with these unlearned lessons of history.

Identifying Our Enemy

We delved into the Marxist doctrine to explore the intent behind the madness. What if you were invited to attend a social gathering with some friends, and you overheard parts of a conversation next to your group? Do you know how to identify a Marxist through their vernacular? Most people are unfamiliar with their phraseology and terminology. Marxists uses the key terms "socialist" and "communist" interchangeably, as well as the free use of the terms "revolution," "comrade," "fascist," "imperialism," "power," insurrection," "equality," and "fraternity." The CCP and Klaus Schwab's "fourth industrial revolution" describes their nefarious deeds as a "revolution" to enhance global "fraternity." Lenin had stated, "the goal of socialism is communism."[33] "Union" is another term used to describe a Marxist revolution to attain some form of gain. "Boycotts," "strikes," and "demonstrations" are all tools used to overthrow a body of authority, like the government.

In every Socialist-Communist government, there has been internal, factional fighting. You're probably saying, "But every political party has internal conflict!" I agree; however, there tend to be factions within both parties, at every level of government, that tend to lean more to the extreme than the party is willing to entertain. Socialism always pushes the envelope to tyrannical governance against the people they represent. It is comparable to cancer that "slowly eats away at people's freedoms through legislation," and it makes people "numb" until their rights are stripped to shreds.[34] The strategy Marx and Lenin promoted turned out to be tyranny disguised as a promise to achieve equality, distracting the people from focusing on their deprivation of freedoms, property, and morality. President Harry S. Truman said, "When people fear the government, that's tyranny. When the government fears the people, that's liberty." During a 1987 speech, President Ronald Reagan said, "How do you tell a communist? Well, it's someone who reads Marx and Lenin. And how do you tell an anti-Communist? It's someone who understands Marx and Lenin."

Battling The Propaganda Machine

In Romans, the Apostle Paul wrote the letter to the Roman house churches about the practical application of faith. The problem was that the Jews would hear the Gospel message, but would not believe, while the Gentiles heard the same message and would believe. Therefore, Paul placed the Jews "on blast" for their continued rejection of the truth. Paul writes, "So then faith cometh by hearing, and hearing by the Word of God" (Romans 10:17). The Greek word, *pistis*, means "to believe." Put another way, what you hear is pretty much what you will accept and believe, and how you perceive life is evidence of what you believe. What you believe is credited for how you live your life, but the question is, "Do you believe the messages from the servant of God is of the Lord?"

Jesus answered Nicodemus about the message from God that "verily, verily, I say unto thee, We speak that we do know, and testify that we have seen; and ye receive not our witness" (John 3:11). Are you like the Jews whom heard a Word from God and rejected it, or do you take an opportunity to listen to what is heard, then apply Scripture to test the spirit behind it? No matter the message, check the spirit of both the messenger and the message delivered for truth. "Beloved, believe not every spirit, but try the spirits whether they are of God: because many false prophets are gone out into the world" (1 John 4:1). For a lie will not stand forever, because it is prone to change, as it is weak, lacks integrity, and must conform to whoever is speaking it. However, the truth will stand forever. Jesus made this known by saying, "My word shall not pass away" (Luke 21:33). The truth, no matter who is speaking it, is bound by God, because it is not a lie. Those who deliberately deceive with propaganda, misinformation, disinformation, and the omission of truths are all liars. Jesus warned of those who mischaracterize facts:

Ye are of your father the devil, and the lusts of your father ye will do. He was a murderer from the beginning, and abode not in the truth, because there is no truth in him. When he speaketh a lie, he speaketh of his own: for he is a liar, and the father of it. And because I tell you the truth, ye believe me not (John 8:44-45).

We are living in desperate times. The last hours are counting down before the Rapture of the Church, and Satan knows the time is drawing near without knowing the day nor hour. "But of that day and that hour knoweth no man, no, not the angels which are in heaven, neither the Son, but the Father" (Mark 13:32). Therefore, Satan has corrupted many, as God has given them over to a reprobate mind. There is information Satan does not want people to know. He will twist, spin, and hide facts to deceive you as appropriate, even if that need is temporary and eventually exposed. In his eye, it was a "no harm no foul" situation, because he achieved what was sought. How does Satan pull the wool over the world? There are three effective methods that have never changed since the Garden:

1. **Propaganda:** "Any systematic, widespread, dissemination or promotion of particular ideas, doctrines, practices to further one's own cause or to damage an opposing one."[35]

2. **Disinformation:** "Deliberate false information leaked by government as to confuse another nation's intelligence."[36]

3. **Misinformation:** "the supple of false or misleading information."[37]

In March 2020, the *Media Research Center* measured the mainstream media's (ABC, CBS, and NBC) coverage of former President Trump. The results suggested the coverage was biased, with "94% negative," and "coverage reaching an unprecedented 99.5% negative in May."[38] It was reported that the networks' daily reporting was negative over 90% of the time. As Americans, we live in a country where the media is supposed to deliver the facts about what is being reported and allow the consumer to analyze the data to make our own decision. What is seen in the news today meets the definition of propaganda, while they avoid calling it that for fear that their proposed doctrines will be boycotted and sabotaged.

It is my understanding that the obvious anti-American agendas were designed by Satan to eliminate President Trump before his presidential campaign was even announce to the nation. President Trump did not have a chance, based on the Senate's investigation which proved that the Obama Administration was in cahoots with the FBI. The illegitimate investigation was enforced within minutes of Trump taking office. Thus, the misinformation machine went into "manufacture mode" with accusations of him consorting with Russia, which proved all along to be a lie, but the narrative was spoken in concert by the various news outlets favoring Hillary Clinton.

I'm a firm believer in the idea to give credit where credit is due. If someone earns the giant clown hat for foolishness, then he wears it. Corrupt or not, everyone deserves a chance, particularly if it was earned. Thomas Sowell, a famous economist once said, "some things are believed because they are demonstrably true, but many other things are believed simply because they have been asserted repeatedly."[39] I refer to the Communists, the Socialists, or the Marxists interchangeably, for they are all the same. The reason why many Americans shake their heads with disbelief regarding the socialist propaganda is because it is a challenge to discern its true intentions because of it being disguised as political correctness. We see the media using political correctness as a weapon "to attack our moral discernment and artificially force everyone to be the same."[40] Socialists claim to be an advocate for the voiceless poor, much like the Chinese Communist Party labelled themselves as the "savior" of the people. A much more accurate statement is they are the oppressor of the people.

How Biden Won, Or Did He?

During the 2020 election, America was arrested by a constitutional crisis in the most contested election in our country's history. Millions of Americans have doubts about the true outcome of the election, and only time will reveal the truth. What is mysterious, according to *The Epoch Times*, is that Joe Biden won 81,000,000 votes, but the statistics showed something was erroneous with this number.

Obama Victory

Biden had somehow won more votes than the first African-American President during one of the largest Black voter turn out in U.S. history, who had 69,000,000 votes. Obama won 396 more counties than Biden. When looking at the normal "token" states of "Florida," "Ohio," and "Iowa," Obama won them.[41]

Trump Figures

It was the greatest turn-out for a sitting president in history, with over 74,000,000 Americans had voted for Trump during this last election. However, here is where the overall math does not agree with Biden's victory. For example, the number of counties a President must win are always greater than his opponents. ALWAYS. When Biden won, Trump had acquired 2,020 more counties than old Joe Biden. Just like Obama, when looking at the normal 'token' states, Trump, likewise, won them.[42]

Biden's Victory

People tend to ignore the historical validity that voter statistics does verify a victor in any election. During the election, Biden only gained 477 counties. And he lost those same token states, yet somehow still won the election.[43]

Democrats: Instigators of Racism

Even in America, the challenge of racism is seated within the Democratic campaign's weaponizing of racial stereotypes against whites, while simultaneously accusing the conservative base of racial intimidation by requiring voter ID. Contrary to belief, African-Americans are not placed at a disadvantaged because of these new laws in Texas, Florida, Georgia, and Arizona. I'm confident the contesters of those voting laws have never read the Democrats HR 4 Bill nor read the states' legislature bills. I challenge everyone to acquire both and compare them. You would be surprised at the amount of misinformation being pumped into your brain.

I take an offense to the Democrat's claim that implies African-Americans are perceived as incapable of obtaining identification to vote. This is a lie from the devil. This idea makes Black people appear intellectually deficient or inferior, which is far from the truth. Black people love to travel, which requires a photo ID to fly, procure a hotel, bank account, purchase a car, register a vehicle at the DMV, etc. I can go on and on. Finally, in his book, *The Enemy Within,* David Horowitz's exposition on the subject was a breath of fresh air, in total alignment with my belief towards voting and the Democrats. Horowitz explains that such allegations made by the Democrats "is not only false, but patronizing to disadvantaged Blacks... the Democrats' disingenuous claims are also refuted by the fact that minorities have been registering to vote in record numbers, including in states that have introduced ID requirements to prevent voter fraud."[44]

I do not know of any Black person who votes that believes they are being disenfranchised. If anything, we need to make sure the people who are ineligible to vote are not voting. There is substantive evidence from several states that ineligible voters had a field day during the 2020 election. Again, the Democrats are using African-Americans as a cover for their diabolical Marxist agenda, and it is harming Black people in general. This propaganda is lies fueled by racial undertones, sponsored by these supposed "progressive" Democrats. Suggesting that Black people are at a disadvantage to attain an ID is comparable to stating that Blacks are only travelling by horse and buggy! Absurd, right? Any fallacious claim is absolutely degrading and ridiculous! One author writes, "[m]any journalists [and politicians]... push their narratives with lies, or partial truths, or insinuations, or misleading statistics. They exaggerate certain things, while intentionally omitting other things."[45] A 2021 Monmouth poll identified 84% of Non-Whites, 62% of Democrats, and 56% of Self-identified Liberals favor 'voters photo IDs.'[46]

Again, I cannot fathom how many African-Americans hear this nonsense and believe it! They do not research the validity of these "facts" quoted by politicians whose claims fall just short of the threshold of truth. The problem is rooted within the method of acquiring facts from a single partisan news source.

It is in the Script

During the first century, our modern electronic sources of entertainment did not exist for viewing classic shows or new release movies. In Jesus' day, people would attend theaters, known as sepphoris, for leisure. In Matthew 6:2, Jesus taught the disciples about quiet giving, to not "sound a trumpet before thee, as the hypocrites do in the synagogues."

As young preachers, it was important to understand it was unnecessary to be flashy, just to seek attention from the people. Jesus uses the term, *hypocrites*, which in the Greek means "an actor." Actors had a great responsibility to demonstrate current events as a way to educate spectators, but also to manipulate. Thus, it was not uncommon for plays to portray murders, rapes, violence and other iniquities as an attempt to desensitize the horrors exposed in the rise of crimes in their communities, and this process was used to brainwash people to be more patriotic towards imperial worship. For centuries, communities have practiced using entertainment to influence its citizens to honor their emperors and kings, hoping to prevent any uprising. Shows depicting the ruler as "for the people" made people less likely to challenge him, and citizens were then more motivated to emulate the ruler, rather than create factions to overthrow him.

World War II was a period of patriotism. Movies were created as a method to brainwash citizens to view the war effort in a positive light. In the 1980s, it was common for Hollywood to create movies with the Soviet Union as antagonists, like *Red Dawn* or *Fire Fox*, as a method to condition Americans with the possibility of WWIII. The Cold War era produced patriotic films that are now rarely made in the 21st Century. America's military then was much more robust than today's, and more people were interested in serving their country as a duty to protect our liberty and freedom. I remember one recruiting commercial that aired on Saturday mornings, singing the U.S. Army's then-motto "Be all you can be, in the Army." After the singing, it would show a scene where a Soldier sat in the woods and greeted his First Sergeant, while sitting and eating some nasty field-rations for breakfast.

In the 1990s, we watched shows that viewed homosexual activity negatively, and sex scenes were slightly uncommon. In the mid-2000s, violence and sex scenes became more and more prevalent. You can now watch a show rife with profanity and sexual overtones during primetime slots. In 2016, primetime shows became bolder, showing more nudity with sex scenes, while homosexual relationships became more open, particularly in movies.

Today, there appears to be homosexual sex and witchcraft on every television show and movie. Why? There are some who would contend that in order to enact social change, it is necessary to socialize taboo behaviors as a norm. Moreover, what better way to reprogram children and young adults to accept these deeds as a "new normal?" Some producers appear to have a lack of concern as to whether or not children are watching. The same goes for the commercials that advertise HIV drugs, displaying same-sex couples showing public displays of affection. There are even shows that glamorize transvestitism that confound even mature adults.

On the other side of this coin, I have noticed there are more biracial (African-American and Caucasian) people of lighter complexion on television commercials, which is a good thing. There is an increase in interracial relationships being displayed, so that it will be more acceptable in society. However, African-Americans of a darker complexion are seen less in commercials, including representations of the Black family unit. There are more interracial family units of White men with Black women than there are of Black men with White women. Again, this depiction is not an issue. I asked several African-American males if they have seen any difference, and I was shocked by their answer. The majority of the men were perplexed, particularly about the increase in biracial actors over people of darker complexion. A few noticed there were fewer, dark-skinned Blacks seen in a family dynamic. Of course, if one were to watch Black Entertainment Television (BET), one would consume predominately that demographic.

Why does this matter? It is the packaging of the message that influences society to believe that this is normal, especially those in rural areas who are unfamiliar with a demographic of people who look different from themselves. What is happening seeds are being planted to spur curiosity, and this disarms the stereotypes people may harbor about others. For instance, most will agree these commercials have been effective, according to Nelson Oliveria, 24% of singles are "now more open" to interracial dating, since George Floyd's death, and there has been an overall "58% increase among interracial dating in the past 10 years."[47] Therefore, if the media pushes a particular narrative long enough, people will begin to alter their psychology to match that narrative. This is exactly the tactic Satan used in the Garden against Even to shift her God-centered view to an ungodly-centered view.

Hypothetically, if I claim that Hollywood's motives are racist, because of the implied alienation of darker African-Americans in favor of those lighter complexion in commercials, and I repeated the misinformation enough, people will accept my assessment as fact. The entire conversation will devolve into a "scandal" about the elites in Hollywood secretly wearing "black face." It's just that simple, if I was evil and wished to be a false witness. Those men could easily have been misguided and subsequently manipulated into believing there was an attempt to silence the voice of Black America by validating "mixed people" over "Black people." Spreading allegations to influence others deep into the pit of deception, as well as causing damage to the integrity of Black identity, is evil.

The point to be made here is the focus on deceptive practice, such as conflicting the English lexicon as a part of the Marxist propaganda machine, thus integrating this machine as a parcel of the Progressive Left. Marxist sympathizers have exercised, as Catherine Yang contends, a "time worn tactic that if you say something often enough people will come to accept it."[48] When the media began their accusations towards former President Trump about racism, it was confusing, because the "media didn't have to explain his policies or instances of racist error, all they do is repeat 'Trump is a racist' until it [stuck]."[49] Now, we must filter the messages that are disseminated from the propaganda machine (the mainstream media) through truth and analyze the true meaning, according to Yang as:

- The **"Green New Deal"** (it is only a crisis-mill designed to harm citizens),

- **"anti-racist training"** (a program that only further encourages racist behavior), and

- **"Health Care"** (which has more to do with the termination of life through the use of euthanasia (assisted suicide) and abortion than anything to do with your health).[50]

My point is that not everything that you see or hear presents you with the reality of these things. It is important to check the spirit of everything presented to us to ensure we abstain from partaking in the sins of others. Therefore, always ask yourself and others the following questions:

1. How do you know this to be true?

2. What evidence or research do you have to substantiate your claim?

3. Did you test your opinion on multiple sources, definitions, and historical facts, instead of maintaining a partisan hard-line?

4. Did you confer with other races, genders, mature adults, alternate political affiliates, and people of diverse socio-economic status regarding their perspectives?

If you constantly ask yourself these questions as you consume the media around you, you will find it rather hard to be led astray. You can also apply this method to conspiracy theories. Michael Shermer, Ph.D, presidential fellow, and author, was quoted in *Popular Mechanics*, queried "How many people would have to be involved in covering up a given conspiracy? The larger the number, the less likely that the cover-up exist;" and Shermer further suggested, "a conspiracy theory concerns two or more people plotting in secret to gain an immoral/legal advantage over someone else."[51]

The Merchandise is You

As an African-American man, I'm troubled by the amount of deception done to the African-American community over the past decade. It seems to me that not many people are vigilant enough to discern the flagrant disrespect and deception spread throughout the community. Traditionally, though, Black people have been ignored when we are deemed "useless," yet when a crisis or an election necessitates it, Black people are dusted off the shelf and utilized as a potent weapon of ignorance. You can witness this during an election period and candidates pander for African-American votes, while never doing anything in return for our community. For example, Baltimore, Maryland, is predominately African-American with one of the worst school systems in America. 41% of Baltimore high school students have a 1.0 grade point average. Baltimore has been in the clutches of the Democrats for decades, and the children are suffering for it. Democrats present themselves as a savior of the Blacks, yet their cities are in chaos, due to a leadership malfunction, which deprives the city of any ability to solve the high crime rate eating away at the core of hope and the heart of the city.

Another sign of the racist disregard for Blacks is seen at the border. Did you notice how thousands, upon thousands of South Americans have bomb-rushed our southern states, thus allowed entrance – processed – routed to military installations, as reported by new outlets, illegals were then transported in the concealment of night, to cities within the interior of America. But when thousands of Haitian refugees did the same, every news outlet treated the story as an emergency. Even the White House spoke of the episode as an urgent matter to return them home. Many politicians agree with this observation, calling out the Secretary of Homeland Security and old Joe to stop the deportations – thus demanding that the Haitians are afforded similar treatment as the Hispanics. I tell you; when the story was released, the Democrats actions gave inference Hispanics qualify to enter America, but not Blacks. Did you hear of any celebrities being applauded in the Black community over Washington's response?

I want to reiterate here: Blacks are not intellectually deficient! When we are informed, Blacks take action. A great example would be the Civil Rights Movement, which you recall was facilitated by the Church. People just do not pay attention to sound information. However, the problem of being ill-informed allows us to be deceived in staggering ways, something for which many Black folks would, in haste, repudiate. What I'm witnessing now poses great danger and can destroy the gains made by the brave men and women of the past. Right now, African-Americans are little frogs in a pot of slow-boiling water. The late President Ronald Reagan once said, "It is weakness, not strength that tempts tyrants."

A lack of awareness is evidence of weakness. When nefarious groups decide to control citizens' behavior, they usually do this by controlling information through media blackouts, keeping people psychologically and morally suspended in the abyss of ignorance. Hence, this calculated effort will inevitably create the conditions that ultimately will influence people's behavior and decision-making. Imagine they are taking a spiked club, made of historical pain and suffering, and using it to beat the backs of our community with the misrepresentation of facts to arouse a familiar feeling of oppression. Racism still exists. Hate still exists. Liars still exist. Police brutality does exist, though not at the levels being represented to the country. Again, all these false narratives are designed to place people on edge, while those who are using this misinformation for their own gain already know people are too lazy to search for the truth.

People cannot forget that America has experienced two Black Presidents within a decade! We are not even talking 20, 30, 45, or even 60 years ago; although back then, America would have likely entertained those voices of hope, but could not stomach the reality needed to create it. Surprisingly, some members of my family do not see it. Friends do not see it. People in my fellowship fail to see it. Many Americans deliberately drop their heard or close their eyes as ignorant Americans. Perhaps, it would be useful to borrow the term, "useful-idiots," a moniker coined by Vladimir Lenin, and is defined as an "ill-informed people, subsequently manipulated by 'socialists' to support lawlessness in cause'."

What does it serve for a faithful collective body of instigators to adhere to plantation politics? I will tell you: it begins with the good ol' Democratic Party. Remember, this is the party of Lyndon Baines Johnson (LBJ). According to Tod Strandberg, the President was once overheard on Air Force One describing African-Americans as "uppity Negros," because they wanted systematic change with the 1964 Civil Rights Act.[52] LBJ "created the Great Society to bribe Blacks into voting for his party," thus offering, as Johnson puts it, "just enough to quiet them down, not enough to make a difference."[53] After pausing for a breath, he said, "I'll have them (n-word) voting Democratic for two hundred years."[54] The Democratic Party is the party of segregationists. It is well documented that Joe Biden was one; Kamala Harris has alluded to this fact during her debates against Biden during the Democratic nomination process. In addition, it was the Democrats who voted AGAINST the 1964 Civil Rights Act and 1965 Voting Rights Act.

Before you label me as an Uncle Tom, Republican, conspiracy theorist or whatever please know that I'm a Christian, highly-educated Black man, who has served as a military officer. I admit to voting in 2008 for former President Barack Obama as an "independent," because he looked like me. I'm not a Republican, just a conservative African-American man who loves my Lord and Savior, Jesus Christ. I hold a biblical worldview and believe America is the greatest country in the world. If America wasn't the greatest country, then why do millions of people sneak into the country annually? Despite the enormous historical imperfections that embrace this nation, she is a blessing. Thus my military career had afforded me ample opportunities to experience other nations. And by far, there is no other country greater than the United States of America. Still, whenever I listen to the Star Spangled Banner, while simultaneously enjoying fighter aircraft screaming across the sky - I cry. Meanwhile, my heart aches for allowing myself to be hoodwinked into voting for a worthless Democrat - Barack Obama.

For me, this deception arose back in 2008, when the Democrat Party was preparing an aggressive presidential campaign for this vibrant, intellectual civil rights lawyer, and Illinois State Senator from Chicago, named Barack Obama. I was impressed by his swagger and, most importantly, the fact he professed to being a Christian, especially after the mainstream media "skull-drug" his pastor, the controversial Revered Jeremiah Wright, for comments made while preaching. Most of my African-American friends, whom were also officers in the military, were voting for Obama for the same reason. Because I was ill-informed, all the negative press just moved the needle closer for me to vote for this Democrat who apparently came out of thin air. I thought all the derision was racially charged, as politicians made sport of him, accusing him of being a secret Muslim. In my mind, and other African-Americans' minds, how could he be a Muslim after he professed to be Christian, especially after the media showed the Obama family sitting within spitting distance of Reverend Wright.

However, I vividly remember when my view of President Obama began to shift unfavorably. It was my time as an Assistant Professor at three universities, two of them being Historic Black Colleges and Universities (HBCU). The first red flag came to me, as one day, I was lecturing at a state-funded HBCU that was worn-down, and wondered why the government wasn't pouring as much money into this "state" school as it was non-historical Black Colleges. The second red flag was developed when the President had cut the military budget while we were still fighting two wars. I could not believe there were service members deployed downrange, risking their lives, while their families were on welfare. President Obama had failed our Soldiers.

Third, before the Great Recession hit, there was a lot of people who had made a great living, with salaries in the range of $60,000, in the manufacturing, steel, and coal industries. These jobs disappeared after President Obama yoke America with the Paris Climate Accord. All the manufacturing jobs in those industries went overseas to China, with China turning around and selling those goods back to America. It seems you cannot buy anything without a "Made in China" label. I will never forget after President Obama said with a straight face, "manufacturing jobs will never return." I knew something was wrong when millions of other Americans expressed their disapproval of his actions by the results of the 2016 election. Again, President Obama failed.

In Matthew 7, Jesus teaches the disciples how to discern when a person claims they are one thing, when in reality, they are something else. In Matthew 7:16, Jesus asserts, "ye shall know them by their fruits. Do men gather grapes of thorns, or figs of thistles?" A person's character will testify either for or against them Jesus further explains, "[e]ven so every good tree bringeth forth good fruit; but a **corrupt tree** bringeth forth **evil fruit**. A good tree **cannot** bring forth evil fruit, neither can a corrupt tree bring forth good fruit" (Matthew 7:17-18). Let's put the kick-stand down here, and establish what is classified as the evil fruit Jesus is referring to, while looking at the actions President Obama took while in office:

- He was the first President to officiate a same-sex marriage, despite the clear view on this in the Bible;

- He was the first President to quote passages from the Quran, instead of the Bible;

- He said the Islamic call to worship was "the most beautiful sound on earth;"

- He declared that America was no longer a Christian nation;

- He allowed transgenders to use facilities of the opposite sex they were born, implying that men and women were not created as God intended;

- He lit up the White House in the colors of the rainbow in support for the LGBTQ community; and

- He maintained political stances that were hostile to Israel, God's chosen people and a long-time ally of America.[55]

As Jesus stated in Mark 13:33, "take ye heed, watch and pray: for ye know not when the time is." We must pray for our country and its leaders, now more than ever.

CHAPTER 5

CANCEL CULTURE IS CULTURAL MARXISM

Congress shall make no law respecting an establishment of religion or prohibiting the free exercise thereof; or abridging the freedom of speech, or of the press; or the right of the people peaceably to assemble, and to petition the government for a redress of grievances, the press; or the right of the people.

- "First Amendment," U.S. Constitution

On July 11, 2021, the world was inundated with videos of people flooding the streets in Cuba, demanding to be loosed from nearly 60 years of oppressive communism. Frankly, this situation gave the United States a sneak peek of the fate that awaits it, after the iron hands of communism have squeeze the juice of liberty from it. The protests highlighted the depressing facts of continuous food shortages, a lack of proper medicine, and deplorable living conditions. During the coronavirus crisis, it was reported vaccines were non-existent and medical personnel were subcontracted abroad in exchange for monetary support. We cannot understand the life of Cubans in a communist state, unless we understand how no one can escape the elephant in the room: widespread food shortages and oppressive rules. It is reported that every citizen is allocated a minuscule portion of rations: a half-pound bag of beans and rice, two pound of sugar, and one pound of brown sugar. Children under 7 receive condensed powdered milk. However, red meat is illegal, as cows are only designated for dairy.

Betrayed, the people of Cuba had enough, and began carrying American flags in the streets, fighting against the plainclothes authority that symbolizes the spirit of Marx and Lenin. Not long after international media outlets had reported the uprising, the Cuban government, with the help of the Chinese, restricted all Internet access to Facebook, Telegram, WhatsApp, and other messaging apps, reports Mimi Nghyen Ly.[1] Why? For the same reason Facebook and Twitter, with their 220 million users, have restricted American conservatism. When any message antithetical to the politics of the censors appears, it must be canceled, just like those liberty-hungry people shackled to a Marxist dictatorship. Organizations, like the Human Rights Watch, mention that any spread of information which harms the reputation of the Communist regime will subject the person to: "harassment, violence, smear campaign, travel restrictions, internet cuts, online harassment, raids on their homes and offices, confiscation of working materials, and arbitrary arrests."[2]

On July 14, 2021 Fox News reported Cuban police fired into the crowds and protesters died. On another day, a YouTube personality was allegedly apprehended during a live interview. This is just like the people who participated in the January 6, 2021, Capitol Protest, who were met by FBI agents kicking in their door and arresting them. The same thing has happened to the Cuban protesters. Imagine, the people in Cuba are being subjected to tireless forms of torture and who knows what else. There are images online that show secret police severely beating a man with batons in his home, then dragged and taken away to prison. Similarly, the January 6 protesters were also detained in a "secret" jail, without due process, until it was exposed by the media. Seven months later, our Justice Department has agreed to pay a firm $6.1 million to create a server, according to *The Epoch Times*, to "host the reams of data that prosecutors are gathering" against the people identified in the January 6 incident.[3] Excuse me, are we talking about America or Cuba?

Cubans in the United States were marching in solidarity with their kinsmen. They accused the Biden Administration of imperiously refusing to denounce the brutality of communism. Despite sanctioning the agencies within the Cuban government, (we do not know the effect these sanctions will have since Cuba has been sanctioned for 60 years) for suppressing the people's voices, it is one thing to provide statements that say: "America stands with you," but it is another to condemn the communists for their brutality. Instead, politicians have asserted to any Cuban refugees, "Do Not Come Here!" Why have the Democrats opened the Southern border, inviting "millions of people" from South American, but deny those living under horrific conditions in Cuba? The answer is the Democrats fear them, and do not want any of the Cuban refugees to speak out and draw a similarity between the Biden Administrations policies to those of Communist Cuba.

Other Democrats have outright refused to denounce the Marxist regime's inhumane treatment of their people. Instead, these Progressive-Leftists, awkwardly sing "We Shall Overcome" side-by-side with the derelict Texas Legislature Democrats, whom left Texas on two chartered jets, costing tax payers $100,000, in "protest." Again, why do the liberals refuse to speak out? They cannot admit the failure of Socialism-Communism. Any rebuke would jeopardize their attempt to pump Marxist ideology into the America tank of political capital, as well as an indictment on their handlers, communist China. Joe Biden does not want to sever any support from the Progressive-Left, even though many of them share the same ideology as the Cuban government.

Cancel Culture Analysis

"Cancel Culture" has been around since the fall of Satan; however, in the end-times, the world will be engulfed in deep delusions packed with apostasy and strife to levels never before experienced in our lifetime. Indeed, in the last days leading up to the establishment of the "beast System," there will ensue a great divide between fact and fiction. People will seek trends that corrupt what's good, consequently lusting for the bad. John James alluded to this and said, "people want good tasting poison over bad tasting medicine." In the end times, people will become intellectual zombies, chasing after rambunctious men who are professional, strategic, manipulators of facts.

These people are servants of corruption, strife-arsonists deputized by Satan to burn a path of discord between the world and the Church. They are of the same caliber as false prophets as, "For when they speak great swelling words of vanity, they allure through the lusts of the flesh, through much wantonness, those that were clean escaped from them who live in error. While they promise them liberty, they themselves are the servants of corruption: for of whom a man is overcome, of the same is he brought in bondage" (2 Peter 2:18-19).

Friend, I cannot assure you how much we will endure before the Rapture of the Church, but rest assured, the diabolical climate is getting hotter. Any time there are competing spirits there will always be envy and jealousy that systematically ignites fierce conflict. The Apostle John writes about this spirit,

> I wrote unto the church: but Diotrephes, who loveth to have the preeminence among them, receiveth us not. Wherefore, if I come, I will remember his deed which he doeth, prating against us with malicious words: and not content therewith, neither doth he himself receive the brethren, for forbidden them that would, and casteth them out of the church. Beloved, follow not that which is evil, but that which is good. He that doeth good is of God: but he that doeth evil hath not seen God (3 John 9-11).

Diotrephes was a leader in the Church who apparently lusted for power and disregarded the apostles' authority. Like any true leader, John needed to inform their church, that should he ever visit, he would not hesitate to confront Diotrephes for disparaging them with malicious talk. Not only was Diotrephes a slanderer, but he deliberately prevented or opposed people from speaking within the assembly of believers. Another example is within John 5, where the Jews sought to "cancel" our Lord and Savior for "calling God His Father, making Himself equal to God" (v.18).

Even the prophet, Micah, found himself in the center of the cancel culture of the seventh century B.C. He had to stand firm during a time when the secular culture had invaded the Israelite community. Micah's ministry preached God's message- a promise of salvation for the remnant of Israel, which contradicted the false prophets' message of "love" and "patience." Micah, being a man of integrity, spoke the truth, thus rebuking them for their wicked efforts to "covet fields, and take them by violence; and houses, and take them away: so they oppress a man and his house, even a man and his heritage" (Micah 2:2). Frustrated and angry, the false prophets were not going to hold their tongues, therefore foolishly voiced their desire to cancel God's messenger, stating: "prophesy ye not, say they to them that prophesy: they shall no prophesy to them, that they shall not take shame" (Micah 2:6). These men were vexed and did not want Micah to preach a message on God's holiness to the people! However, Micah was not shaken by their intimidation, because he was a man of holy confidence. There are many more examples throughout the Bible where "cancel culture" is used as a casual tactic of evil men. We can concede there is nothing good that comes from silencing a dissenting view. In doing so, you just prove there is something seriously wrong. It is no wonder why the Framers of the Constitution insisted on establishing Article 1 of the Constitution, as a means to prohibit abridging freedom of speech.

Cancel Culture

I remember the first time I heard the term, "cancel culture," used to describe the political jujitsu employed by the Democrats. We hear about it, but no one seems to have provided a definitive definition. What does this word really mean in context? To "cancel" something or someone is to "Destroy the validity; bring to nothingness; to strike out for deletion; and to remove."[4] Cancel Culture is censorship on steroids; an elusive device employed asymmetrically to annihilate ethics, history, traditions, religion, and according to David Horowitz, the "reputation of dissenting individuals."[5] Many victims have experienced professional isolation from various platforms and harassed to the threshold of depression.[6]

Historically, the perpetrator's goal is to crackdown on dissent to the point that information becomes scarce. Such behavior is anti-American and antithetical to the Founders' vision of their experiment of the blessed republic, the United States. Such radical ideology is processed and distributed through mainstream media and politicians, with "Big Tech" being the biggest threat to the First Amendment. Liberal media companies, such as NBC, ABC, CBS, MSNBC, and particularly CNN (with 914,000 viewers) are the original fake-news traffickers of all the cable networks. Twenty years ago, CNN was a trusted source of breaking news. Once Fox News joined the industry in the mid-1990s, Tod Strandberg affirms, CNN suffered the loss of over 80% of its viewership.[7] All of this was due to their liberal spin which alienated their larger demographic of conservative viewers. Throughout the years, most media platforms have bent to the left, resembling the "leaning tower of Pisa." Today, the delivery of the news from CNN and MSNBC have been compared to "Radio Moscow" during the 1960s as a "revolt against America's 243-year-old political system" consistent with Communist flavor, noted Horowitz.[8] During the 2016 election, CNN anchors' countenances fell as reality set in as their candidate was beaten by Donald J. Trump. I was concerned about them being seconds away from the hilarious "Two Minutes Hate" as depicted in George Orwell's novel, *1984*.

Within moments, the assault on America was unleashed by the censorship machine. After the election, whenever President Trump spoke, a contradiction was released in an attempt to discredit his assertion. No matter what was said, the former President was made out to be a liar or just plain incompetent. It did not matter if there were sufficient facts to support the message. Do you recall a time when the media used "fact checkers" as a weapon to slander him as a pathological liar? 99% of the time, smiling reporters would emphasize that Trump's message "was debunked," "was false," or asserted that "what the President said was not true." Even months after the election, Trump made statements about the perilous times ahead for America, and the gears of the fact-checker machine would immediately crank out a contradiction.

Americans have short memories. During the summer of 2020, then-Senator Kamala Harris and Joe Biden were the first guilty parties to spread disinformation against Operation Warp Speed. Although their administration has since changed their irresponsible claim, the truth of the matter is that neither of them trusted the "Trump vaccine," just because it was Trump's plan. Now, the Biden Administration must take responsibility for planting the seed of doubt when people do not trust the vaccine, especially from the beginning where the now-President and Vice President had disapproved the validity of the treatment.

It did not stop there. Between CNN and Democratic politicians, it was weird to hear them quote the same talking points, to the letter, as if they were all reading from the same script. According to the Edelman Trust

Barometer poll, 52% of Americans do not trust the media, while 80% of Americans' perception of "the system," is a collection of "government," "media," and other enterprises that maintain an incapacity to cure the calamities which afflict America.[9] Another example of this distrust is that slightly over half of Americans dislike the Leftist media, because of their integrity deficit. Ivan Pentchoukov suggests, in Biden's first ninety days in office, the "evening news coverage" was 59% positive, compared "to Trumps' 11% positive coverage."[10]

Politicians have a major influence on the climate of cancel culture viewed during the evening news. During a rally in Los Angeles, California Congresswoman Maxine Waters held a megaphone, demanding her antagonists to "show up where we have to show up" and "create a crowd" to harass the conservatives, which means Christians, no matter the location. What person would provoke people to incite violence, causing innocent people to fear for their lives? It is evil, vindictive, and irresponsible for a seasoned politician to behave in such a manner. Ms. Waters was one of the main voices claiming Trump was an illegitimate president.

Senator Minority Leader Chuck Schumer, during a protest in front of the Supreme Court, angrily demanded the highest court of the republic to exercise impartiality in legal interpretation, because the shift of the political leaning of the court scared him. He exclaimed: "I want to tell you, Gorsuch. I want to tell you, Kavanaugh; you have released the whirlwind and you will pay the price! You won't know what hit you if you go forward with these awful decisions," recalls Julie Musto.[11]

Congressman Adam Schiff (I hope the Lord changes his heart) was caught in so many lies, deliberately misleading the public about facts to the Russian Collusion hoax. During an interview with CNN, Mr. Schiff testified to have seen "bombshell" evidence proving Trump's guilt. Surprisingly, after both Senate and Congress received declassified documents proving no such evidence ever existed, the FBI confessed there were insufficient evidence to even begin an investigation, let alone to obtain the FISA warrants required. On numerous occasions, Mr. Schiff continued to spread the same lies, as if to silence the president. Even after President Trump launched a series of text messages in his defense, Twitter, and its "fact-checkers," instantly flagged his messages. This made it look like Twitter and Facebook had superior sources than the President of the United States, despite his robust intelligence network. It doesn't make any sense!

However, after the investigation and documents were released, Trump's claim of being a victim of a "hoax" was true. Actually, the scandal was a result of crimes committed by Hillary Clinton's campaign. According to the investigation, a fake dossier was paid for by her campaign with the collusion of the White House, the FBI and the DOJ. These people were complicit, Musto argues, "for these slanders were the same people who had peddled (and were still peddling) the discredited 'Russian hoax' designed to undermine and destroy him. The analogy was exact."[12]

In the summer of 2020, Facebook and Twitter had initiated their assault on politicians, businesses, and the President. An Internet platform called Parler, a conservative alternative to Facebook, was denied access to its shared-server with Amazon for 90 days. Google, Facebook, and Twitter were flagging any conservative accusation about voter fraud or of the Biden's. It was purported their main goal was to silence the "MAGA leader" and his "supporters" in the 2020 election.

The Leftist mainstream media did everything they could to suppress details of Hunter Biden's laptop scandal which indicted his father, Presidential candidate Joe Biden, in things from corrupt business acquisitions to cash-in-hand Federal violations. Once Trump started to direct focus on the Biden's and the election, Trump's Twitter account was placed on suspension. From there, an immediate assault by the tech giants on the conservative base was so aggressive as to silence companies like "My Pillow", which many major chain stores have discontinued selling their merchandise.

After Trump's second impeachment, on January 18, 2021, Leftist Congresswoman Alexandria Ocasio-Cortez (A.O.C.) suggested employing a Communist method of "reeducation camps" in order to "reprogram" conservatives and their associated media outlets to a fundamental Democrat "political orthodoxy." Terrified, A.O.C. and her cohort wanted NewsMax, Fox News (with its 2.1 million viewers), and ONN eliminated from their platforms. Immediately, other new personalities began to question whether Verizon, AT&T, and Comcast should even host these news entities.

In the state of Washington and nationwide, there are camps in the middle of nowhere, surrounded by barbed wire, with warning signs, that are managed by the U.S. Government, and not by the Department of Defense. Perhaps A.O.C. is referring to using these facilities to embark on their wicked scheme. These people, like A.O.C., might believe their way is righteous, but do not realize that their deeds are in line with Satan preparing the way for his Beast System. Those involved are preparing to enslave millions of Americans not willing to concede in surrendering their liberty.

These Orwellian-Communist ideas insinuates their need to remove conservatives from their platforms, where they can no longer influence the population. Who would imagine that in 2021, the Democrats' methods resemble the "thought Police" in Orwell's novel?

In Orwell's book the Ministry of Truth handles every aspect pertaining to public media – news, entertainment, education, and the fine arts – much like how the Democratic Party and Big Tech now operate. For instance, citizens were afraid of being accused to what amounts to a "Thought crime," which was any act of sabotage, heresy, and deviation from the One-Party-State objective. No matter what, they are pushing the idea that a "Thought crime does not entail death: thought crime Is death."[13] How does anyone know what you're thinking, unless it is asserted? Twisting, bending, or plugging words into your mouth is pure evil. Calling someone a "racist" because their views are antithetical to yours does not meet that standard. It is not right to confuse American patriotism and Christianity for a method of supremacy.

For one, this anti-American attitude troubles me, considering I lost a friend in Iraq, and I suffered overwhelming stress due to the possibility of being killed every time I departed Bagram Air Base. To this day, memories about the numerous battles my unit supported within theater of operation are triggered by hearing of this destructive push by the Leftist. In Afghanistan, you cannot imagine the horror of hearing the gruesome back briefs, which detailed how some of our heroic men died during battle. I even remember several of my Soldiers begging me to take them off convoy security out of fear of death. Afghanistan, Iraq, Vietnam, World War II were fought for what? For Freedom. Liberty. These wars were fought for ungrateful anti-Americans to enjoy the liberty of ransacking the fabric of this nation. We fought so these ungrateful people can have the liberty to disregard those who sacrificed their lives and shed their blood. You know, God blessed this great republic as the city on a hill. Imagine, if America was not so great, there would not be such a mighty force attempting to destroy her, and what she stands for. You know why: "Blessed is the nation whose God is the Lord" (Psalm 33:12).

I personally struggle with these politicians who swore an oath to "protect and defend" America from her "enemies foreign and domestic." I love my Lord and Savior Jesus Christ, my family, this nation and her people, and if duty ever calls, it would be an honor to lay down my life for all four. No questions! Do you sense Americans are beginning to understand the upside-down-twisted intentions of the Left? If you take the time to listen to politicians and big tech, from Bill Gates to mainstream media, they will tell you everything that's in preparation to happen. What is being talked about reminds me of a twisted slogan in Orwell's novel that depicts the direction of misinformation and disinformation into conflicting views, like:

War Is Peace
Freedom Is Slavery
Ignorance Is Strength.[14]

These slogans show how the one party within the world of the novel flipped the definition of words to better maintain control of the population. Sound like anything you know?

In China, the late Liu Shaoqi, Chairman from 1959-1968, was a type of President Trump. No matter the time of day, *The Epoch Times* noted, Shaoqi suffered abuse, with the media blasting away at every meter of his credibility until he was finally removed, thus forcing him to die in isolation. After being cremated, China celebrated his demise with great social gathering as a tribute to those in power.[15] Shaoqi felt the wrath of lawlessness that eventually destroyed his life and drove China into being the most diabolical regime in the world. The same methods used to control Shaoqi was the same strategy Hitler exercised as the leader of the National Socialist Workers Party (NSWP) in Nazi Germany. He desired a way to control the people, which meant any control of the economy had to be heavily regulated. To accomplish this goal, industry leaders would fall into compliance through reinforced methods of intimidation, even deposing weak leaders for stronger NSWP members.[16]

Censorship was not foreign to Nazi Germany. Hitler used the "Brown Shirts" as brigades of young anarchists to limit and manipulate the information flow, through violence and intimidation, to silence his opponents.[17] It is not uncommon for Marxist-spirited leaders to import "tactics [that] parallels the often successful efforts to 'cancel' and 'shut down' public speaker by activists and violent actors as Antifa."[18] In 2021, John MacGhlionn explains, there were two respected biologists, Heather Heying and Bret Weinstein, who were viciously targeted, harassed, and censured for having integrity to speak out and questioned the coronavirus origin.[19] Every day, it seems there is something new that enables the government to tighten down on citizens. For instance, the Biden Administration has discussed restricting text messaging and social media activities of anyone labeled as an "extremist" or a "nationalist." Likewise, many within the Democratic Party has officially joined in the censorship attack on Americans.

Dinesh D'Souza mentions, on July 15, 2021, it was announce the White House partnership with Facebook to screen for conflicting COVID-19 and vaccine narratives that are spread through social media platforms. White House Press Secretary, Jen Psaki, boldly asserted: "We're flagging problematic posts for Facebook that spread disinformation."[20] She has since provided Facebook with a list of accounts to ban from all platforms.

History has taught us one thing, Socialist-Marxist regimes have the propensity for internal battles, and will, on occasion, figuratively, eat their own. For instance, Petr Svab of *The Epoch Times*, in July 2021, interviewed a well-known liberal journalist and CEO of DailyClout, Dr. Naomi Wolf, joined former President Trump in a class-action legal battle against Twitter, Facebook, Google. She wrote a story about the alarming discovery of documents, one from Moderna and another from the Food and Drug Administration (FDA) warning about potential Viral RNA (ribonucleic acid) products which may be "detected in waste water."[21] Wolf has a reputation for aggressively tackling tough health issues in the past against government entities on defective product and procedures for women.

It began on June 4, 2021, when Wolf's spouse, boldly exposed truths about funding being pipelined to the Wuhan Institute of Virology (WIV), through sources, such as EcoHealth Alliance funding, which is generated from the U.S. National Institute of Allergy and Infectious Diseases (NIAID).[22] Wolf explained to Svab, during which her spouse was on video exposing the "biography" of coronavirus expert, "Professor Ralph Baric." In his "curriculum vitae (CV)," it indicates having received millions upon millions of dollars to fund unbelievable gain-of-function projects in partnership with the infamous WIV with funding from the NIAID.[23] First, I must state that Dr. Anthony Fauci, Director of the NIAID, testified before Congress that his organization did not, in anyway, "fund any gain-of-function research referring to experiments that enhance viruses, such as by modifying them to infect a different species."[24] Obviously, Fauci's testimony was far from the truth. What really took place, as identified in Prof. Baric's CV:

> Several NIAID grants that have been disclosed as a source of funding for gain-of-function research in a 2015 paper co-authored by Baric. That paper described an experiment in which a bat virus spike protein that didn't work on humans was grafted onto the SARS virus, resulting in a new virus that was capable not only of infecting humans, but was also resistant to treatment. The research was funded by the EcoHealth Alliance group, which in turn received millions of dollars in funding from NIAID.[25]

Twitter reaction to this video resulted in Wolf's account being "deplatformed" in June 2021. Wolf noted that the media began to apply pressure through censorship by publishing "one-way" stories that labeled her as being "anti-vaccine." My question is: why would Moderna Pharmaceutical Company, the maker of a COVID-19 vaccine, publish on their website that the COVID-19 vaccines' mRNA is the "software of life?" Perhaps the most reasonable person would become concerned about the meaning and motive behind it. Whereas in reality, Moderna's terminology has a nefarious sound to it. Moreover, Wolf wrote on her Twitter account, calling "a COVID-19 vaccine a software platform."[26] The Bible teaches us that from the overflow of the heart the mouth speaks. I once heard a recording of the Moderna CEO stating that after vaccine inoculation, the human body becomes an "operating system." Here is a possible reason why; in the Massachusetts Institute of Technology (MIT), there is a growing field called bio-digital interfacing. The place is for people to "wear or ingest biodigital technology to monitor and enhance our health and lifestyle."[27]

During another posting on Twitter, Wolf was aghast by the findings, and stated that the waste of vaccination people should be "separated from general sewage," because of the spike protein composed by the body after vaccination. As recorded in FDA documents, there is a health hazard from the "shedding" of "gene therapy" through human waste, which could likely contaminate drinking water."[28] Wolf provides the

FDA's definition for "gene therapy" as "product that mediate their effects by transcription and/or translation of transferred genetic material and/or by integrating into the host genome and that are administered as nucleic acids, viruses, or genetically engineered microorganisms."[29] There are many questions wrapped around the transmissibility of the coronavirus and its effects. There is a quote from one of China's premier scientist, Jin Qi, who has declared the coronavirus "is very likely to be an epidemic that coexists with humans for a long time, becomes seasonal and is sustained within human bodies."[30]

Each week, it seems as though the level of surveillance around the U.S. becomes tighter and tighter. Beloved, the Chinese model of surveillance has been adopted by the Biden Administration. Throughout history, it has always been the bad guys who spy on their citizens and punished them for their thoughts. Even the Surgeon General, Dr. Vivek H. Murthy, spoke during a White House press conference about "Confronting Health Misinformation," writes D'Souza.[31] Murthy complained that social media was not doing enough to control the spread of misinformation.

In contrast, Dinesh D'Souza's criticism of the Biden Administration's role in the restriction of Americans, through its surveillance state agents in Big Tech, he writes:

> But what if the government, which is constitutionally prohibited from restricting speech, directs private corporations to carry out what the government itself is prohibited from doing? This is what's at issue here, no direct government restriction but government collusion with private platforms to achieve the same result.[32]

It took only seven months from the time of the inauguration to when the Biden Administration has admitted to spying on American citizens to establish their Marxist surveillance state. Such hypocrites. During the summer of 2020, both Biden and Harris were guilty for spreading disinformation, asserting they "did not trust" the Trump "vaccine;" now, all of sudden they have grown halos, and eagerly want Americans to trust the same thing they were adamantly against. How does the White House determine fact from fiction? Who defines it? What is the standard? It is obvious there is only "one" ideology that buttresses the one party standard: totalitarianism.

Facebook just sent you a new message:

Do you know anyone who is an extremist?

The answer might be you.

CHAPTER 6

THE GREAT RESET: BEAST SYSTEM RISING

And I stood upon the sand of the sea, and saw a beast rise up out of the sea, having seven heads and ten horns, and upon his horn ten crowns, and upon his heads the name of blasphemy… And they worshipped the dragon which gave power unto the beast: and they worshipped the beast, saying, Who is like unto the Beast? Who is able to make war with him?...And he causeth all, both small and great, rich and poor, free and bond, to receive a mark in their right hand, or in their foreheads: And that no man might buy or sell, save he that had the mark, or the name of the beast, or the number of his name.

-Revelation 13:1, 4, 16-17

"Welcome to the year 2030. Welcome to my city – or should I say, 'our city.' I don't own anything. I don't own a car. I don't own a house. I don't own any appliances or any clothes. It might seem odd to you, but it makes perfect sense for us in this city. Everything you considered a product has now become a service."[1]

These words were contributed by a Marxist named, Ida Auken, of the World Economic Forum (WEF), who provided insight into the new normal – where life as you know it, will no longer exist. Currently you are witnessing the intense "crisis building" that is necessary to bring their 2030 plan to pass. The full execution was determined at the Devos, Switzerland meeting in 2022 – whereas such changes will require an implementation of a national currency that is to replace the tangible US dollar to an intangible digital currency. Keep watch for China, from the rise to superpower status to an oppressive social scores as examples for other nations to emulate. Today, China has plans to implement a digital currency that is being proposed as the replacement for the U.S. dollar. Once that happens, it will not be long until America adopts the Chinese model as her new normal. Do you think it is possible, after 2025 people will begin to go from owning to renting and borrowing the least essentials, such as clothes?

Indeed all of this sounds like a nightmare, a conspiracy theory enlisted by some 30 year old, tin-foil-hat wearer living in his parent's basement. However the hair-raising words spoken by Ms. Auken is evidence to a diabolical 8 point plan, and was devised by the master-mind, Klaus Martin Schwab. According to *Wikipedia*, he was born in Ravenburg, Germany on March 30, 1938; the founder and executive chairman of the world-renowned **Devos Summit**, the World Economic Forum.[2]

Many people have not heard of this man, nor his plan, in an alliance with many global leaders (predominately millionaires, billionaires & politicians) such as Bill Gates, George Soros, Prince Charles and Joe Biden with the intent to establish the "Great Reset Initiative". In fact, do you know where Biden's presidential campaign slogan: **Build. Back. Better.** originated? He appropriated the slogan from a 2015 "United Nations Sendai Framework Risk Reduction" document adopted by the G7 and WEF; and used it as a wink-and-nod certifying his dedication to the Great Reset agenda – a theme song to his presidency. In 2020 Dr. Schwab published excerpts from his Great Reset Manifesto, dictating the Reset, according to *The Epoch Times*, will be satisfied after "revamping all aspects of our societies and economies, from education to social contracts and working conditions" affecting "every industry from oil and gas to tech, transformed."[3]

According to Dr. Schwab the Great Reset, or **Fourth Industrial Revolution** (4IR) will be a forced assimilation into the Cultural Revolution. John MacGhilonn mentions that this revolution demands "every country, from the United States to China, must participate" in this plan.[4] What a bold statement coming from a German that appeared out of nowhere and resides in Switzerland. How can someone dictate to a sovereign country that has a robust constitution, and demand its participation in a scheme antithetical to American principles? I have pondered on this thought, and even considered: How will the antichrist be revealed? Like the author of Revelation claimed, "the beast rise up out of the sea"; which may suggest the beast may be less renown, however could he come from among the sea of successful people, nations or organizations (Revelation 13:1)? What concerns me is that in one of his observations, Dr. Schwab explains how the fourth industrial revolution will impact global governments.

Dr. Schwab predicts, under the Great Reset, a nation-state (government) is known as a "macro-power". During the Reset there will be a redistribution of power "from [the] state (macro-power) to non-state (micro-power) and from established institutions to loose networks."[5] You might ask: what is considered a non-state entity or loose-network? On the following page of his book, Dr. Schwab highlights the WikiLeaks debacle as an example of a "tiny non-state" which successfully contended with a powerful giant; plus, any entity that is identified as a macro-power has the potential of being dominated by a micro-power.[6] The bottom-line, a nations sovereignty, at any time, is in jeopardy of being overthrown during Dr. Schwab's "stakeholder" democracy (a fresh coat of paint for communism). When you read his book, the details are obscure because in certain parts of the book, Dr. Schwab quotes Karl Marx and R. Buckminister Fuller. The language used in context encourages a sharing economy (redistribution of wealth); Skynet (micro-chip in human brains); monitoring landowners (surveillance state); loose networks to seize power from nation-states; from recycle to up-cycle; social grouping and so forth.

In all, whenever he explains the impact of the fourth industrial revolution it is easy to get lost within literary eloquence of his prose. I'm convinced the Great Reset is the system Satan will use to establish his Tribulation kingdom. Many believers will transform into unconscious slaves by drinking from a steady stream of deceit. In Proverbs, the psalter insists, "When the righteous are in authority, the people rejoice; but when the wicked beareth rule, **the people mourn**" (29:2, emphasis added). Just as the cunning serpent, in the garden, persuaded the first husband and wife to buy into his scheme, it was all fun and games until the ecstatic deceit filling their bellies had dissipated; when the damage is done, it will be too late to change the life altering consequences.

I want to be clear; I'm not claiming, nor do I think Klaus Schwab is THE antichrist of the Tribulation. It is my bold opinion, he is a special agent whom Satan is using to facilitate the establishment of the initial phase, of the Beast system. When I was introduced to United Nations (UN), and the WEF agenda, the first thing that occupied my mind: What does "all" of this mean? In his book *The Fourth Industrial Revolution and COVID-19: The Great Reset,* Dr. Schwab describes, in-depth, how technology (digital revolution) will be the vehicle to usher in the "transformation of humankind."[7]

Dr. Schwab withheld not one detail explaining the Reset agenda, as it translated to the New World Order – Beast system. First, it is important to note, the beast system will convene once the antichrist is identified during the Tribulation (Revelation 13:1-18). I like to call this Reset the: *Abaddonist Society* (comes from the Hebrew name Abaddon which means destroyer) because the world has never encountered anything as evil as this destructive agenda.

Quite frankly, it is the gateway for the Beast to rule the entire world "and deceiveth them that dwell on the earth by the means of those miracles which he has power to do in the sight of the beast" (Revelation 13:14). In my bold opinion, I believe it is possible that the power that is described in the text will have much to do with "technology", considering the roll-out of quantum computing, with the interface of fifth Generation (5G) and Sixth Generation (6G). Further making it possible for some supernatural-type of capabilities that will allow for the Beast to rule, without much opposition. It appears that the global elites, so far, have had very little resistance for a global takeover – and example is the willfulness of people to lock themselves down despite losing their jobs and basic freedoms. It is when the freshest technology or App, rolls-out that people will easily relinquish their privacy for the latest gadget. It is possible that the Reset takeover will be easy and seamless. Interestingly, though, this scheme must intersect a variety of technological platforms that consequently generate paradigm shifts in every industry. Hence the grand scheme is visualized through an underlying intent to change, as Dr. Schwab suggests, "who we are…" and our self-concept through technology.[8]

Anthony P. Mueller, a professor of economic describes "the main thrust of the forum [the WEF] is global control. Free markets and individual choice do not stand as the top values, but state interventionism and collectivism."[9] You might ask - what is **collectivism?** It is defined as "the ownership and control of the means of production and distribution by the people collectively."[10] In other words, it is sacrificing your individual needs to accommodate the good of the majority. It sounds good - somewhat Christian; however this pertains to your livelihood, and welfare; from the food you eat, to your ability to have a family, and the way you worship Christ Jesus within the Communist construct. **No longer will you own anything,** because that is capitalism; to function in a collectivist world requires a dependency upon one entity (usually a communist government) but this will be surrendered to the Beast. What we are dealing with is "communism on steroids"; for instance, in order for Dr. Schwab's plan to work, capitalism must be a thing of the past.

Capitalism is defined as an "economic system in which all or most of the means of productions and distribution, as land factories, railroads, etc. are privately owned and operated for profit."[11] We are accustomed to capitalism being the backbone of America, yet envied by other nations like Russia and China. But in reality, the envy that has overtaken these nations is built upon a much greater scale – it is spiritual-in-nature. It is extremely important, thus, for believers to see matters for what they are, instead of being bamboozled by distractions.

George Orwell's novel, *1984,* gives us a sneak-peak into a socialist-communist world that is controlled by a system similar to the Great Reset. The evidence suggest, first there must be a revolution or revolt against something that represents a state of "oppression". A **revolution** is always in opposition to the alleged "oppressor". Orwell wrote: "It has long been realized that the only secure basis for oligarchy is collectivism. Wealth and privilege are most easily defended when they are possessed jointly."[12]

In a comparison, Dr. Schwab, with the Project MainSteam initiative, will facilitate the transformation of the world into a "circular economy" that will enmesh two humanist fields of study: "economics and psychology"; henceforth being a model to reprogram the world through an establishment of fresh universal values and ideas, aimed at reshaping enterprise models. A global community will greatly benefit from the shared commitment of this collectivist objective.[13] It is no longer about the importance of what you value; which is textbook socialist theory, where you're willing to surrender your personal desires for the fulfillment of the majority.

What is the Fourth Industrial Revolution?

Dr. Schwab defines *revolution* as simply "abrupt and radical changes" that has influenced societies throughout history.[14] Conversely, the justification for the Great Reset revolution is the same spirit that aligns with Karl Marx's philosophy, except with the institutional framework integrating technological innovation and individual. Dr. Schwab describes the fourth industrial revolution shadows the previous class of revolutions:

- First Industrial Revolution   1760-1840

- Second Industrial Revolution   19th century

- Third Industrial Revolution   1960-1990[15]

In another chapter, under the subtopic: *The Way Forward,* the fourth industrial revolution according to Dr. Schwab "may be driving disruption" that culminates from challenges that we will encounter, however they "are of our own making."[16] He admits to having no definitive answer as to where the Great Reset will lead; which is rather deceptive considering Dr. Schwab is the mastermind behind the movement. Yet, all throughout his book are explanations detailing how people's welfare and "living standards" will be affected for either the better or worse, as they are ushered in through the revolution's technological advancement.[17] The expectation presupposes that people will live longer under the fourth industrial revolution – live healthier and vibrant lives. With one exception, the "aging" population will be an "economic challenge" once their retirement age has been met.[18]

Considering the world population is projected to balloon to 9 billion people within two decades; there will exist more elderly than young adults to contribute to the employment pool and stabilize the economy with purchasing power. It is suggested the only way to mitigate any disruption is to increase the retirement age. Of course, for years this has been the discussion about the future of social security because there are more people reaping from the entitlement than investing into the program. However, Dr. Schwab suggests having a major jump in productivity that is driven by the "technology revolution" is the solution for people to contribute longer, while not working as hard. Likewise - when you hear that social security is on the verge of being bankrupt; just remember the plan is to keep the elderly productive by working. How is this so? When, as Dr. Schwab explains how those painful disruptions may cause a major "destruction effect" due to "innovation" and "automation" implementations, thus increasing unemployment.[19] At the time of this writing, the world is experiencing Schwab's destruction theory; where massive disruptions in logistics and manufacturing have caused major economic breaches. These breaches are contributing to incremental stages of inflation and scarcity being a token sample of the fourth industrial revolution.

According to the author, this revolution will create fewer jobs compared to any revolution in history.[20] One must ask, how can there be such exuberance for this fourth industrial revolution, notwithstanding this coveted technological revolution destroying millions of the middle-class?

Researchers from Oxford University studied hundreds of occupations within the next two decades which are at high risk for elimination as part of the technological revolution. Dr. Schwab suggests: "research concludes that about 47% of total employment in the US is at risk... characterized by much broader scope of job destruction (Real Estate Brokers, Legal Secretaries, Insurance Appraisers, etc.) at a much faster pace than labor market shifts experienced in previous industrial revolution."[21] In all Communist regimes, the middle class (or middle-man) is the target for elimination in order to forbear the total issuance of the Marxist system. In America "employment will grow in high-income cognitive and creative jobs and low-income manual occupations, but it will **greatly diminish for middle-income routine and repetitive jobs**," according to Dr. Schwab (emphasis added).[22] This is exactly what the Biden Administration has dedicated in their role as investors into the Reset. How is this "Build. Back. Better" initiative positive, when the plain-of-success is based upon the destruction of the (middle-man) middle class? Remember the middle-man is evidence of a capitalist society; which is a threat to globalism

Dr. Schwab said: You will own nothing in 2030

Earlier I mentioned Dr. Schwab had devised an elaborate, 2030 comprehensive, 8 point plan that will establish a global plantation. It is necessary to list them and provide a brief commentary that will translate certain aspects, with evidentiary signs to his global predictions. Kenan Kolday observes:

1. "You will own nothing… you'll be happy about it".[23]

You may, at one time, heard of immigrants whom divorced their parent country, often times escaping dangers to share in the American dream. They may have dreamed of owning a business that will sustain their families. Some may have dreamed of owning property or a home that was once impossible in their native country. Likewise, many Americans grew up being encouraged "if you work hard, one day, you can marry and have a house with a white picket fence." What is so significant about these dreams? It boils down to these opportunities exist for "everybody" who has the fortitude and the ability to achieve the goal of ownership. It doesn't necessarily have to be a home; it could be a vehicle that was purchased for the first time, and it is your possession. Well – it has been determined, in a decade, ownership will be a thing of the past. Unfortunately, Americans do not have a clue to what is waiting for them in a short period of time. When people are asked their opinion on the predictions prophesized by Dr. Schwab, often times their responses are dismissive out of disbelief. But in essence, their disbelief is the result of being uninformed. I'm a true believer: what you do not know can hurt you. Why is it important for us to have this 8 point plan? It is so we can consume the information to become stewards of sound decisions. When we know better, we do better – and make sound decisions that will ultimately change our lives.

At this point, many people will consider it important to inquire who will own these goods and services in this "sharing-economy?" Furthermore, who will manage the logistics of such a gross network? To rent goods, does the consumer need to accumulate enough points, let's say,

2000 points to rent a house; 500 point to rent furniture, and less points – for tooth paste and soap (3 points)? Is it possible that entities like Amazon, Wal-Mart, and other online platforms will provide on-demand system of production? To support this assertion Kolday reasoned, "what if they [WEF] do not let you rent anymore or increase the price?... What if you have to sacrifice your freedom to improve your credit history to continue" to survive?[24] For instance think about the resistance to the coronavirus vaccine ID, in Italy and France it is mandated for citizens to present verification of vaccination or else – be denied access to practically everything from buying groceries, entertainment, and working. Likewise, we have witnessed similar restrictive measures in America through incremental phases. At this rate, vaccine passport restrictions are seen gripping Europe, soon, America will desperately grapple; which is to be expected during the implementation of any communist program.

In my bold opinion, I believe by 2030 it will get to a point where the ability to rent will become impossible if citizens are out of tolerance. Dr. Schwab actually refers to this topic as part of the "sharing economy" and "leasing model" bearing the primary purpose of "making it easier to capture, reuse, and 'upcycle' materials" as applicable.[25] Think of this process like the rent-to-own stores where you sign a lease for a time. When you no longer desire the item, the service provider recovers the item and then it is repurposed. The item is reused by the next sharer in a revolving cycle which I like to call a "U-sharer".[26] In the novel *1984*, "individually, no members of the party owns anything, except for pottery personal belongings.[27]

You have to ask yourself, then how will this happen? The Schwabian –Orwellian spirit insist "Capitalist class were expropriated, socialism must follow."[28] The act of expropriate is to take something of significant value away from the people. Much was taken away in this communist world such as "factories," "Mines," "Land," "Houses," "transportation" – everything had been taken away from [the people]."[29]

Orwell's novel is spot-on with the current events of 2022 and likely in the following years. I must be clear and restate that I'm not a prophet – so I'm unsure of the future. Anything I suggest is based upon prayer, my appetite for eschatology, research of history, and current events to make any claim. I'm evidence based; thereby provide only facts to build this case, allowing you an opportunity to make your own decision grounded by substantive evidence. In all cases, take what has been presented, and conduct your own investigation for yourself.

You will not own Property

Remember in Chapter 4, the Vancouver Declaration defines land ownership as a major deficit which is seen, by Marxists, as standing between them and accomplishing their task of controlling the populous. Even Lenin's hanging order was about the wealthy farmers being perceived as an obstacle to the maturity of Communism. Indeed land ownership is a staple of capitalism; which is still an enmity to the collectivist dogma.

Based on what has been presented to you in this book, do you think the government will ever achieve Dr. Schwab's plan to confiscate U.S. citizen's land? Did you ever imagine in your lifetime a situation where America citizens would be forced to lock down and relinquish their liberty? I did not! Did you ever imagine pastors forbidden to have church service, to the point of being threatened with fines or confinement in 21st century America? I did not! Did you ever imagine the racial division manifest as quickly as it did in America, to the likes of 1960s? For one, I never thought it would happen in my life time – it has happened!

In June of 2021, Joe Biden issued a conservation plan embedded in Executive Order 14008, known as the 30x30 Land-Grab. Peter Svab, reporter for *The Epoch Times*, wrote the purpose of "tackling the climate crisis at home and abroad"… with the "goal of conserving at least 30% of our lands and waters by 2030."[30] Conservation plans are nothing new; the United States Departments of Interior, Agriculture, and Commerce are managers of these programs and currently has 12% of water and land in the program. A problem arose for the Biden administration, 15 governors have great interest and concerns with how the administration would achieve this goal of 30% of land by the year 2030.

On June 24, 2021, Svab had interviewed Nebraska Governor, Pete Ricketts. Mr. Ricketts explained that in April 2021, several governors forwarded a letter to the Biden Administration, to request clarification on why it is necessary to restrict private land, thus placing it in conservation? In the foreseen future any deliberate action will cause considerable harm to farmers and ranchers. The governors understood the long-term effects such an ambitious plan would generate. In the letter they explained, "we are deeply concerned about any effort to enlarge the federal estate or further restrict the use of public lands in our states… infringing on the private property rights of our citizens and significantly harming out economies."[31] The administration had provided a generic report that was insufficient; lacking any specific details able to quench their concerns. One thing is for sure, the Administration made it clear the 30x30 need no specified law to achieve the goals set by President Biden. Some believe the first attempt of the Biden Administration will be to inspire land owners to comply on a voluntary basis before the government takes matter further.

Notably, Svab's response to this approach was to assert: "To achieve the Biden Administration's goal of placing 30% of U.S. land under conservation, a chunk of land roughly the size of Nebraska would have to be added every year for nine years.[32] Governor Ricketts points out that 97% of land in Nebraska is privately owner. Agendas to accomplish the goals set out by the Biden Administration would likely destabilize these small communities in order to increase the federal real-estate by 2030. Listed below, Svab provides 3 distinctive courses of action accessible to the Biden Administration to achieve their 'Land-Grab':

1. **Eminent Domain.** Government right to purchase your (private) land for public use.

2. **Regulate.** Create an administrative gauntlet of restrictions to remove owners' rights.

3. **Cajolement.** Smooth talk and trick people into signing the dotted-line and relinquish their rights.[33]

Finally, Governor Ricketts asserted: "Your personal property rights are being eroded when the federal government has the ability to start regulating."[34] Under the Great Reset, citizens will no longer own any land – or anything that reflects the strength of capitalism.

It Will Cost You To Own A Vehicle

The Great Reset will require fewer owners of private vehicles in 2030. One might ask, how can this be done where millions of American drivers will have to relinquish their personal transportation through conformity?

Originally what came to mind was Germany and their social concept of vehicle ownership. Public transportation is widely used in the form of mass transit: commuter buses, trains (subway systems), taxis and very popular – bicycles. For one, the process for procuring a driver's license in Germany is an experience feat. Imagine paying, in the ball-park, a thousand dollars to learn and test for a certificate. Another challenge is that most cars are much smaller than American vehicles. The biggest reason for this is that the cost of fuel was then and remains outrageous compared to American standards.

I would like to use a quasi-socialist country for an example; hence in Germany gasoline is sold at the pump by liters; albeit in the early 2000s, a liter of gas was around $3 dollars. The average American citizen would be unable to afford to pay for, let's say, filling the tank of a 3-series BMW, which costs in excess of $200 for a full tank of gas. However the solution, Americans can purchase "gas coupons" at the cost, per gallon, at the American fair market value. This cost differential is made possible due to treaties that forbear any transfused tax from the German government over to U.S. service members and civilians.

My point – we may begin to experience such tax trends here, in America, to deter us from driving. Even though there is a push for electric vehicles to replace the traditional gas automobile, this does not mean that our government will not find some method to persuade its citizens to abandon vehicle ownership. Thus encouraging our citizens to utilize the money they saved to call an uber-driverless-cars to work. We must keep in mind the Resetter's goal is for you and I to own nothing – this includes privately owned vehicles. What else is on the drawing board that aligns with this evil - Dr. Schwab's prophecy? We do not have to look far – in *The Epoch Times*, Mark Tapscott mentions that contained within the Biden Administrations Trillion dollar "Infrastructure Investment and Jobs Act" is an authorization for Pete Buttigieg, U.S. Secretary of Transportation, to implement a federal pilot program, through the Department of Transportation (DOT), to "tax drivers for every mile driven."[35] The goal is to have volunteers subject themselves for a user fee. A fee that allegedly will be allocated towards the Highway trust fund to pay for infrastructure (roads and bridges).[36] Look – I can't stress enough, the Marxist signs are springing up like crabgrass again and again – all happening in increments until America bows-down.

2. "The U.S. won't be the world's leading superpower."

Here we are - COVID has caused so much suffering; where people have lost loved ones, careers disrupted, an estimate 3 million Americans at risk of being evicted because of a debt surge, and children suffering from emotional or psychological effects from peer-to-peer isolation. And now, if America hasn't been beat-down enough, the WEF has placed an expiration date on this Christian nation, claiming the world needs a change in leadership. There are several factors that contribute to Dr. Schwab's bold statement, as reason to dethrone America. In essence it is of no surprise to many prophecy watchers, for over 60 years the globalists and communist have expeditiously infiltrated every industry in America from academia, the private sector, and all the way to our government. Within the Abaddonist society, there is a desperate push to integrate a silent control-platform for the inaugural installation of a global plantation. Like any communist system; such as the early 1900s Soviet Union, the 1970s Poland, and the 21st century North Korea, all have panted, in ecstasy, for power over a naïve population. Thus every building block related to this scheme erects an hour-glass of categorical strongholds, soon to be instituted by some small fraternity of aristocrats, through the shaping of inadequate resource management.

Interestingly, though, Dr. Schwab made this bold prediction as part of the plan for the fourth industrial revolution; to develop a Geopolitical Reset. I'm amazed by how this global misery has been portrayed as the remedy to the "perfect crisis" for global elites to destroy capitalism and establish their communist utopia. *The Epoch Times* reports how Prince Charles believes COVID-19 is an opportunity to reset ourselves. While the Canadian Prime Minister Trudeau, believes the coronavirus is "an opportunity for a reset..." and to "reimagine economic systems that actually address global challenger like extreme poverty, inequality, and climate change."[37]

Now, the word "utopia" in its literal form means "nowhere"; in other words, whatever the fantasy is – it doesn't exist. When people speak of a utopia, they have self-induced themselves into ignorance, believing in a fictitious world; where every citizen is happy and every disparity is remedied and so forth. I compare this to believing that an Alice-in-Wonderland world can actually exist. In no form or fashion will that ever happen because it was a fantasy of the human mind. Again, what they champion does not exist, however, when Christ returns to establish His millennial Kingdom, the Edenic curse will be removed and earth will return to its natural state: the Garden of Eden.

Why is there a global demand for America to no longer rein as the world's leader? The answer to this question is broad, considering this mission was set in motion by globalist-communist alike between the Korean War and Cold War to erode the American structure inside-out. For one, we cannot forget about President Franklin D. Roosevelt's environmental plan called the "New Deal"; which is the inspiration to the Democrats Green New Deal (GND) – a chest of environmental legislation that is allegedly designed to tackle climate change. In 2019 the GND was made famous by Congresswoman Alexandria Ocasio-Cortez. Additionally it became the inspiration for the Biden Administration's $3 trillion-plus infrastructure bill.

Reason to Overthrow America

In his chapter *Macro Reset,* Dr. Schwab misrepresented the facts about China's global aspiration to rise as the world superpower. He said, "unlike the Soviet Union, China is not seeking to impose its ideology around the world."[38] What!? Are you kidding me? Where has he been for the last 5 years? In no way is Dr. Schwab's statement hyperbolic language or a misprint – it is absolutely a twisting of the truth. This claim, asserting the CCP has not been seeking to spread their demonic – ideology globally, is nothing short of mind-bending propaganda 101. Let's start in America; in their article "China's Boast Deliberate Plan to Take-over Steps to Overthrow America," Nicole Hao and Cathy He, revealed a nefarious plan delivered during a speaking engagement by Jin Canrong, a professor from the Renmin University, in Beijing, whom boldly prophesized that China will become the global superpower simply by: "interfering in U.S. elections, controlling the American market, cultivating global enemies… stealing U.S. Technology, and influencing international organizations."[39] Basically, this is called a soft-hit – when no one will hear the ideology but can see and feel the impact of the ideology in action. We must diligently look closer at the substance of any ideology that rests within its intent; ever since Biden has been in office the CCP has boasted of their 2030 proposal to leap-frog over America. Perhaps, meditate on this question; how can the CCP accomplish this objective without firing a missile? Of course, the Chinese communist are not flamboyantly holding above their heads communist banners in our cities. However we should ask ourselves, who is funding Antifa and which politician's palms are being adequately greased by CCP influence – money? Another example to debunk Dr. Schwab's statement, back in June of 2020, *Associated Press* reported Twitter had intercepted an enormous number of accounts, created by the CCP, disseminating steady streams of misinformation beneficial to the communist agenda.[40] More so, the CCP has spent millions of dollars to influence the young minds at our colleges and universities through their Confucian Centers. Many people do not know the history of Confucius, a Chinese philosopher in 479 B.C., and his ideology which is interwoven into the fabric of the CCP. We cannot forget about the continent of Africa; specifically locations that are trapped within the giant CCP footprint. One particular nation is Ethiopia (known as little China) which regularly prints a communist newspaper courtesy of the CCP. In fact, this African nation prides themselves because of the enormous investment made by the CCP has endowed them with technological advances that surpass any of their neighbors. With the sustainable investment and pipeline of money, China has ultimately entrapped them into an economical slavery.

Is it possible that Dr. Schwab may have been deceived with misinformation pertaining to these activities? The likelihood of this happening is very low indeed. We should understand that Marxist do believe their deeds are righteous. The Bible even affirms this claim, as it says, "there is a way which seemeth right unto a man, but the end thereof are the ways of death" (Prov. 14:12). The "end thereof" is the seed of deception that is planted in the hearts of those who walk in step with the Great Reset.

Let us evaluate some of the reasons, according to Dr. Schwab, why America will not be the leading superpower:

Nationalism

The definition of nationalism or nationalist depends upon the flavor of news one consumes or their worldview. I have heard nationalism being compared to white supremacy or some form of dogma that spurs hate. It is my earnest opinion, with urgency, to establish a definition for nationalism as a patriotic identity upheld by someone that is willing to defend the integrity of a national independence. A nationalist is someone

who is dedicated to support and defend the policy of national independence (such as the U.S. Constitution).

In contrast, globalism seeks an interdependence of world nations in
cooperation of resources, education, wealth, finance, service and trends.
Apparently it has been and continues to be the belief that a globalist
serves as a stepping stone – to successfully overcome global hunger and
homelessness. What these globalist forget is that American, a capitalist
nation, is the most generous, among all of the wealthiest nations, to spend
tax dollars to improve impoverish countries. The globalist absolutely hate
nationalism; but why? We can think back to the founding fathers of this
experiment called America; for it was by the grace of the One true living
God for a Republic structure of governance, to be a blessing to the people. Patrick Henry stands out the most in which he said:

An appeal to arms and to the God of hosts is all that is left us!...
Sir, we are not weak if we make a proper use of those means
which the God of nature hath placed in our power... Besides,
Sir, we shall not fight our battles alone. There is a just God who
presides over the destinies of nations, and who will raise up
friends to fight our battles for us... is life so dear, or peace so
sweet as to be purchased at the price of chains and slavery? Forbid it, Almighty God! I know not what course others may take;
but as for me, **give me liberty or give me death!**

Even past presidents spoke on the relevancy of nationalism because
of how synonymous it is to being a Christian. George Washington mentions: "It is the **duty** of all nations to acknowledge the providence of Almighty God to obey His will, to be grateful for His benefits, and humbly
to implore His protection." John Adams maintained a nationalist view of
America as being Christian, and he said:

We have no government armed with power capable of contending with human passions unbridled by morality and religion...
Our Constitution was made **only** for a **moral** and **religious people.** It is wholly inadequate to the government of any other.

The strength of America is the result of the blessings given from our
Lord and Savior Jesus Christ. The Founders intent was for America's

Constitution to be a reflection of our reverence to God, through our Christian faith; which has paved the streets of influence for centuries by establishing schools in China, hospitals in India, and seminaries in Africa; while all in some form, has reaped the endowments handed down from Heaven. The foundation of America, the Great Reset objective is to demand Americans to shift their beliefs in God for an atheist, nation-state government as their god. In Matthew 6:24, Jesus warns believers that no man can serve two masters. He said, "for either he will hate the one, and love the other; or else he will hold to the one and despise the other. Ye cannot serve God and mammon." The Great Reset worships possessions because after 2030, nobody will own anything of significant monetary value because it will belong to the government. God cannot be mixed within this equation because worshipping Him would sever the globalist "connection"; and this is contrary to their bottom-line. Dr. Schwab explains some reasons for America's dominance fatigue through a theory developed by a Harvard economist named, Dani Rodrick, called "globalization trilemma." The main-idea of this theory explains how globalism and nationalism are incompatible and cannot ever co-exist; which is shocking but it gets better. He asserts:

> The trilemma suggests that the three notions of economic globalization, political democracy, and the nation state are mutually irreconcilable, based on the logic that only, two can effectively co-exist at any giving time… Democracy and national sovereignty are only compatible if globalization is contained. By contrast, if both the nation state and globalization flourish, then democracy and globalization expand, there is no place for the nation state. Therefore, one can only ever choose two out of the three – this is the essence of the trilemma.[41]

We can compare the trilemma to what is written in the Book of James 4:7-8, that says, "Submit yourself therefore to God. Resist the devil, and he will flee from you. Draw nigh to God, and he will draw nigh to you." What came to mind reminds me of a person involved in witchcraft, after the individual realizes his or her error, then draw close to Christ Jesus in repentance. Once this happens, Satan and his imps must flee! According to Dr. Schwab, "the rise of nationalism makes the **retreat** of globalization **inevitable** in most of the world – an impulse particularly notable in the West."[42] In reality –nationalism is a good thing, especially when the loose entities like the WEF suggests a total control of society.

The trilemma is rather appealing, considering that through the years a number of American leaders, who peddled the globalist agenda, were in essence pushing a demonic sweep through America. When we examine their intent (as we are now doing), their efforts were no help to this country, but rather painfully weakened the structure that the Holy Spirit led the Framers, of The Declaration of Independence, to craft as a commandment, of sort, to protect the United States from dominance fatigue. The "dominance" reference only signifies America's place as the world leader; which is under attack.

Now we can understand the reason why there is a push for a one party system in America. For instance the Republican Party, is known typically as conservative, Christian, and patriotic; yet, often, referred to as an enemy to the globalist agenda. This is why since the 2020 election an idea has been circulating-malicious and accusatory talk claiming White American males are "White nationalist" or "White evangelicals" and being cast as these boogie-monsters. When in fact, what is really being suggested is that Christians, including those of whom seek to preserve a capitalist society, are the number one threat to America - when it is really a threat to globalization. And now, this slander depends on the demonization of Christians whom oppose taking the coronavirus vaccine, seek fair elections, and contend against critical race theory has caused the Leftist-Democrats to panic. Such actions "triggered," according to Dr. Schwab, "the rise of populist and right-wing parties around the world… which, when they come to power, often retreat into nationalism and promote an isolationist agenda – two notions antithetical to globalization."[43]

Many believe the months ahead are going to get worse, particularly as time draw closer to the mid-term elections. We may see more slander and disparaging accusations towards Christians as many are waking up to the folly that is invading our lives, and they are becoming energized towards taking action. This is why the Democrats will accelerate the call for a removal of the Senate filibuster and a mad-dash to pass HR 1, "For the People Act," and now, HR 4 at the time of writing this, HR 4 as a sign of desperation. Without these pieces of legislation, it will be impossible for Democrats to implement the "one-party system" needed to push their global agenda.

Therefore, be prepared for the vice-grips to tighten down on our liberties and the free expression that is a right for all to proclaim the call of righteousness and holiness. As for you nationalists- there is a plan for you to be silenced. Be aware!

US Hegemon

In the section called *Geopolitical reset,* Dr. Schwab writes about the end to what he calls "the chaotic end of multilateralism."[44] What this encompasses is the rise of nationalism that affects the performance of nations to eliminate, such things as, the pandemic. But instead, in his opinion, nationalism became the author of instability that gave birth to stressors defined as the "Thucydides trap."[45] Dr. Schwab, however, labels the United States as the hegemon because for many decades America has been the global superpower leading in, just about, every spectrum of finance, technology, industry, medical, entertainment, religion, and military. However, rivals like the nation of China, an up-incoming superpower, has caused much global tension, as Dr. Schwab calls "global messiness."[46] However the central theme to Thucydides suggests countries that heavy depended upon America, let's say, for security, are now having to reconsider their strategic dependence for national defense. These nations are said to be in a vulnerable position, at the hands of China. For instance in Asia, China has claimed sovereignty over the surrounding islands in the South China Sea and Taiwan, the main manufacturer for 92% of the global high-end micro-chip market; which America strongly needs for technology. In 2021, the level of aggressive towards CCP's neighbors (both India and Japan) are a testament to the CCP's motive for global dominance. It is my opinion America does not have the leadership nor the stomach for a full-blown sea battle with the CCP, particularly if they invade Taiwan. However, a way to deter any further aggression towards nations in Asia, require an amendment to the post-WWII treaty made with Japan. Doing so would allow growth and modernization of Japan's military and its offensive capabilities, with some limitations, instead of their current Self-Defense Force. Immediately, America should provide Japan with a sufficient number of F-35 Stealth Fighters, to include essential military technology that China stole from the United States to level the playing field. In doing so, makes sense. Most importantly, the CCP will be deterred from invading any nation, because they would know Japan has the capability and the will, to single-handedly defeat them. For now, Japan-Taiwan are engaged in security negotiations to bolster military ties. Often I tell people that the Chinese government does not think like Westerners; they are willing to allow the western half of China to be destroyed (millions of their own people would perish) in order to carry out a nuclear strike on 3 American cities. However, the question; before the 2024 election, will the Biden administration give China the greenlight to invade? I believe America will ignore it and do nothing. Biden, cowardly, will make a statement affirming Taiwan was always a part of China. But in the same breath condemn China, which will be part of a script his handlers will direct him to read.

Now, countries that depend on America for defense (European Union bloc nations) have voiced their concerns about the global volatility and America's ability to protect them. Perhaps Dr. Schwab was thinking, along the lines of, the hegemony expiration is, in part, the concern of a future power grab executed under diplomatic and economical alignments. An example of this could be Germany's oil pipeline with Russian that has the ingredients to deepen NATO's alliance, rendering them acceptable to manipulation and severance. Another example is Israel's discovery of an abundance of natural gas off their coast that has appealed to both Turkey and Russia. President Vladimir Putin had once invited the former Israel Prime Minister, Netanyahu, to craft a joint-proprietorship; for which Netanyahu rejected the offer in totality. We will explore threats to Israel further in chapter 8.

Special Drawing Rights (SDR)

In order for Dr. Schwab's prophecy to come to pass the dollar must be weakened and replaced as the world's reserve currency for a global digital currency. So you ask; How will that happen? In a scheme, the International Monetary Fund (IMF) will inject $650 billion in SDR in an effort to increase global liquidity and trigger reform of the global financial system. It has been reported this SDR is double the amount allocated in the IMF's history. Alex Newman, wrote a piece in *The Epoch Times*, where he explains that the SDR refers to a "sort of proto-global currency, based on a basket of leading currencies dubbed an 'international reserve asset' by the IMF."[47] Newman succinctly states that, "each government receives an amount of SDR proportional to its stake in the international organization."[48] Such governments (CCP and under-developed nations) are the prized beneficiaries to this enormous issuance of funds. William Middlekoop, founder of Commodity Discovery Fund, contends:

It is clear the Biden Administration is in favor of working together with the IMF and China to start using IMF's balance sheet to create more 'stimulus'... by allowing the IMF to create $650 billion worth of new SDRs, central bankers are able to create another layer of fiat money to an already unstable financial system.[49]

A Global Scam

It is disappointing to learn the Biden Administration is colluding with the IMF to arrange the SDR allocation to fall just short of the threshold that would require congressional approval. For now the Great Reset has the momentum it needs to devalue the dollar thus removing the United States as the premier global reserves. New York Times published an article criticizing the Biden Administration and IMF intentions to provide debt relief to "dictators" hence "accusing the IMF and the Biden Administration of scheming to divide up a $1 trillion SDR issuance" in 2 phases: 1) "$65 billion in 2021," and 2) "$350 billion in 2022."[50]

The impact of this blitz, to dethrone the U.S. dollar, is an erosion of the purchasing power that has been a strength in America. I have mentioned before, Dr. Schwab's Great Reset agenda boosts the CCP to surpass America as the global leader. Bretton Wood Institution (BWI) echoes this fact and says, "[the] CCP's digital currency is set to benefit to the point it has huge potential to dethrone the dollar" (emphasis added).[51] In addition, BWI indicated senior executives in the IMF and other global financial institutions, absolutely despise the dollar. As BWI explains what centers around the IMF and Biden Administration ideology is set because "they believe in real globalism...a lot of them believe we should be ruled by global equivalent of Brussels, where technocrats make decisions for everybody."[52] Many believe the worse mistake former President Trump made was not acting on his threat to return America to the gold standard. Doing so would have offset this current collision we are on with evil.

3. "You won't die waiting for an organ...they will be made by 3D printers"

Health care has been a topical issue for many Americans reaching far into the political realm. This issue is exacerbated as the country's aging baby boomers and Gen. X (my generation) are the predominate populace and populations growth reduced to a crawl. According to Dr. Schwab, although people are living longer, thanks to technological advances, there are 2 billion citizens that share insufficient health care. There are those needing lifesaving solutions but are disqualified due to individual finance deprivation. What if an inexpensive manufacturing trend could be injected into medical treatment to increase the availability of prosthetics and organs at a third of the cost?

Needless to say, 3D printing (also known as: additive manufacturing) has increased in the past five years in both production and manufacturing in most industries. The whole process encompasses creating any product from start to finish with precision. Using almost any raw material, 3D printers build one layer at a time with each subsequent layer being added directly to the former, according to its Computer Aided Drafting (CAD) blueprint specifications. The object is thus built, one layer at a time, to form the final product. Andrew Zaleski explained the process as:

> General Electric's Lear jet engine is not only one of the company's bestsellers, it's going to incorporate a fuel nozzle produced entirely through additive manufacturing. The process, popularly known as 3-D printing, involves building layers of material (in this case alloyed metals) according to precise digital plans. GE is currently completing testing of the new Learengines, but the benefit of additive manufactures parts has already been proven on other models.[53]

By the year 2030 there will be more products created through the use of this form of manufacturing. But what about within the dental or medical field, where human organs are created layer by layers, just like the GE process of the jet part? 3D printing of human organs exist, known as bioprinting. Researchers and scientist have developed material that may be used from stem cells to grow body parts from aborted fetus' (with ethical concerns) to animals that appear close to human organs, for example pigs or mice. The extraordinary advancement came about, as the world population grew, with an increase in diseases and immune deficiencies that may weaken organs. Consequently this problem required organ replacement; in most cases, fast. Therefore the objective was to develop a solution to overcome the enormous shortages to quench the demand.

For years, many patents have suffered while waiting for their life saving operations. Hence as a solution 3D printing is, now, integrated to eliminate the organ insecurity. According to Dr. Schwab, people on the organ waiting list often face imminent death; for instance, over 20 people perish daily because of the organ shortfall.[54]

Popular Science published an article, Chinese doctors had a young patient with cancer of the spine. The surgeons took the affected vertebra and made history by creating a synthetic vertebra to reintegrate as the original.[55] According to Dr. Schwab, by 2030 bioprinting will be more common and will eventually eliminate the wait for an organ; It is my bold opinion; we will see who will benefit from bioprinting, as it may only be for the privileged citizen.

Science Fiction Technology

The fourth industrial revolution will prescribe to the world innovation once seen in movies as fiction, but not anymore. August 2021, Elon Musk announced the developing of a 5-foot-8, 125 pound humanoid to relieve humans of "repetitive" tasks. Musk is working on bioengineering that includes transhuman-conjoining nanotechnology and AI as part of cranium implants, thus transforming the human body into a type of super-human computer. This technology will interface with Internet of Things (IoT) that includes (home appliances, and lights); to start your vehicle as it identifies you. During the Great Reset, people will function as an operating system as a person's thoughts and body are digitally configured to receive upgrades, report illnesses, prevent heart attacks, and including altering DNA through 6G or Artificial Super Intelligence (ASI) platform for preventive medicine. A technology modification called "CRISPR" has developed genetic modification technology that can grow human organs in pigs (appendages: eyes, ears and etc).

In 2011, the first ever, glow-in-the-dark cat was born and resistant to an animal type diseases (HIV). The objective is to edit human genome within an embryo for designer babies.

4. "You'll eat much less meat…An occasional treat, not a staple…"

Did you ever imagine a day when you are prohibited from eating pork or beef products? Get ready. It is coming. At the time of writing this, there is a shortage of just about everything, including bacon. Equally important it is the classical inception of Marxism. Did you know the Bible confirms a time of food shortages? The Beast system will regulate what people eat and the quantity. In Revelation 6:5-6 during the third seal judgement, people will be afforded "a measure of wheat for a penny, and three measures of barley for a penny; and see thou hurt not the oil and the wine." Indeed this Revelation account resembles these days, we are living in consequently will incrementally grow worse, like a gangrene infection. It will get to a point, people will only have a days' worth of food. Poverty will be the majority, where a penny worth of digital currency will get you a days' worth of wheat and barley.

It cannot be stressed enough, calamities are slowly but steadily increasing with shortages metastasized to, just about, every "goods" industry. Throughout history, the commencement to every Marxist nation is shortages.

For instance, after the devastating 1963 Hurricane Flora, the Cuban government made it illegal for farmers to sell meat from their cattle, because of a sizable reduction in herd population. Fast forward 58 years later, one would think the communist government would have rectified the issue generations ago, but has not. Imagine there are Cubans that have grown up drinking powdered milk as a substitution for cow's milk. No wonder the pictures of Cubans protesting has not one obese person.

Perhaps, today, this is likely the globalist psychology to gently enforce an agenda, first, by claiming "climate change" is the culprit for the mandates. Thus with all the intentions of raising the prices on meat, and legislate laws; which would influence a reduction in cattle ranches in America. Considering America is a major exporter of beef and pork, however once the restrictions are implemented, the rest of the world will feel the effects from the shortages. One must ask the question; why is there, all of sudden, this effort to prevent people from consuming animal meat? Since 2017 commercials for meat alternatives has increase, where fast food restaurants are conforming to the trend. During her 2020 town hall meeting, then Senator Harris was asked about this very issue. Her response left people perplexed and alarmed; Harris went on to say how much she enjoys eating a hamburger from time-to-time, but it is the responsible thing to eat burgers – beef in moderation. Why did she make such a statement? It all falls backwards to the Democrats in the World Economic Forums, British monarchy, and United Nations agenda.

In essence how does meat contribute to climate change? For one, everything points over to the abaddonist society's lust for control. Also could this be why Bill Gates is the largest owner of farm land? Does Gates farm land ownership have anything to do with Biden Administrations 30 x 30 conservation plan, both, being aligned with Dr. Schwab's (Great Reset) where's-the-beef agenda? Why is the average American citizen becoming an incredulous consumer of the climate change lie? Or is it about animal cruelty?

Perhaps this is why many are believing the methane gas produced by cow flatulence and belches are a reputable cause for global warming. It sounds crazy- believe me; no part of the Great Reset plan makes any sense. But you have to ask; what does a cow belch or flatulence have to do with eating beef? For example, let's explore how crazy these leftists are leaning; Kristen Painter wrote an article about a company that created a "wearable device that is fitted on a harness and hangs over the cow's nostrils like a window awning…" for the purpose of "absorb[ing] methane [gas] released by theirs burps and exhales."[56]

Let's be realistic – if you say that a large demand for pig and cow meat contributes to climate change then perhaps. However, what would happen if we stop slaughtering cows and pigs? In the long term would the animal population theoretically increase thus discharge more methane gas then before? It sounds crazy – believe me; no part of the Great Reset plan makes any sense. We have to retain the thought: what doesn't make sense, don't make sense.

In the state of Oregon there is an initiative petition (proposal) called IP-13 arranged as a petition for voters to consider in the November 2022 elections. This vote will be on whether to ban the slaughter of animals and essentially animal husbandry as a whole. Mary Anne Cooper, Vice President of Public Policy at the Oregon Farm Bureau (OFB) wrote the following regarding IP-13:

"Specifically, the petition: adds 'breeding domestic, livestock, and equine animals' to the list of activities that constitutes sexual assault of an animal, effectively making it a sex crime to artificially inseminate animals, and potentially targeting preg-checking and even planned breeding of animals. [Also, this petition] removes nearly every exemption that prevents common activities from being considered abuse or sexual assault, including transportation, rodeos, commercial poultry, good animal husbandry practices, slaughter, fishing, hunting and trapping, wildlife management practices, scientific or agricultural research, pest, and vermin control, and handling and training techniques."[57]

In Nebraska, stakeholders and farmers have taken an initiative to establish their own meat processing and packing plants to counter the disruptions in slaughtering cattle. This disruption has caused a beef shortage, thus contributing to beef prices sky-rocketing by more than 30 percent. We know what happens when grocery stores soak up the increase, it is trickled down to the consumer's wallet. These mysterious "black swan" events – some series of compounding catastrophic anomalies affecting everything from meat processing and packing to economics, such as inflation. For instance the mass COVID shut down of major meat packing plants and others, the May 2021 cyber-attack on JBS meat processing plant, government mandated lockdowns, and unemployment benefits that make it more advantageous for low-wage workers to not work.

However, many "red states" (conservative states) have realized the infiltration of Marxist agendas by the globalist and have prepared by passing laws to protect and preserve farmers, to include meat, thus preserving an America staple –hamburgers and steaks.

Protein Substitutes and 3D Printers

According to Dr. Schwab, in the fourth industrial revolution the number of nations that will suffer food insecurity because of famines, force migrations, and "plandemics" will increase within the next 8 years. One solution being discussed is the introduction of Genetic Modified Organism (GMO) in foods, making insects a protein substitution (crickets, roaches and grub worms) for western nations. GMOs are nothing new, in many foreign countries, Coca Cola and other snack foods have integrated crickets in soft drinks and potato chips. In different locales a population's diet consists of inexpensive food sources and is often high in protein bugs. There have been discussions on whether Americans would deviate from what is considered culturally appropriate foods, to be willing to consume insects as a protein alternative. This is a concern even though worms are safe to eat. However, a prolong consumption of worms is disruptive to the "gut" (digestive tract). Regardless, I can assure you, we will gradually see this form of GMOs integrated in health conscious snack foods and they will have an artificially appealing taste, to win supporters; thus possibly, scarcity targeting common products such as sugar, flour, bananas, vegetables, breads, you name it – may give people no choice but to adjust their selection of food to GMOs.

Then there is beyond meat or "faux meat", made from 3D printers that is becoming popular and realistic. Israel has a company called Redefine Meat Ltd. Which uses "3D printing facsimiles of beef cuts, from fillet to rump and brisket" with the look of real meat.[58] The process, for the meat to look real, utilizes a plant-case ink which is loaded into a 3D printer. This printer in turn will "print meat countless times and deliver a complex layers of muscle and fat to re-create the right texture."[59] There are leading venture capital investors and other interested parties pouring millions in to this process, for example, McDonalds Corporation with many more investors drawing interest to this market.

5. "A billion people will be displaced by climate change"

What is the truth? Is climate change the same as global warming? Why, within several years, has global warming hypothesis reshaped into climate change? Why has this global policy become the banner for politicians, predominately the leftist-Democrats? What is the position of the church on the issue of climate change? According to LifeWay Research, 53% of Protestant pastors believe "global warming is real and man-made" compared to with 49% of American adults holding the same view.[60] Scott McConnell, executive director at LifeWay Research, believes every year churches are becoming more tolerant to global warming. McConnell contends:

"Climate change can be a difficult issue to address because the causes and effects are not always easily seen where you live. Much like the current coronavirus pandemic, environmental mitigation efforts require trust in the scientists measuring the problem and finding the best solutions that balance all of the concerns involved."[61]

Does this trend indicate the church is melting away into an apostate church? What effect does an acceptance of climate change has on the church?

We have explored extensively Dr. Schwab and fundamentals to his prophecy (predictions) into the decade of 2030. It would be unbecoming for me not to identify other actors implicit in the shaping of the Great Reset – Abaddonist society; primarily the United Nations Intergovernmental Panel on Climate Change (IPCC) is the leading agency that collaborates global scientific and socioeconomic data pertaining to risks induced by carbon emissions (translates to air pollution), along with other international entities. It is hypothesized by global alarmists that climate change occurs when greenhouse gases attract and absorbs heat which in turn increases the Earth's temperatures. Many claim human activity: automobile and trucks exhaust, trains, boats, industries, and electricity are credited to the size of carbon emissions polluting the atmosphere for over five generations. During the coronavirus lockdown many climate alarmist anticipated the level of the carbon dioxide emissions to dissipate by large numbers because people were not driving or working. In light of this assertion, the International Energy Agency (IEA) predicts, according to Dr. Schwab, the global lockdown will have reduced carbon emissions by 8 percent.[62] Thus if the IEA's emissions estimate holds true, these draconian measures (lockdown and restrictions) would translated to the most comprehensive reduction in history. Dr. Schwab believes, "it is still miniscule compare to the size of the problem and it remains inferior to the annual reduction in emissions of 7.6% over the next decade that the UN thinks is necessary to hold the global rise in temperatures below 1.5°C."[63] He did not view these statistics as an accomplishment, but rather as a disappointment. In fact, if the lockdowns did not reach the 7.6% goal marked by the UN, that would mean, on the horizon, more drastic communist measures waiting for implementation. What was interesting about his response is that it was comparable to a "head-nod" of support for more lockdowns to reach the IEA's goal. This is where Americans need to pay close attention! Dr. Schwab insists that to accomplish such an expectation, Americans must get comfortable with "consuming much less" electricity to agriculture (beef). In 10 years, the globalists are determined to end Western dependency on fossil fuels (natural gas). That will make it impossible for farmer and ranchers to operate equipment needed to harvest food. This agricultural production not only feeds billions but is a critical economic component in various regions. Not to mention, it will be essential to have transportation, independent of fossil fuels, for mobility sustainment in partnership with the United Nations (UN) agenda 2030. Dr. Schwab said:

"It seems to suggest that small individual actions (consuming much less, not using our cars and not flying) are of little significance when compared to the size of emissions generated by electricity, agriculture, and industry, the "big-ticket emitter" that continued to operate during the lockdowns (with the partial exception of some industries)."[64]

Just in this last quote support Dr. Schwab's 8 predictions to control, on a Marxist scale, the consumption of the goods and services by the global population, disguised as climate change. Many globalists, like Schwab, believe extreme "strategies" are needed to address a series of challenges. These strategies include the implementation of nontraditional modifications to how energy is generated and enmesh with global communities sustainment ability. Another strategy, (I must use his words) will require:

"structure changes in our consumption behavior. If, in the post-pandemic era, we decide to resume our lives just as before (by driving the same cars, by flying to the same destinations, by eating the same things, by heating our house the same way, and so on), the **COVID-19 crisis will have gone to waste as far as climate policies are concerned"** (emphasis added).[65]

Schwab continues with this draconian idea to impose on our great country, "[c]onversely, if some of the habits we were forced to adopt during the pandemic translate into structural changes in behavior, the climate outcome might be different."[66]

In essence, the whole point is to sustain the reduction in carbon emissions which will require people to remain at home for the unforeseen future with office work being predominately fulfilled from home. Dr. Schwab even suggest "walking instead of driving to keep the air of our cities are clean as it was during the lockdowns;" in addition you will no longer be allowed traditional vacations but instead, according to Dr. Schwab, "vacationing nearer to home: all thee, if aggregated at scale could lead to a sustained reduction in carbon emissions."[67]

There is a problem with the conclusion to this hypothesis- it makes the assumption that man is solely responsible for any climate changes. This is an assumption that is unproven by peer reviewed scientific methods. One would ask; how is this so? Humans do contribute to climate change, right? I do not deny the human factor, to a certain degree. However, there are additional factors that are out of man's control and it is imperative to include these factors in any studies or discussions about climate change. It is important to note, global temperatures always remain in a constant state of change because of the unpredictability of climate cycles that drives the fluctuation. Climate alarmists would want you to think otherwise, however these are natural occurrences that, even, Dr. Schwab did not pay homage to.

Cheng Xiaonong provides four of the most common causes to temperature fluctuation that are under-recognized: 1) Drift of the continental plates, 2) Sun (solar), 3) Orogenic movement of the Earth Crust, 4) Ocean currents, all of which needing to be explored:

1. **Continental plates.** The first thing that comes to mind are the science classes in high school where we watched videos of the plates altering the landscape and ocean floor. When the plates are disturbed they simultaneously stimulate the atmospheric circulation; which triggers climate fluctuation.[68] In August of 2021, Haiti suffered a 7.2 earthquake and in May of 2020, Nevada experienced a 6.5 earthquake that was felt in Salt Lake City, Utah, and in California. In 2019, there were an estimated 151 earthquakes. Comparatively May of 2020 had slightly more (59) compared to (54) for the previous year.

2. **Sun (solar).** In the Genesis account, God created the sun for heating the earth and for providing light. Ever since the introduction of sin into the world it was the firmament that protected the earth from the radiation levels that beams upon earth until the Great Flood in the days of Noah. Through the years, the earth continues to die and as a consequence, radiation fluctuation will eventually intensify during the end-times. "It's short-term radiation fluctuations such as sunspot activity with an 11 year cycle and a radiation change with a cycle of 20 plus years, all have an impact on the Earth's Climate."[69] The author adds, "changes in sunspots will induce a change of 1.5 degrees Celsius of the Earth's Stratospheric temperature making high latitudes colder and low latitudes hotter."[70]

3. **Orogenic movement of the Earth's Crust.** People do not realize natural alteration to topographical terrain features causes changes

in temperature. These natural occurrences are very common. Volcano eruptions are increasing; since July 2, 1774, there have been over 45 eruptions.[71]

4. Ocean currents. Since the earth is 80% water, the Earth's temperature is affected by flow of the sea current; which has an effect on hotter than normal temperatures. For instance, have you wondered why the Gulf of Mexico is warmer? In short-order it is because "the stream it produces emits more heat than the world's annual coal-burning heat," said Xiaonong.[72]

Meteorology expert, Christopher Landsea, from the National Oceanic and Atmospheric Administration (NOAA), believes with the advancement in technology has contributed to systems capable of detecting more severe storms. For example when there are more laws and police, more crimes are detected, hence translating to an increase in the prison population. Equally important, there is a government report that was collaborated by 30 scientists which the UN often quotes its numerous climate reports. These quotes and reports will make you scratch your head in disbelief. Jean Chen describes in an amazing article that Steven E. Koonin, the former undersecretary for science for the U.S. Department of Energy, wrote a bombshell piece in the Wall Street Journal that criticized scientists for deliberately distorting scientific facts by taking climate data out of historical context. He directs attention to the U.S. Government Climate Science Special Report, published in November 2017, which contends "the report ominously notes that while global sea level rose an average 0.05 inch a year during most of the 20th Century, it has risen at about twice that rate since 1993. But it fails to mention that the rate fluctuated by comparable amounts several times during the 20th Century."[73]

He draws further attention to the deliberate misrepresentation of facts by scientists and media; needless to say – after a meticulous examination of "the same research papers the report cites show that recent rates are statistically indistinguishable from peak rates earlier in the 20th century, when human influences on the climate were much smaller..."[74] The purity of fact exposes the misleading climate change theories, which Koonin bravely debunks by declaring how "the report's executive summary declares that U.S. heat waves have become more common since the mid-1960s, although acknowledging the 1930s Dust Bowl as the peak period of extreme heat. Yet, buried deep in the report is a figure showing that heat waves are no more frequent today than in the 1900s."[75]

In a 2010 interview, Ottmar Edenhofer, an IPCC official, debunked the climate change scheme by accusing climate alarmists for:

"Basically, it's a big mistake to discuss climates policy separately from the major themes of globalism… One must say clearly that we redistribute defacto the world's wealth by climate policy… one has to free oneself from the illusion that international climate policy is environmental policy. This has almost nothing to do with environmental policy anymore, with problems such as deforestation or the ozone hole."[76]

Yet you have Marxists, like Dr. Schwab, hoping for people to avoid or reject pre-coronavirus reports from reputable, academic-qualified scientists. But instead prey on the misinformed to follow their "disinformation of lies" while not listening to the science (as the Leftist-Democrats always exclaim). Another report from the IPCC affirms climate change is not causing extreme weather as climate alarmist maintain; IPCC concludes "there is only low confidence for the attribution of any detectable changes in the tropical cyclone activity to anthropogenic influences."[77]

In a Global Warming Policy Foundation report, published by an Oxford physicist, says that evidence suggests there is a downward trend in extreme weather. The report indicates, "if there is any trend at all in extreme weather, it's downward rather upward. Our most extreme weather, be it heat wave, drought, flood, hurricane or tornado, occurred many years ago, long before the carbon dioxide level in the atmosphere began to climb at its present rate."[78]

6. "Polluters will have to pay to emit carbon dioxide… There will be a global price on carbon…"

There is a regulatory plan that has been discussed by climate alarmist, former Vice President Al Gore, to launch sophisticated satellites. These satellites will function as a type of police that monitor CO2 emissions in the atmosphere, albeit to establish a standardized baseline, to identify as well as police the farmer and industry violators. Imagine having the capability to view a satellite image of the state of Texas through an infrared scan. In this image a certain color, let's say, a purple tone, may signify an extreme amount of gas emitted in a general area, in contrast to other areas perceived in a normal range. The purple will be considered a violation of the baseline set standard by an alphabet agency (i.e. U.N.). Just think, any result from an investigation into the company or farm that has been found out of tolerance may receive a large fine or other sanctions. Be vigilant! One thing believers can do is remain steadfast in prayers while staying educated on current events and watch for potential regulations and laws that will affect our lives. You can do more than you think – start by learning who's your state and congressional representatives. Create a Christian grassroots organization to spread what you have discovered through research and analysis. You will be amazed at the response from like-minded Christians, and maybe, non-believers. Therefore do not knock small beginnings because it is in those small beginnings that greatness is born.

Volcanoes and CO2 Emissions

Currently there are an estimated 45 active volcanoes in the world. One subject less heard, is the amount of CO2 that an active volcano can deliver daily. I can assure you, globalists thrive on people who are more willing to triage information disseminated to them through officials they believe are an authority: United Nations, World Health Organization (WHO), or technocrats (like Bill Gates), when they are imposters. I have never heard technocrats or our legislative representatives in D.C. argue about the effects of "volcano's" CO2 emissions. Doing so would exceed the alarmist standard preached by the globalists. Perhaps, the reason for their "tight-lips" on volcano's CO2 delivery may be that it doesn't fit their diabolic, global plantation narrative.

Jonathan C. Brentner contends, "an active volcano can spew over 150,000 tons of CO2 daily into the atmosphere."[79] This also includes the "900,000 sea floor volcano-hydrothermal vents" that are pouring into the sea.[80] When there are active volcanoes delivering close to this volume of CO2 then they should be part of the climate discussion. What about non-erupting volcanoes? Brentner asserts, "recent geological research by the University of Leeds and others prove that non-erupting volcanoes can emit massive amounts of CO2 into Earth's atmosphere and oceans."[81]

One researcher, David Kupelian noted in 2019, 500 scientists sent a letter of admonishment to the United Nations for fraudulently spreading statistical data, claiming climate change (CO_2 magnification) contributes to an increase in natural disasters. These brave scientists proclaim:

> There is no statistical evidence that global warming is intensifying hurricanes, floods, droughts, and such like disasters, or making them more frequent. However, CO_2-mitigation measures are as damaging as they are costly. For instance, wind turbines kill birds, and bats, and palm-oil plantations destroy the biodiversity of the rainforests.[82]

The letter further explains that the issuance of climate mitigation factors are worthless and are causing more harm than good. First, the same people whom globalists claim are repressed – living without electricity and water, under their proposal – are the same people being denied opportunities for affordable and sustainable energy.

We are constantly hearing about threats of climate change, however when the climate alarmists speak of "mitigations factors," this term is ambiguous to most of us. What is really happening? I believe God has opened the window for believers, in Christ Jesus, to see first-hand the evil motives held by the globalists to control nations. Albeit climate alarmists remind me of the Pharisees and the Sadducees. In Matthew 16:2-4, they sought out Jesus for a sign from Heaven. Our Lord knew their curiosity was grounded out of an evil heart. He said to them, "when it is evening, ye say, it will be fair weather: for the sky is red. And in the morning, it will be foul weather today: for the sky is red and lowering. O ye hypocrites, ye can discern the face of the sky; but can ye not discern the signs of the times?" Indeed, Jesus' final remarks, in verse 4, are a designated moniker to describe those who are lost within a pseudo-reality, like a cult-ritual (climate change) are "a wicked and adulterous generation seeketh after a sign." These charlatans could read the weather but could not discern that Jesus' miraculous works were evidence of the Kingdom of God. Even now, these people are blinded because of their lack of faith. And because of this deficit, do you think people will treat the predictions from Schwab as something pious, similar to the Pharisees seeking attention through their piety? Either way, his idealism is taking root as fragments are being launched into every spectrum of society.

Remember, Schwab's first prophecy gave emphasis to a world where its citizens owned no vehicle or house, and they weren't permitted to enjoy airline travel because of the anthropogenic emissions (that you and I are to blame) that increases CO_2. People fail to discern how systematic the "goal-post" is incrementally being shoved back to meet the globalist's goal to have the people grow fatigue, and fall into submissions.

Did You Know the Government Manipulates Weather?

The U.S. Government… has begun a top-secret program of operational **cloud seeding** in and around Vietnam… the code name of the field trial was **Project Popeye.** In October 1966, Project Popeye, a clandestine, all-service military – civilian experimental program, **seeded the skies over** southern Laos to evaluate the concept of impeding traffic on Viet Cong infiltration routes by **increasing the amount of rainfall** and the **length of the rainy season** (emphasis added).[83]

In his book, *Fixing the sky,* James Rodger Fleming gives a wake-up call for those seeking to understand how climate change has influenced technological fixes to manipulate weather to save the planet. Several case studies shed light onto many of the secret governments and corporate bodies who share capabilities to "ecohack" or "geoengineer" global weather. Perhaps, after reading some of the large-scale atmospheric manipulations schemes, this may lead you to never view the trailing vortex from high altitude aircraft the same. I need to be clear – the purpose for writing this section is not to suggest that governments or organizations are the cause of devastating climate events. The purpose is simply to educate and make aware that weather controlling experiments have been and likely continue to be performed. Furthermore it is to bring to light the effect planetary weather manipulation may have in the end-times. For example, the "Dark Winter" in late 2020 had record freezing temperatures in Texas, and into many southern states with extremely high humidity. Weather manipulation is nothing new. In fact, it has been around since the mid-19th century with silly rainmaking practices by James Espy, Climate alarmist – Niles G. Ekholm, Joseph Black's discovering of carbon dioxide, to WWII fog removal for allied bombing against Nazi Germany.[84] There have been numerous policy-driven discussions into the installation of weather fixes, however, I want to focus briefly on 4 specific controls that are least heard of in conversations: geoengineering, ecohacking, cloud seeding, and chemtrails.

Fleming defines a "geoengineer" as someone "who contrives, designs, or invents at the largest planetary scale possible for either military or civilian purposes – a layer of snares at the global level."[85] Next there is "ecohacking" which refers to the application of "science in very-large scale [planetary scale] projects to change the environment for the better – stop global warming (e.g. by using mirrors in space to deflect sunlight away from the Earth)."[86] There are those who exaggerate climate models with the ridiculous, according to the author, "when people propose to cool the Earth by 2°C (3.6°F) using a technical fix, they are overlooking the fact that Earth has not yet warmed 2°C in the past century".[87] On the contrary, not all people believe ecohacking is practical. Fleming indicates this practice as nothing more than "geo-scientific speculation." I challenge that view! Perhaps it is possible since the publishing of his research, the technological outfit has grown expeditiously. About 10 years ago technology surpassed the imagination envisioned with the first dinosaur "I-phone". Today, there is Netflix's use of Artificial General Intelligence (AGI) to predict movies people desire to watch, smart phones can direct advertisements (ads) to ones phone from eavesdropping on conversations. Cyrus Paras, an AI expert and author, suggests 5G will be the first phase to connecting the world in preparation for 6G infrastructure along with Google Deep Mind AI. Further, Elon Musk made it reality to connect people with technology through his company called "Neuralink," which specializes in Neuralace brain implants.[88] Just this summation of technological advancement should convince anybody the ability to influence weather is not impossible. For instance, "cloud seeding" refers to the ability to inject into clouds a cocktail of chemicals ranging from: dry ice, salt, lead and silver iodide to create a desirable chemical reaction that artificially influences the weather.

In the mid-1940s General Electric corporation's (GE) seeding experiment, led by scientists Vincent Schaefer, Irving Langmuir, and Bernard Vonnegut successfully "dropped 6 pounds of dry ice pellets" above 10,000 feet in clouds creating "ice crystals and streaks of snow."[89] There were reports after the cloud seeding that a local airport control tower could identify "streams of falling snow pouring out of the base of the cloud more than fifty miles away."[90] One of the most provocative statements came from Langmuir's future ambitions associated with this technology, saying:

Of one pellet of dry ice, 'about the size of a pea,' could precipitate several tons of snow, he predicted that 'a single plane could generate hundreds of millions of tons of snow' over mountain ski resorts, possibly diverting the snowfall from major cities. Or, depending on conditions, perhaps the seeding technique could be used to clear fogs over airports and harbors or prevent aircraft icing problems.[91]

Scientists frequently use geoengineering concepts as methods to control climate on a global scale. A common cloud-seeding treatment is "silver iodide" (AgI); which is harmful to plants, wildlife and humans. I think it is important to note, many of the silver iodide experiments were mysteriously followed by devastating events. However, cloud seeding was unable to be proven as the cause.

In her book, *Chemtrails, HAARP and the Full Spectrum Dominance of Planet Earth*, Elana Freeland explains "in April 2013, Weather Modification, Inc. listed 37 cloud-seeding operations in 17 states, and 66 such operations in 18 countries."[92] Every year it seems more evidence is developing relating to cloud-seeding and chemtrail operations. For instance, Rosalie Bartell, wrote, about an incident that transpired in 1989, where "two Black Brant X's and two Nike Orion rockets were launched over Canada, releasing barium at high altitudes as creating artificial clouds… observed as far away as Los Alamos, New Mexico."[93] It must be noted, aerosol delivery systems can be difficult to distinguish. Indeed, when we look up at the sky and observe aircraft leaving behind contrails, what we see, somewhat, can be confusing. Clifford E. Carnicom, in his *Contrail Distance Formation Model*, explains contrails are "persisting spray" or "condensation" that "typically forms one wingspan behind the aircraft." However not so with chemtrail formations, which appear "nearer the engine."[94]

In May 5, 2008, the Council of Foreign Relations (CFR) discussed Project Cloverleaf operations under the stratospheric aerosol geoengineering (SAG) and solar radiation management (SRM), thus authorized the release of "micron-sized particulates" covering "NATO populations" with such hazardous chemicals as "sulfur dioxide, aluminum oxide dust, self-levitating aerosols, and sulfuric acid."[95]

Seeding technology is an extremely dangerous technique to alter atmospheric conditions. Particularly when hazardous chemicals (silver iodide, sulfites, or nanoparticles), are being released at high altitudes, where eventually absorbed in the human body. It is mind blowing for the Government to knowingly permit the release of hazardous chemicals, without its citizen's knowledge and consent. Absolutely, those who promote such dark activities have no regards for people's lives. Yet, in their patents, claim these technologies are for the sole purpose to control climate change. Fleming suggests "critics say it [ultimate technological fix] has unlimited potential for planetary mischief. Shade the planet by launching a solar shield into orbit. Shoot sulfates or reflective nanoparticles into the upper atmosphere, turning the blue sky milky white. Make clouds thicker and brighter."[96]

I challenge you – the next time you look to the sky and see a jet, at a high attitude, leaving contrails or chemtrail in the sky, to think about the experiments that have been performed and imagine, in the end-times the Beast system will have advance technological packages as instruments to control the world. For now, geotechnology is not so far from ones imagination. The capabilities exist to create droughts and famines in specific regions, just by spraying a cocktail of chemicals. It is important for Christians to be wise in this age of wickedness and resist the plots exploited by wicked men.

Just assume there will be a time evil men will have their hands on the switches to cause drought, flooding, or inclement weather conditions by cloud seeding or chemtrails; the same technique used against America's enemies in Vietnam with Project Popeye. It is impossible to refute this Pandora's Box of dangers because the government has delivered these as weapons in history – more than one time. I reflect back to my military experience; what I can tell you, whenever there is a weapon system that is effective – the military does not scrap it; they perfect it in secret. You better believe governments have been utilizing these and other unknown programs to their advantage. China and Iran are suffering droughts and flooding, while in America, the West coast and Mountain States are on fire. Wouldn't it be normal to ask ourselves, given this knowledge of past experiments, are these events natural? Have our enemies created them? We really do not know the capabilities of those wanting a one world government. I'm just saying.

For the last decade, the United Arab Emirates (UAE) has worked on a Rainfall Enhancement Science project reaping impressive results; while using drones to release electric shocks in clouds. The UAE government's intent is for the drones to release an electrical pulse to function as a type of magnet, which will consolidate water droplets creating larger forming clouds. Keri Nicoll, Meteorologist, at Reading University, explained during a CNN interview: "What we are trying to do is to make the droplets inside the clouds big enough so that when they fall out of the cloud, they survive down to the surface."[97]

Russia and China have used similar technology to melt Arctic ice for shipping routes and during the Olympic Games for atmospheric changes to create favorable weather conditions. Just think, in the 21st century, America's military has managed weather modifications programs for a half century. As laymen we don't know what conditions must be present to reproduce some of these weather modification techniques. What we do know is that despite the government's sophisticated capabilities for climate restoration, it has done nothing to relieve the West Coast from drought, especially with many wild fires burning thousands of acres. We also know that the government has reportedly been successful in artificially producing rainfall utilizing various chemicals and methods of seeding the atmosphere. Perhaps it is likely that geoengineering is a quick fix for cooler temperatures and lacks effect in hotter temperatures or arid environments. It sounds good; however, the act of helping is far from their design.

In closing, with Project Popeye the U.S. Military Industrial Complex's goal was to attack "68 clouds" and cause enough rain to maintain a high level of precipitation. This precipitation was needed to keep the soil extremely muddy and effectively hinder enemy movement.[98] The project was created by an atmosphere scientist for the U.S. Navy, Pierre St. Amand, an expert in blowing stuff up (pyrotechnic). He had developed the "seeding flares" for the operation.[99] St. Amanda stated, "[the] first cloud we seeded grew like an atomic bomb explosion and it rained very heavily out of it and everybody was convinced with that one experiment that we'd done enough."[100] I would like to provide three additional sites to enhance your personal study on weather fixing at: weathermodificationhistory.com, climateviewer.com and geoengineeringmonitor.org. After considering the information provided in this section on geoengineering, if you wanted to make people extremely afraid, to the point, they will accept the Great Reset, New World Order – What would you do differently?

7. "You could be preparing to go to Mars."

Did you ever imagine, after the year 2030, the government would instruct you to pack up your belongings to colonize Mars? NASA, particularly, Elon Musk, are devising plans to colonize the red planet that has summers as warm as Alaska's winters. It appears, though, that every nations that has the capability to launch objects into space are landing rovers on the planet for "alleged" research. Once the data proves human-life can be sustained on the planet indefinitely, structures and planetary systems to grow food will be created for the long space voyage. Be not surprised to hear countries like, China, will militarize their Martian footprint.

It is written in the Bible, God created the Earth for the inhabitants of His creation for this purpose to "be fruitful and multiply, and replenish the earth, and subdue it" (Genesis 1:28). Even the Book of Psalms embraces this truth, "the heaven, even heavens, are the Lord's: but the earth hath he given to the children of men" (115:16). Nowhere in the Scriptures does it indicate there are any other created beings in this solar system. It is obvious, those who do not know Christ are desperate in their struggle to discover a utopia to quench the fear aroused by Satan's deception. Look how ridiculous this Mars escapades sounds. For a moment let's assume, hypothetically, that climate alarmist claims of the Earth overheating, being overpopulated, has a food shortage, and so forth – is legitimate. Would you be willing to leave this planet, which is free of any life support apparatus, for Mars where it is impossible to breathe without artificial implements? We are continuously lectured there is not enough food to feed the world. Right now, on Mars, food sources don't exist. What size budget is needed to sustain a logistical operation for importing resources in an artificial, Earthly environment on Mars? Think about this – considering other nations have the same idea of colonizing the Martian planet, each global government must produce enough sustenance to feed their colony. It doesn't make any sense; hence there is a desperation to reduce meat consumption. This is being done by injecting into our psyche the strategy for people to acclimate to eating 3D printed fake meat or insects. Perhaps it is the perfect exercise for preparing a people for life absent of traditional methods of feeding.

8. "Western values will have been tested to the breaking point"

Western values must be pushed to their breaking point – this is believed by many leaders Dr. Schwab's, WEF philosophy, which is defiantly stalking American values. Throughout the life of our illustrious nation, it has been the world's pulse for morality and Christianity that stood against all strong-arms of totalitarianism like Schwab's Great Reset. Any time something is tested to its "breaking point" it gives inference to taking this thing and bending it past the point of no return. Once that point is reached the material would have to be reduced to its constituent parts and reformed anew. In fact remember Dr. Schwab referred to testing being executed through a total "revamping" the way we live, while eliminating practices common to our lifestyle. Yet he insists "check and balances that underpin our democracies must not be forgotten."[101] Absolutely, the underpin of Western societies is the exercise of Christian faith. He believes, like many of the globalists, we are to forget not the fabric of our moralistic reform (Christian values) but to apply self-abasement to our religious fervor. To break their psychology down further, the reseters bottom-line is for society to assimilate out of "obedience." This is the planned schematic to accepting the radical changes of the Abaddonist society. It is like having "blind-faith" which says, even though things sound complicated or does not make sense, just trust us at our word, even if, the evidence contradicts our claim. But oh no, (globalist reseters would stress) do not maintain the "radical norms" of the Bible, because it infringes on the success of the Great Reset.

The underlining of the revamping western values, has much to do with a reduction of consumers' purchasing power. For one, consumer prices are increasing in the mist of this era of scarcity. The supply chain disruption has tripled for companies to ship goods to box stores. Company walk-outs and exodus' are increasing, leaving company's without truck drivers to move product. Thereby leaving the nations crippled with shortages.

Gas prices have increased to over 30%. In the Democrats Trillion-plus, Build.Back.Better bill (an actual pseudonym for the Green New Deal); did you know one of the main objectives of this bill is to eliminate oil, gas and coal, with the thirst to put the oil and gas industry out of business? However, though, you are safe for now; any pain and suffering from the teeth of this bill, expect to feel the pain in ten to twenty years from now.

It will be long after the Biden administration is in the history books for its radical shift of America from her superpower status. Does it seem Washington D.C. is a clown car? More issues upon issues keep circulating from this administration? For now, expect all prices to soar. Gas prices of 2020 is a thing of the past. In November 2020, it was reported, for, the first time in history, America was the number one exporter of oil. Until the Biden Administration became a bull in a china shop, slowly dismantling the wealth of the middle class. Here is the reason for my assertion; those of whom are being greatly impacted by this increase, the middle class. There are people who must make the hard decision to buy fuel for work or buy food to feed their family for a week. What is so crazy about this crisis; it is manufactured. It is self-inflicted. America is rich in natural resources to, now, having to beg "Russia" and "OPEC" to release more oil for the consumers, in return YOU will feel it in the wallet. It is unfair. It is not right. Especially when there is cleaner energy like, fossil fuels and nuclear energy. Americans are being prepared for another "Black Winter" in the northeast and southern states. It is projected there will be similar 2020 blackouts because of certain states having converted their energy to windmills that freeze in extreme weather. Do we reap what we sow? People sowed a vote to reap poverty.

Many Americans have short memories; so allow me to refresh it. Gas prices in 2020 reached as low as $1.80 a gallon; whereas in 2022, gas had reached, in some places $7.00 a gallon. In addition consumers are guaranteed to see their energy bill increase to top it all off. Even if you are current on your bill; municipalities will decide, on one's behalf, to sequestrate power during extreme cold. More to come…

Beloved, the method to expose the reset scheme, requires believers to "test" the reset elements with the fire of the Word of God. Glory to God – if you want to know why the Marxist are dogged to temper the church, God's word says this:

> For it is written, I will destroy the wisdom of the wise, and will bring to nothing the understanding of the prudent…but we preach Christ crucified, unto the Jews a stumbling block, and unto the Greeks foolishness (1 Corinthians 1:19, 23).

In Psalm 9:15-16, David praised God for His judgement over the wicked that wanted to thwart our lives. He said, "The heathen are sunk down in the pit that they made: in the net which they hid is their own foot taken. The Lord is known by the judgment which he executeth: the wicked is snared in the work of his own hands.:

Indeed God's Word is truth and the truth is sprayed upon the world's wisdom, exposing the lie constructed from the children of Satan. One thing the world hates most is being exposed of their great lies.

Do not touch these things (Colossians 2:8, 18-22)

Beware lest any many spoil you through philosophy and vain deceit, after the tradition of men, after the rudiments of the world, and not after Christ… let no man beguile you of your reward in a voluntary humanity and worshipping of angels, intruding into those things which he hath not seen, vainly puffed up by his fleshly mind, and not holding the Head, from which all body by joints and bands having nourishment ministered, and knit together, increaseth with the increase of God. Wherefore if ye be dead with Christ from the rudiments of the world, why, as though living in the world, are ye subject to ordinances, (Touch not; taste not; handle not; which all are to perish with the using;) after the commandments and doctrines of men?

Apostle Paul wrote this letter to respond to a dangerous philosophy that was wrecking the church in Colosse. Like many Christians, they were under a deep spiritual attack to disqualify them of Heavenly rewards. There were duel attacks from Jewish and Gnostic teachings that focused on worshipping of elements or "elemental spirits" that refers to the creation (earth, fire, and water) and the zodiac signs over the Creator. It was common practice for the church to pray for angels to endow them with answers to prayers for protection, instead of committing prayers to the One-True-Living-God. In their minds, God was too big for their small faith to access. So in the Greek, verse 8, Paul warns the church, "See to it that no one takes you 'captive' [refers to the Greek word, sylagōgōn – means '*to make you victim of fraud*'] by means of philosophy and empty deceit according to traditions of men, [whereas, these traditions are what is handed down from human teachings], according to the elemental spirits of the world, and not according to Christ" (emphasis added).[102]

And elemental spirit is simply rudiments of an intellectual perfunctory system, which is fueled by an earthly way of thinking. But also are interdimensional entities (demons) that materialize and feed off the thoughts and emotions of its victim. Emphatically, Paul writes against this destructive spirit in verse 20 and asserts: "Wherefore if ye be dead with Christ from the rudiments of the world, why, as though living in the world, are ye subject to ordinances?" Apostle is suggesting why do you **submit to regulations?** The bold clause derives from the Greek word, "dogmatizō," which means to suffer laws imposed on oneself. In context, global warming, through the disguise of climate change, is born from an elemental spirit of the universe; as it is a Marxist philosophy crafter herein an empty deceit that has been around for half a century.

These global elites are deeply rooted – antichrist, dedicated, Marxist ideologues who flirts with the core principle of scientific knowledge, ground into rich, tiny pieces of lies to deceive the simple majority in the end-times. We are given warning in 1 Timothy 4:1-5 as "the Spirit clearly says that in later times some will abandon the faith." Paul uses the Greek verb "apostatize" in the future tense, to say "they will have stood away from the truth." Paul continues with some believers will "follow **deceiving spirits** and things **taught by demons** such teaching come through **hypocritical liars,** whose conscience have been seared with an hot iron" (emphasis added, NIV). In Colossians asceticism – enforcing rigid rules in every spectrum of one's lifestyles as a method to draw closer to God – instead of trusting in Christ Jesus as Lord, was a common practice.

Verse 3 provides sufficient details to some of the rules being imposed by the enemy as "Forbidding to marry, and commanding to abstain from meats, which God hath created to be received with thanksgiving of them which believe and know the truth." Unfortunately in the 21st Century, we are bumper-to-bumper with the same evil at the intersection of Deception and Truth. It appears the reason for people's ignorance of the truth has much to do with their devotion to deceitful spirits. Those who promote these evils are liars and hypocrites invested in discouraging people from anything good. All the while they are encouraging people to not marry or have children in order to reduce the strain overpopulation has on climate change. Instead, Bill Gates made an omission during a Ted Talk, thus explained his desire to improve global health care, but in the same breath, suggests wanting to reduce the global population. How can one improve global health care with immunizations, simultaneously reduce the global population?

It makes sense to improve health care because people live longer; but to reduce the global population means people must die. Does this make any sense to you? It is the doctrines of demons. Conversely, to test Western values to its breaking point will require global asceticism through sufferable draconian laws; which restricts us from anything that God has created as good (See 1 Timothy 4:4).

As history has shown – totalitarianism always start small then rules and restrictions incrementally gets worse. During COVID-19, governors, politicians, and experts called for citizens to give up socializing, eating out, and working for lock downs, social distancing and wearing a useless mask for the greater good. Even Dr. Fauci did not agree with the wearing of COVID-19 masks. He mentioned back in February 2020, in leaked emails: "why are masks mandated even when the data showed that they made no difference."[103] Yet on mainstream news Fauci's message was the lie: "wear masks" to "protect" your neighbors.

Evidence has shown, all of the regulations and rules were instruments of social engineering – a method to condition the population to change societal norms. God's Word tells us, "Ye therefore, beloved, seeing ye know these things before, beware least ye also, being led away with the error of the wicked, fall from your own steadfastness" (2 Peter 2:17). Beware of the tricks and deceptions that circulates on the internet, and challenge the statements made by those in authority. I tell you, there is a lot of inconsistencies that only points to fabricated facts. Franklin D. Roosevelt said, "if it happens in the government, it was planned that way." Even today, people still believe in the lie that a mask saves lives, when it really does not. Melanie Hempe, recalls an old fairy tale about *The Emperor's New Clothes,* and asserts:_

"Charlatans come to town and convince the emperor to purchase the most magnificent clothes – that are invisible to the stupid or incompetent. The emperor, unable to see the clothes, but too proud to admit it, struts through the town naked, and everyone goes along with the ruse. It's not until a young child, his voice ringing above the crowd, declares, 'But he hasn't got anything on!' That the townspeople finally take notice. Their pre-set bias got in the way and blinded them – the crowd wanted so badly to believe that something was true that they did."[104]

I believe this fairy tale speaks for itself. For one, regarding the draconian mask mandates – people will go along with practices that is obviously wrong, pretending it's right. But even after someone, with good intentions, expose the lie, amazingly people will still reject the truth – out of fear, for the substance of the lie. An example would be Dr. Fauci's (February 2020) email to Sylvia Burwell. He claimed data suggests wearing masks made no difference in protecting you and I from contracting COVID-19. The virus, so tiny, will easily penetrate the material. Even now, it is inconceivable people grip this lie for truth, while deep – down – inside knows a mask does not protect you and I from contracting this virus. I know people vaccinated, wear masks, and still caught the virus. Why are we wearing them still? It is ultimately up to you, but don't be a fool and fall for these evil schemes.

Please Do Not Submit Yourself To These Evil Schemes!

The apostles' question, in verse 20, conveys if we are in Christ then "why do you live as if you still belong to the world... [Or submit to its regulations, to its rules?]" We, who are in Christ, why do many believers celebrate the idea of this wicked Reset scheme that makes God out to be a liar? Like the Scripture says:

"God is not a man that he should lie; neither the son of man that he should repent: hath he said, and shall he not do it? Or hath he spoken, and shall he not make it good" (Numbers 23:19)?

If you are in Christ, we have died to the basic demonic principles of this world to: 1) trust in man, not God; 2) trust in nature (science); and 3) listen to men rules as key to liberate the world. No matter the decisions we have made from a reservation of lies that pervades our lives will always come with eternal consequences. Most times people fail to count the cost but instead fasten themselves to the seat of deception for a journey into unnecessary hardships.

Paul asserts the remedy in Colossians 2:21 and 22 when he states that it is for godly wisdom to reform the Colossians thinking; look at what the apostle said: "Touch **Not!** Taste **Not!,** Handle **Not** (which all are to per-ish with the using), after the **commandments and doctrines of men** [these are worldly rules as obligations]" (emphasis added).[105]

1. Do not touch!

There was a problem with the Colossian church asking questions to first seek to understand the "silver-lining" herewith these human pre-cepts. For Paul wasted no time to refer to these doctrine-rules as worth-less because of the effort to disqualify members of that church body. For these purity and dietary laws were disguised as pseudo-morality imputed by ruthless community leaders. Even though it was evil, perhaps in the corrupt minds of these leaders they thought their actions were done for purity. Indeed, what is being hyped-up today by fake-news is the constant "food insecurity" to "overpopulation" of the world. It appears the blame has shifted, somehow, to a land deficit for the growing global popula-tions that is antagonistic to the global climate. Yet, in hypocrisy the CCP amended their Population and Family Planning Law allowing families to have up to 3 children as an antidote to avert the low birth rates.

While the climate alarmists have an earnest need to reduce the carbon footprint, they have this idea of diminishing the world population by 6.3 billion people. In Elberton, Georgia, there is a monument called the Georgia Guidestones, it is known by many as the secular "ten command-ments" to globalism written in eight languages: English, Spanish, Swahili, Hindi, Hebrew, Arabic, Chinese and Russian. For the purpose of educa-tion, these ten, what I call abaddonist commandments, are for people to enforce in their daily lives to:

1. Maintain humanity under 500,000,000 in perpetual balance with nature.

2. Balance personal rights with social duties.

3. Be not a cancer on earth – leave room for nature.

4. Unite humanity with a living new language.

5. Rule passion – faith – tradition – and all things with tempered reason.

6. Protect people and nations with fair laws and just courts.

7. Let all nations rule internally resolving external disputes in a world court.

8. Avoid petty laws and useless officials.

9. Prize truth – beauty – love – seeking harmony with the infinite.

10. Guide reproduction wisely – improving fitness and diversity.[106]

Christians are commanded, by God, to abstain from partaking in, devising, adding to, or even, influence people to accept these doctrines (Psalm 50:17-22; Romans 1:32). Many Americans believe the "plandemic of 2020" is the first step to totalitarianism. Thus where a repressive governing body (state and Federal) require from its citizens unremitting subservience. People have been jailed; fined, churches were prohibited from meeting in fear of being labeled "super-spreaders", while strip clubs, Casinos and abortion clinics are left operational. People were encouraged to practice impractical restraint from intimacy – married couples were told to wear masks during sexual intercourse, to even being told in some locations to desist from having any intimate contact, just to eliminate any spread of COVID-19.

There is legislation imposed to ban non-vaccinated people from domestic travel, eating at restaurants, entertainment, grocery shopping, denied enrollment in college classes; hospital – dental treatment, renting housing, and denied employment. Even though these coronavirus mandates are not the mark of the beast – it should give you the chills because of the similarities in the restrictions (like a shadow that gives reflection to what follows behind it). Revelation 13:17 describes "that no man might buy or sell, save he that had the mark, or the name of the beast, or the number of his name."

As citizens we are to obey authority; however, when there is conflicting facts on the transmission, and tightening restrictions that prevent us from enjoying basic constitutional rights, we are to resist! Think about the Black Robe Regiment – a cadre of pastors united to fight during the Revolutionary War to resist tyranny. Let us pray in this time for God to raise up religious leaders and believers to stand up and to speak out.

2. Do Not Taste!

Previously in this chapter. I have described how climate change is the vehicle for the mass production of GMO foods and so buyers beware. Many of the foods people consume are packed with GMOs and chemicals that are found in plastics and metals.

Another excuse for Americans to readjust with GMOs is in an area that is gradually making news is global overpopulation and anti-masculinity, what I call, "de-boy." There is a company in California that has created a GMO that injected spermicide into a gene of a corn seed. The results are simple – a man who eats this GMO brand of corn – he cannot produce children. There are so many foods that have been altered with a higher level of hormones such as estrogen (birth control) aimed to suppress the hormone testosterone in males. Vaccine administration (mRNA) will be made simpler by synthesizing fruits like bananas with this technology.

Many of these contaminated products are then provided to poor, third-world nations because whenever it comes to GMOs being vetted, many countries have little to no standards compared to the U.S.F.D.A. scrutiny. These foods carry with them a dual purpose: (1) provide cheap food sources and (2) most importantly, a proving ground for efficiency in averting fertility. Hypothetically, if I wanted to reduce the fertility rate in Africa or India, I would send foods engineered with GMOs that is capable of accomplishing this goal.

Feminization of men, or to "de-boy," has been increasing since the #Me-To Movement began. On television, there are cereal commercials where a girl's appearance changes into a Tiger, while a boy morphs into what appears to be a feminine version of a Fruit Loop hero. In support of this claim, several well-respected individuals have suggested the cereal commercials delivers this message. So, the effort to "de-boyitize" men is everywhere from commercials, movies, and the food we eat.

Did you know Burger King's "Impossible Whopper" can cause men to develop breasts from consuming too many? This is due to the enormous quantity of estrogen in each Impossible Whopper. James Stangle, a veterinarian, explained this unknown, horrific fact during an interview and contends:

> The Impossible Whopper has 44mg of estrogen and the Whopper has 2.5ng of estrogen. Now let me refresh your metric system. There are 1 million nanograms (ng) in one milligram (mg). That means the Impossible Whopper has 18 million times as much estrogen as a regular Whopper. Just six glasses of soy milk per day has enough estrogen to grow [breasts] on a male. That's the equivalent of eating four Impossible Whoppers per day. You would have to eat 880 pounds of beef from an implanted steer to equal the amount of estrogen in one birth control pill.[107]

Beloved, it is important to know "who you are" in sight of all the hysteria. Let me say this – men need to be men and act like men. It is one thing to respect the opposite sex; which every man should do. Yet it is another to relinquish your responsibility to raise your children, lead your family in the ways of God, and be an example to other young boys. We (men) take for granted the significance of manliness, especially for those without a man to emulate those manly characteristics. It all comes down to if anyone ever asks you this question: "Who are You?" Providing a response should not be challenging, but rather render an articulate and though provoking answer to spark an opportunity for the gospel message.

One day, several of my brothers in Christ had a conversation about this very subject. When one of the guys shared an experience about his time stationed in Japan for several years, he said, "my experience being immersed in Japanese culture showed younger men are effeminate." He then went on to comment on their physique. He explained that it is in the younger men that eschew from the manly traditions and seek a softer look.

3. Do Not Handle!

As believers, we are not to entertain these evil plots, nor yoke together with anyone supporting doctrines of this kind. Moreover, facts indicate what we are experiencing today – the rise of the fourth industrial revolution, climate change, and the Green New Deal (GND). The GND is defined as "a proposed package of United States legislature that aims to address climate change and economic inequality," are a pavilion for scandalous crimes of the century.[108] Where did all of this start? It all had its start from the deep secrets of Satan. All of this perceived wisdom is the offspring of worldly knowledge such as Gnosticism. *Gnosis* is a Greek word that means to be "special" or "superior" as in spiritual knowledge. In the Latin, the word gnosis is translated as *scienta,* hence derives the word *science.*[109] The bottom-line it is the "knowledge covering general truths or the operation of general laws…tested through scientific methods."[110] Many evangelical churches have joined hands with Gnosticism while adopting a foundation centered upon steady streams of Pagan philosophies, with origins adopted from the Greek and Eastern customs. This was nothing new, Apostle Paul addressed the church regarding a system that managed to spew its toxic philosophies; thus insisting followers, as a Gnostic "stipulation," to abstain from consuming meat and follow a rigid lifestyle that included abstinence between married couples. Further pagan practices were premised on "deeds" over "faith" and these maintained that whosoever abided by these strict "stipulations" – meant the adherent cleaves closer to God of the Bible.

Vegetarianism was the result of pagan practices that was born from a "stipulation" adopted by Gnostics, then eventually, assimilating the church. In comparison, the Thyatira church in Revelations 2:18-29, resembles the moral crisis within society today. Its name tells a lot about who they were, as it related to the church condition as an "unweary sacrifice." Indeed, everything looks good on the outside, but on the inside are broke, busted, and disgustingly wicked. Thus there appeared a sort of love in the church to "help others" and be "good" citizens.

Yet, in reality, many members of this community were cowardly and empty. The problem was extensive – for the church was married to the things of the world. Here is a warning: you have to be very careful who you follow. Not everyone with a smile on their face and speaking about unity is of the Household of God. Likewise there was one person, a woman, in the community who Christ gave the moniker "Jezebel," due of her wicked acumen. According to Jesus, the church was tolerating this self-appointed "preacher" operating outside the authority of God. Jesus tears into this church saying, "notwithstanding I have a few things against thee, because thou sufferest that woman Jezebel, which calleth herself a prophetess, to teach and to seduce my servants to commit fornication, and to eat things sacrificed unto idols" (Revelation 2:20). She encouraged the church to practice idolatry and immorality which encompassed sexual rituals to fertility gods. We are talking about sex with temple prostitutes which included extramarital sex acts being acceptable.

The whole idea is insane – right; just like today, Thyatiran believers were naïve to Satan's deep secrets (verse 24). Here is how Jezebel deceived them by the deep secret of Satan – she taught it was acceptable to participate in pagan rites, citing there is no harm, since these pagan gods do not exist. Further, by teaching morality was not a factor because Christ dwells in them. Even today, the Classical Social Theory being the DNA of the GND and the Marxist Great Reset are tightening the Gnostic screws declaring their actions as being good for humanity. In Colossians 2:23, NIV, reminds us: "such regulations indeed have an illusion of wisdom with their self-imposed worship, their false humility."

I remember hearing about a teacher telling an academically challenged student, who is now a news anchor, "lift up your head – you are not stupid, just uneducated." Conversely, the detriment of the Christian church is not that they are stupid, just uneducated. The anecdote to the madness is to lift their heads and see what is going on around them, then commit what they see to prayer. Solomon did just that in the Book of Ecclesiastes 7:25, asserting, "I applied mine heart to know, and to search, and to seek out wisdom, and the reason of things, and to know the wickedness of folly, even of foolishness and madness." Solomon wanted to know the why? The Bereans in Acts 17:11, were called "more noble" for their due diligence to receive Biblical instructions, while taking the time daily, to verify everything against the Scriptures.

Be Careful of Self-imposed Worship of Demons

It is easy for people to be deceived, not knowing they are worshipping idols. I want to provide for you 3 Gnostic deceptions that has a form of godliness, but in reality it is a doctrine of demons:

1. **Nature, science, and animals will be an excuse for lifestyle modifications.** In the Colossians church worship had members practicing astronomy and the zodiac, which some synagogues had floors covered with these inscriptions during the 2 and 3 AD. Even Israel fell into worshipping animals and nature with

the pagans. Therefore in Paul's epistles he eluded to the perils of idol worship that followed over to the European churches during Apostle John's letters to the 7 churches.

2. **Eastern philosophies and religious practices.** Today practitioners argue there is no harm in doing yoga poses – even though each pose symbolizes one of their million (demon) gods. I have heard Christians defend these poses as mere exercises, or yoga gods are not being worshipped. Another lie of the enemy!

3. **Science is the answer to the world's problems, not God.** During the early stages of the COVID-19 crisis all over mainstream media, and politicians, incrementally placed emphasis for leaders and American citizens to "listen to science," means – listen to "Scientia," listen to "Scientia, means – listen to *gnosis*, listen to gnosis, translates to – listen to the "Marxist", listen to the Marxist equals – obey the Great Reset.

Likewise, we were told to "listen to the experts" who are the "neo-priest" of knowledge. Do you remember the former governor of New York, Andrew Cuomo, of whom boldly elevated science above Christ's miracles. Even to mock and revile former Vice President Pence for declaring "we need a miracle." Yet, the former governor's message was for all New Yorkers, not knowing any better, to listen to us, who knows what is best for you.

In conclusion, all of the philosophies of the globalist and politician are nothing more than deceptions to the secrets of Satan. Those who broker the GND, to include the New World Order within the Great Reset, have the Jezebel spirit. Like the Cretans in Titus 1:12, whom were "always liars,' "evil beasts," and "lazy gluttons" these are what you have been called to standup on lookout as a watchman. We are called to the teachings of sound doctrine, all the teachings of the grace of God. It is through Christ "teaching us that, denying ungodliness and worldly lusts, we should live soberly, righteously, and godly, in this present world."

"Looking for that blessed hope, and the glorious appearing of the great God and our Savior Jesus Christ" (Titus 2:13). Our Savior is waiting for those who claim to be in Christ but hold to the deep things of Satan to "remember therefore how thou hast received and heard, and hold fast, and repent. If therefore thou shalt not watch, I will come on thee as a thief, and thou shalt not know what hour I will come upon thee" (Revelation 3:3). You cannot touch, taste nor handle the deep things of Satan. It might be possible, if you receive those simple lies – what will stop you from apostasy?

CHAPTER 7

THE GREAT DECEPTION: TAKE HEED
THAT NO MAN DECEIVE YOU

"And Jesus answered and said unto them, Take heed that no man deceive you. For many shall come in my name, saying, I am Christ; and shall deceive many."

- Matthew 24:4-5

Our foundation text, Matthew 24:4 & 5, takes us back to the Mount of Olives, when Jesus provided a warning to His disciples regarding how men from the 1st century to the Tribulation shall claim to be the Messiah. He said many (GK. *polloi*) will come masquerading, saying, "I am Christ." Like a child listening to a parent, each disciple held onto His instructions to "go ye not therefore after them" (Luke 21:8). Unfortunately, many people throughout history did not take heed to this warning; even now, there are people bending to all forms of deception. For prophecy watchers, the rise of false messiahs have always been of great concern, yet expected. According to the Bible, the end of the Church Age is near. For many believe within every generation, Satan has had someone ready to occupy that unholy vocation, the false messiah. Moreover, many of these imposters whom Satan chose are charismatic and wacky characters, easily disguised behind church growers or social justice movements. It is extremely important to note that identifying them is not a difficult feat. For one, they claim to be Christ, while lacking any of the power that accompanies the name of Jesus. Indeed, a time will come when the false messiah and false prophet will display "great signs" and "wonders" people have never before seen. Does it seem possible that any great sign and wonder will function as a tipping point for people to fall for their spiritual hoax and wither away?

In the Gospels, the Jews and Pharisees were seekers of viable signs for "evidence" to (dis)prove that Jesus was who He claimed to be. All it took was for a sign to coincide with an Old Testament prophecy, such things as raising people from the dead or instantly growing arms back. All these signs were for people to comfortably accept Jesus.

Three years ago, a very popular magician, whose name I will not mention, did several public illusions while on television. Believably, the people present were in shock after witnessing this man levitate off the ground. I have heard of credible eyewitness accounts where people levitated during deliverance events. However, we also understand that Hollywood has the editing technology to manipulate scenes to deliver a scripted outcome. Concerning this magician, I discerned something about him that was demonic; for anyone to levitate is not of God. Did you know Satan can endow his own to perform superhuman acts, such as levitation? Undoubtedly, something as simple as this magician-illusionist performing his art, in the face of hundreds of spectators, will convince people with great signs and wonders. In an article published in *Popular Mechanics*, Courtney Linder, wrote about Microsoft creating a "2D or 3D simulacrum of a person that is dead."[1] It was simply designed for families to apply "images, voice data, social media posts, text messages and written letters to create or mortify a special index in theme of the specific person's personality."[2] In 2019, *60 Minutes* aired an episode introducing this technology and conducted interviews with chatbots of deceased Holocaust survivors in real-time. These are examples that reflects the spirit of the Beast, after he suffers his fatal head wound and "heals" from it.

Nathan E. Jones, in *Exposing Evil Seducers & Their Last Days Deception*, alludes to Jesus' warning for signs of false messiahs, and he writes:

> Jesus lists false messiahs as the very first thing. He did not just mention this sign once, but three times throughout His Olivet Discourse. False teachers are actually the most prolific end-time sign Jesus taught. Not only in Matthew 24:4-5 does He mention them, but then in verse 11, He does so again: "Then many false prophesy will rise up and deceive many." Again, in verse 24, Jesus warns. "For false [c]hrists and false prophets will rise and show great signs and wonders to deceive, if possible, even the elect. Three times in this passage, Jesus stated that false prophets and false christs would come claiming to be Jesus, and they would mislead many people with their heretical teachings.[3]

People Who Have Been False Messiahs

Throughout history, there has been several people who claimed to be the messiah. In this section, I want to identify three men whom many have heard of, but know less about.

Jim Jones

Jim Jones was the founder of the Temple Christian Church, located in the jungle of the South American nation of Guyana. Jonestown was the utopian village, far away from the corrupted oppression that troubled America. Somehow, over 900 people were brainwashed to leave their lives in America, to surrender their freedom to this master manipulator. You might have heard the analogy, "You've drunk the red kool-aid," implying someone partaking in some activity that had unfavorable consequences. It comes from the following incident.

In 1978, after receiving their last and false revelation, Jones stressed to his victims that it was the will of God to commit suicide together by consuming poison. There were some who, at that final moment, understood Jones did not have their best interest in mind. Therefore, those brave few mustered enough courage to escape, but were eventually captured and murdered. Sadly, during the recovery of the bodies, an audio recording was found and revealed a horrific moment, with many women and children heard wailing out of fear.

David Koresh

Founded in 1955, its cultic practices was made known by a leader named David Koresh, for whom was responsible for the Branch Davidians siege, in Waco, Texas. He preached a false doctrine, claiming the Book of Revelation was the foundation of salvation.[4] On April 19, 1993, an extremely hot day, Federal law enforcement raided the Branch Davidian compound. I remember this day well, as I was stationed at Fort Hood, and it was my birthday. I distinctly remember watching footage of armored vehicles and Federal agents exchanging gunfire with the Davidians. When agents attempted to breach the second-story windows, many were shot in the raid. All of sudden, a fire ensued, eventually destroying the structure. Consequently, Koresh died in the inferno, along with many other members of his cult. The image of this building in flames will be engraved into the memory of history, aware women and children were trapped in a burning lie.

Sun Myung Moon

Sun Myung Moon was born in Korea (1920-2012), and was the founder of the Unification Church that is a part from the New Age Movement. At an early age, Moon experimented with the spirit world, through his "ancestral veneration," according to Walter Martin.[5] He eventually grew into hyperspiritualism with visions of Jesus that became the center of controversy towards the authenticity of his claims. Many of Moon's claims of Christ visiting him were in question, due to the changing facts of at least five alleged visits. For instance, Walter Martin, in his book *The Kingdom of the Cults*, delivers a bombshell during his investigation into Moon's claims, and asserts: "the most devastating blow to Moon's credibility for his vision is that April 17, 1935 was not on 'Easter Sunday' or 'Easter morning'… because Easter Sunday was on April 21 in 1935."[6] Martin concludes that in 1935, Moon was fifteen, further invalidating his claim. However, Moon was sixteen on Easter Sunday on April 12, 1936.[7]

False messiahs are men with little self-control. Indeed, Moon was a devoted sex addict, accustomed to having sex with members of his congregation. Women were encouraged to have sex with Moon three times to escape the "original sin" through a spiritual cleansing rite called "blood cleansing."[8] There were many accounts of Moon's evil behavior that not only included the manipulation of women, but he also served two years in prison for bigamy and thirteen months for tax evasion.[9]

Moon's theology was fragile, teaching that Christ's work on the Cross only supplied a partial salvation; claiming that the only way to experience complete salvation was through the Unification Church. Even though he believed Jesus came in the flesh, Christ's deity was undermined, and at the same time, it implied God is a liar. This all qualifies Moon as a false messiah. The Apostle John wrote in 2 John 7-11:

> For many deceivers are entered into the world, who confess not that Jesus Christ is come in the flesh. This is a deceiver and an antichrist. Look to yourselves, that we lose not those things which we have wrought, but that we receive a full reward. Whosoever transgresseth, and **abideth not** in the **doctrine of Christ**, hath not God. He that abideth in the doctrine of Christ, he hath both the Father and the Son. (emphasis added)

The Antichrist

"Little children, it is the last time: and as ye have heard that antichrist shall come, even now are there many antichrists: whereby we know that it is the last time" (1 John 2:18).

The Apostle John gives us ample warning about the end-times, when there will appear a man, known as the Antichrist or the first beast. Revelation 6:1-2 is the beginning of the Tribulation, with the occurrence of the Seven Seals Judgement. John's account gives us the indication that the first seal is an inauguration for the Antichrist, whom is fully possessed by Satan and will terrorize this godless world. John wrote, "And I saw when the Lamb opened one of the seals, and I heard, as it were the noise of thunder, one of the four beasts saying, Come and see. And I saw, and behold a white horse: and he that sat on him had a bow: and a crown was given unto him: and he went forth conquering, and to conquer" (Revelation 6:1-2).

The Antichrist will come on a counterfeit white horse, symbolizing a man who will imitate Christ and his message of peace, as Revelation 19:11 suggests. In contrast, Jesus will return on a white horse with a significant difference; "He that sat upon him was called Faithful and True." Moreover, Jesus will come to judge and make war in righteousness. However, the Antichrist, as described in Daniel 9:26 & 27, will "destroy the city and the sanctuary... and he shall confirm the covenant with many for one week: and in the midst of the oblation to cease, and for the overspreading of abominations he shall make it desolate." He will desecrate the restored Jerusalem temple and prohibit Jews from worship. This man will make a deceptive covenant with Israel for one week, then forfeit the agreement to murder the nation of Israel, along with the Tribulation Saints; causing this time to resemble the Holocaust on steroids (Revelation 13:7). He will establish the one world government (Abaddonist Beast financial system and the UN combined) that encompasses a full activation of a global currency. Interestingly, could the Great Reset and the United Nations 2030 agenda be the staging ground for the Abaddonist Beast System? What does this mean for the Church? Does this mean the previously mentioned agendas are an unconscious, preparatory instrument for the Antichrist? Many prophecy watchers think so!

We do not know when the Tribulation will happen; although, there are signs that validate the end of this age is here. We do not know when the Rapture of the Church will happen; however, I want to be clear, the Rapture will precede the Tribulation (See 1 Corinthians 15:51-52; 1 Thessalonians 4:17; Revelation 3:10). The Rapture will designate the end of the Church Age, consequently propelling the world into chaos as millions of people instantly vanish. Imagine, young children vanishing from the arms of their mothers, spouses vanishing while the other is left behind, and most megachurches are still full.

During the Tribulation, no one will own anything, because it will all belong to the Antichrist. The establishment of a global surveillance state will turn the planet into a slave plantation. If you want to know how this will look, look at China. China is littered with millions of cameras in their cities to spy on their citizens, and gauge citizens' loyalty through a Social Credit Score, which means you have more privileges for travel, employment, and financial comfort. A low score suggests a less loyal citizen (Christians, Muslims and journalists) with restrictions regarding employment, travel, et cetera.

Every nation will surrender their sovereignty to this man for seven horrific years, as the calamities will become unbearable, thus making the seven years seem like thirty years. People do not realize the greatest impact during the Tribulation will be the judgments destroying vast amounts of "physical earth," while those who receive the Mark and reject the gift of salvation will share in this judgment. Those who are wise and repent of their sins and confess Jesus Christ is Lord, they shall be saved.

Some may incredulously ask, "Are you saying, people can receive salvation during the Tribulation?" Yes, there will be Tribulation Saints, because God grants (GK: *doreomai*) salvation through Jesus Christ to the Jews and Gentiles during the Tribulation (See Luke 10:32, 12:32; 2 Peter 1:3). Therefore, the Holy Spirit does not depart the earth. What does occur during this time is that the hand of God is removed, which means He will have stepped aside, turning the world over to consequences of its actions. Nevertheless, we do not hear about the Church after Revelation 4 until chapter 19, which is the time Christ returns to establish His Millennial Kingdom. Amen! You can view the evidence written in Revelation 7:14, that says, "And I said unto him, Sir, thou knowest. And he said to me, These are they which came out of great tribulation, and have washed their robes, and made them in the blood of the Lamb." This text can be viewed in two ways: 1) the great multitude refers to the raptured believers, or 2) these refer to those martyred during the Tribulation. I believe the latter view sufficient, for no one knows the actual time period this will occur.

Where Does the Antichrist Come From?

In Revelation 13:1, as I previously mentioned earlier in this book, the Antichrist will come out of the sea of humanity, which refers to people in general. There is evidence to this claim found in Daniel 7:7, which implies this evil man will rise out of the revived Roman Empire (European Union) and will likely be a Jew. He may have none, or some, political experience, similar to how former President Obama was thrusted into national status. It is possible the Antichrist may come on the scene like former President Trump, a non-politician with celebrity clout that gives him leverage. Mr. Antichrist will gain notoriety for having the sophisticated solution and will become the voice that unites the world beneath him. It will likely be so impressive that a Nobel Peace Prize will be granted to him out of amazement.

The False Prophet

And I beheld another beast coming up out of the earth: and he had two horns like a lamb, and spake as a dragon. And he exerciseth all the power of the first beast before him, and causeth the earth and them which dwell therein to worship the first beast, whose deadly wound was healed.

-Revelation 13:11-13

John's following vision describes another coming from the earth (just like the Antichrist), and this will be the second beast, the False Prophet. He is a powerful religious figure who appears to be godly, Christ-like, and meek, but his tongue speaks lies and is evil as Satan's. His mission, however, is to enforce a global worship of the Antichrist. Can anything be more disturbing then when millions of people will come to worship a man because of an exhibition of signs and wonders to the world? John says, "and he doeth great wonders, so that he maketh fire come down from heaven on the earth in the sight of men" (Revelation 13:13). Boldly, the false prophet will order people to "make an image to the beast," so he can "give life" to the image (Revelation 13:14-15). The False Prophet will perform "miracles" with the "power" granted to him, "that the image of the beast both speak, and cause that as many as would not worship the image of the beast should be killed" (Revelation 13:15).

In May 2021, did you see the world's largest talking and moving statue, named "The Giant," which stands at ten stories high? Elizabeth Montgomery wrote about it in the *Arizona Republic*: "The Giant's arms and head can move in multiple directions and would change shape every hour as crowds gather below. The Giant can **take on any image** so you could even find yourself featured, talk about the ultimate selfie. The statue can also sing and speak" (emphasis added).[10] The world is moving closer and closer to worshipping an image that will become a fountain of solutions to a dying world: the Antichrist.

The Mark of the Beast

Currently, prophecy watchers are on the look-out for signs of any technology that remotely resembles Revelation 13's "Mark of the Beast." Some believers have inquired if the COVID-19 vaccine is the Mark of the Beast. My answer to this question is an emphatic NO! Here is some consolation: the Rapture hasn't occurred yet, people are not being murdered for refusing the shots, nor has any of the bowl judgments been unleashed upon the planet. Therefore, no, the vaccines are not the Mark of the Beast.

Now, I will say this, the spirit of the Mark is there. Vaccine mandates being imposed, where unvaccinated people cannot travel, work, buy, sell, and so forth, is a forerunner of the Mark! We are witnessing prominent pastors refusing to provide members with an exemption based on their subjective view, rather than the sincere view of the member. I view this as wrong, and it needs to be checked. If the member is sincere about their doubts and beliefs, then give them the exemption. I have wondered if the churches left behind during the Tribulation will become agents for the Beast, making strides to convince the "sincere" elect to accept the Mark, claiming it to be safe or asserting, "This here chip is not the Mark of the Beast."

John gives us details to measure current events against actual Tribulation events, and he said, "And he causeth all, both small and great, rich and poor, free and bond, to receive a mark in their right hand, or in their foreheads: and that no man might buy, sell, save he that had the mark, or the name of the beast, or the number of his name" (Revelation 13:16-17). Now, in the 21st century, we understand technology better than previous generations because of the rapid advancement in capabilities. It is possible that technology like, according to Cyrus Parsa, Neuralink's Neuralace implants will connect people with machines by chip implants into the brain.[11] Even a hybrid mark in the forehead or hand may contain nanotechnology that operates as a sensor, thus linking to the brain implant, which can remarkably interface with Internet of Things (IoT) and stored in the cloud.[12] Once the implant is operational, the recipient will lose sovereignty over his – or herself. They will become an operating system where, at the mercy of the Antichrist, ASI (Artificial Super Intelligence) can instantly download data or upgrade software in chips, which in the worst case can make the person appear to be possessed by a demon.[13]

There are countries racing to be the first to implement this technology. For example, Sweden is scheduled to fully implement a cashless society by 2023 with an implant microchip, the size of a grain of rice. The implant will go, just underneath the skin of the hand, which will render cash and credit cards obsolete.

However, there will be many Antichrists and False Prophets who will sum up the Church Age. Many of them are engaged in deceiving the world, dividing societies, and spreading lies, while making gains in preparation for the Beast system implementation. Since the 2020 election, their voices have grown louder and more spirited in their intentions for a One World Government. All the while, their lust for power is fomenting discord and hatred against Jesus Christ.

Even today, we are witnessing in America a diet-sized oppression inflicted upon Christians during the "plandemic." I often wonder what will be the magnitude of the violence towards Christians during the Tribulation. It is possible to compare such violence to that occurring in Nigeria. For example, 43,000 have been killed and 18,000 are missing in just over a decade. On June 6, 2021, Islamic Jihadists murdered 160 Christians and receptive Muslims in Burkina Faso, West Africa, which is known as the Muslim Sahel region.

A Decade of the False Prophets

Once upon a time, a wolf resolved to disguise his appearance in order to secure food more easily. Encased in the skin of a sheep, he pastured with the flock deceiving the shepherd by his costume. In the evening, he was shut up by the shepherd in the fold; the gate was closed and the entrance made thoroughly secure. But the shepherd, returning to the fold during the night to obtain meat for the next day, mistakenly caught up the wolf instead of a sheep and killed him instantly. Harm seek, harm find.

- Aesop[14]

This post-coronavirus world has afforded us an opportunity to witness, first-hand, the character of many individuals claiming to be representatives of God, but who in reality are destructive. In Aesop's story, the determined wolf saw an opportunity to satisfy his hunger by disguising himself as one of the sheep. Deep inside, his wisdom took him to a place where his character could not keep him – the Kingdom of God. He diligently exercised being disciplined among the sheep, which required adopting the vernacular, the behavior, and the walk of a sheep, so none were afraid to be around this wolf in sheep's clothing.

The Apostle Paul said, "for such are false apostles, deceitful workers, transforming themselves into the apostle of Christ, and no marvel; for Satan himself is transformed into an angel of light" (2 Corinthians 11:13-14). They will come on the scene speaking of love and Jesus, but will deny the whole counsel of God. We are given warning after warning to take heed of the imminent dangers believers face, that seek to destroy the body of Christ. For our Lord and Savior, Jesus Christ, insists:

Beware of false prophets, which come to you in sheep's clothing, but inwardly, they are ravening wolves. Ye shall know them by their fruits. Do men gather grapes of thorns, or figs of thistles? Even so every good tree bringeth forth good fruit but a corrupt tree bringeth forth evil fruit. A good tree cannot bring forth evil fruit, neither can a corrupt tree bring forth good fruit (Matthew 7:15-18).

A Dangerous Man: Jorge Mario Bergoglio (aka Pope Francis)

Warning! There is a charlatan that goes by Pope Francis, the 266th pontiff of the largest Christian denomination, the Roman Catholic Church. When we think about the qualities of a religious leader, the books of Scripture that teach about these are 1 Timothy 3 and Titus 1. However, if there is one religious leader that definitively has a spirit of the Antichrist, it is this man, Pope Francis. He has "departed from the faith, giving heed to seducing spirits and doctrine of devils" (1 Timothy 4:1). Why has Pope Francis caused so much confusion within the Catholic Church, and it is still unconscionable to discuss removing him? Regardless, in this section, we will expose three areas Pope Francis has given heed to the doctrines of demons and seducing spirits: doctrine error, homosexuality, and universalism.

Doctrine Error

Through discernment, our Bible teaches us how to operate as fruit inspectors, and we ought to take serious this danger and study God's Word, so that our discernment is strengthened and for identifying these tricksters. All believers have the responsibility to confront these men and women who deliberately speak lies, deceiving people, and twisting Biblical Truths. Does an apple tree produce oranges? No. Does a banana tree have apples? No. Does a good tree produce bad fruit? No. Jesus teaches us to identify these destructive ideas, "which cause divisions and offences contrary to the doctrine which ye have learned; and avoid them" (Romans 16:17). There is a deep well of evidence that testifies Pope Francis is spoiled fruit. Think back to the first two chapters of this book, in which the premise encouraged you to develop a sound theology in Biblical doctrines, and among such doctrines, we discussed the Doctrine of Sin and Hell.

Considering the integrity of these doctrines, his understanding of Hell contradicts the Christian Bible and Catholic doctrine. Pope Francis had the nerve to proclaim, "There is no hell where sinners suffer in eternity." How is that so, when the Bible clearly describes Hell as a real place? In fact, in Revelation 20:14, John wrote, "Death and hell were cast into the lake of fire. This is the second death."

Jesus was clear in Matthew 10:28, for everyone to "fear him which is able to destroy both soul and body **in hell**" (emphasis added). We can find more evidence in Luke 16:19 & 22-24, which depicts Hell as the locale where the rich man cried out: "for I am tormented in this flame." The only place there will be flames is in Hell and the fiery pit – nowhere else.

Regardless of the evidence, the Pope's rebellious nature steadily deceives 1.3 billion people by saying, "after death, those who do not repent cannot be pardoned, and they disappear." Alright, where do the unpardoned go, then? This is the type of confusion that Satan desires for people. According to the Bible, a person whom dies in their sin is forever separated from God; however, the Pope disagrees with these Scriptures. Conversely, a question must be raised: where does the unrepentant go for eternity? "Hell does not exist, but what does exist is the disappearance of sinful souls," said Pope Francis. What a bold statement to contradict Scripture, which draws into question his belief in the God of the Bible.

The Word of God tell us, "For if God spared not the angels that sinned, but **cast them down to hell,** and delivered them into chains of darkness, to be reserved unto judgment; and spared not the old world, but saved Noah the eighth person, a preacher of righteousness, bringing in the floor upon the world of the ungodly" (2 Peter 2:4-5, emphasis added). Moreover, even the writer of Hebrews asserts, "For if we sin willfully after that we have received the knowledge of the truth, there remaineth no more sacrifice for sins, but a certain fearful looking for of judgment and fiery indignation, which shall devour the adversaries" (Hebrews 10:26-27). Anyone reading this must know that those whom uphold the Pope's belief system is calling God a liar! God is not a liar, for He cannot lie (Hebrews 6:18). The Apostle John follows up with, "little children, let no one deceive you: he that doeth righteousness is righteous, even as he is righteous. He who committeth sin is of the devil; for the devil sinneth from the beginning" (1 John 3:7). In the Greek, when it says, "doeth righteousness" the word, *poion,* which translates to "make it a practice to do" right, as it requires a person to practice to refrain from a homosexual lifestyle.[15] Likewise, the Pope has failed to practice proclaiming God's Truth, but instead sins by proclaiming the doctrine of demons. Right now, if you follow Pope Francis' teaching, you must repent and turn away from this evil man.

Homosexuality

During the 2020 *Francesco* documentary, Pope Francis gave an interview pertaining to civil unions and said, "Homosexual people have the right to be in a family. They are children of God. You can't kick someone out of a family, nor make their life miserable for this. What we have to have is a civil union law; that way, legally, they are legally covered."[16] Christians are called to love our neighbors and treat all people with love, dignity and respect; this includes those whose lifestyle, according to the Bible, are an abomination. We are to share our example in Christ Jesus, in the hope of being a bright example for them to recognize their sin and depart from it. What the Pope's message is stating goes against the authenticity of Biblical truths. During an interview in *America* magazine, the Pope said:

A person once asked me, in a provocative manner, if I approved of homosexuality. I replied with another question: "Tell me: when God looks at a gay person, does he endorse the existence of this person with love, or reject and condemn this person?" We must always consider the person.[17]

The bottom-line: people who do not believe in God's justice and re-demptive plan will believe in anything and will accept philosophies as a main form of belief. A line must be drawn, for Christianity is not social justice, and social justice is not Christian. Lifeway Research conducted a survey of 1,000 Protestant pastors who were asked if they saw anything "wrong with legal civil unions between two people of the same gen-der." 30% of mainline pastors strongly agreed compared to the 9% of evangelicals whom strongly agreed.[18] The Apostle Paul made it clear that any unrepentant person, meaning those who are active in their sexual immorality or corrupt behavior, is grounds to excommunications from the Church. In 1 Corinthians 6:9, the Apostle Paul asserted, "Know ye not that the unrighteous shall not inherit the Kingdom of God? Be not deceived: neither fornicators, nor idolaters, nor adulterers, nor effemi-nate, nor abusers of themselves with mankind." First, we must ask the question: what does Paul mean? Does he speak in the literal, figurative, or allegorical sense? The answer is to articulate Paul's assertion in the literal sense, for three reasons:

1. Elsewhere, in Paul's epistles and John's prophecy (Galatians 5:21; Ephesians 5:5; and Revelation 21:8), refers to the same menu of transgressions that prohibits one from inheriting the Kingdom of God.

2. The Greek verb, *ete* (you were), is in the imperfect tense – a past continuous action that does not indicate when the action was complete.

3. Paul spoke of a tendential action; this refers to a repeated effort.

We can say there were believers within the Corinthian Church whom Paul knew had struggled with these sins, but prevailed against it. This church was a mixture of slaves, aristocrats, Jews, and Gentiles. Many had been pagan priests, priestesses or partakers in the temples' ceremonies, having orgies with male and female temple prostitutes. Paul was not concerned as to when the individual conquered the sin, but the only thing that mattered was that the sin was no longer an issue in their lives.

Also, the word, "unrighteous" (Gk. *adikas*: means a lack of integrity or honesty), covers a wide spectrum of customs.[19] It introduces offenses to which any person whom lacks integrity will rehearse these sins, as a habit, and will consequently not inherit the Kingdom of God. "Now this I say, brethren, that flesh and blood cannot inherit the kingdom of God; neither doth corruption inherit incorruption" (1 Corinthians 15:50).

The Bible is clear that anyone who is a practicing "effeminate" (means a male prostitute or transvestite) or homosexuals (Gk. *arsenokoites*: refers to a male engaging in same-gender sexual activity) are against God's divine plan.[20] In 1 Corinthians 16:13, Paul emphasizes for men to behave manly unto himself (Gk. *andrizomai*; in the middle voice) as being a part of one's faith. According to Romans 1:26-27, Paul explains that male and female participants of homosexual relations are pregnant with "degrading passions." He charged that the women did change the "natural" (Gk. *physikos*: means agreeable to nature) use into that which is "against" nature.[21] We must refer back to Genesis 2:24, when God drew the woman from Adam's side; thus instituting His divine standard for creation, as the process of nature. For one, man and woman were aligned together in harmony, codified as a covenant standard for the marriage union, requiring one man to "cleave to his wife: they shall be one flesh." God's design has never gone void, which is why, in Romans 1, any union outside of this command is deemed unnatural, in error, and a shameful act (Gk. *aschēmosynē*: refers to indecency or shame).[22] Conversely, in Acts 17:30, the Apostle Paul made clear that salvation could not be achieved through one's own intervention, for the time of ignorance has passed due to man's wickedness. He said:

And the times of this ignorance God winked at; but now commandeth all men everywhere to repent: because he hath appointed a day, in which he will judge the world in righteousness by that man whom he hath ordained; whereof he hath given assurance unto all men, in that he hath raised him from the dead.

In this passage, God declared that all mankind must reflect on their sinful actions, and thereby set all their wickedness aside through repentance, to seek obedience in Him. Mankind, for the most part, does not desire to surrender itself, because of how God is represented in one's own imagination. Many have made Christ into their own corrupt image.

A Catholic High School was sued by Lynn Starkey, a homosexual who was terminated for being in a same-sex marriage, has claimed discrimination under Free Exercise and Establishment Clauses of the First Amendment. On August 11, 2021, Michael Gryboski, of *Christianpost.com*, wrote, "United States District Judge Richard Young ruled that the Catholic institution was free to fire Starkley on the basis of its religious standards for employment and that a secular court had no place to interfere in the decision."[23] Does the Church have a right to follow their statement of faith on these matters, and not be force to comply with an unbiblical lifestyle? How has God viewed this behavior throughout Biblical history? Where, in the Bible, does verses supporting homosexuality exist? There are none. Listed below are three Biblical truths that challenge the sin of homosexuality:

1. False prophets lie, affirming people to practice homosexual behavior. (1 Corinthians 6:9-11; 1 Thessalonians 4:1-8; 2 Thessalonians 2:7-12; and 2 Peter 2:1-3).

2. You cannot hyphenate Christianity (there's no such thing as a gay-Christian, thief-Christian, etc. (Isaiah 30:8-13; Jude 7; Romans 1:32 and chapter 6; 1 Corinthians 1:18-31; 5:9-13; 6:9; Galatians 5:19-21; Colossians 3:1-8; Hebrews 10:26&31; 11:6; 1 Peter 4:16-19).

3. People "are not" born homosexual; it is not an immutable characteristic (Deuteronomy 22:5; Romans 5:12-21; 1 Timothy 1:4-11; 6:10).

Did you know that the city of Sodom is mentioned 49 times in both the Old Testament and New Testament? There is a reason for this, of course. Adam's sin was inbred into humanity and because of his sin, disobedience became sin of the heart. The bottom line: any practice of homosexuality originates from the heart, for what the man thinks, so he is. Whatever God of the Bible considers an abomination, even today, is incompatible with Christian teachings. There is a source to this wickedness. Satan has ordained three specific demonic spirits to influence this behavior: the crown of the snake (kundalini), the incubus, and the succubus (both of these demons molest people). For instance, in the first century, Emperor Heliogabalus was known by the people as being mentally ill, because he continually dressed in women's clothing and married a dissolute boy.

Some may ask, what if the person is not an active homosexual and renounces the lifestyle? Do they still not inherit the Kingdom of God? The answer to this question is found in 1 John 1:9, which says, "If we confess our sins, he is faithful and just to forgive us our sins, and to cleanse us from **all unrighteousness**" (emphasis added). I would ask, did the person renounce the homosexual lifestyle and believe Jesus is Lord? Did they ask for Him to be Lord over their decisions and lifestyle? Did they ask Jesus to teach them His ways? The unrighteous are those who do not renounce, nor turn away from their sins. The unrighteous are anyone who accepts, or finds pleasure in, those who live in rebellion against God (see Romans 1:32).

Universalism

Pope Francis believes Christ's gift of salvation is granted automatically to unbelievers and atheists. This is not a hyperbole, nor an attack against this man, but a mere fact presented within this section. In a response to an inquiry made within a newspaper back in 2013, the Pope explained:

> You ask me if the God of the Christians forgive those who don't believe and who don't seek the faith. I start by saying... that God's mercy has no limits if you go to him with a sincere and contrite heart. The issue for those who do not believe in God is to obey their conscience.[24]

Pope Francis' response fits within the scope of universalism – the solemn belief that Christ's love for all mankind will never allow for anyone to perish, regardless of one's acceptance of Him, or their belief, lifestyle, sin, or religion, that all will be saved. There are signs to identify a Universalist: one is their hyper-utilization of the term, "love." No doubt, for God's love abounds much, but so does His justice, mercy, and the remainder of the whole counsel of God. However, Norman Geisler explains that "universalism derives from the word *apokatastasis* (i.e., "restoration," in Acts 3:21), is the belief eventually everyone will be saved."[25]

Let's say, there were two babies born in two different states by two different mothers. As they grow up and become adults, one hears about Christ and believes, while the other person does not hear about Christ and dies. Does the latter person go to Hell? Yes is the answer. Consider this: if Jesus had not discovered the twelve disciples, would each one of them gone to Hell? Yes, but by believing in Jesus as Lord, Heaven became their final destination. How is it that someone who has not heard about Christ will go to Hell? It does not seem fair. However, as Adam is the father of all mankind, and sin is hereditary (passed down to everyone), which requires a blood offering to atone for sin.

Animals will not suffice, therefore God came down in the form of God-Man – Christ Jesus, "and for this cause, he is the mediator of the new testament, that by means of death, for the redemption of the transgressions that were under the first testament, they which are called might receive the promise of eternal inheritance" (Hebrews 9:15). In John 3:3, the Bible says, "verily, verily, I say unto thee, except a man be born again, he cannot see the Kingdom of God." Jesus prayed to the Father, "I have manifested thy name unto the men which thou gavest me out of the world; thine they were, and thou gavest them me; and they have kept thy word" (John 17:6). Here is Scriptural evidence that Jesus will not grant salvation without believing in Him:

For I have given unto them the words which thou gavest me; and **they have received them,** and have known surely that I came out from thee, and they have **believed** that thou didst send me. I pray for them: I pray **not for the world but** for them **which thou has givest me;** for they are thine (John 17:8-9, emphasis added).

Even Ephesians 2: 4-5 mentions:

But God, who is rich in mercy, for his great love wherewith he loved us. Even when we were dead in sins, hath quickened us together with Christ, by grace ye are saved.

And also, evidence is seen in 1 Corinthians 2:14:

But the natural man receiveth not the things of the Spirit of God: for they are foolishness unto him: neither can he know them, because they are spiritually discerned (1 Corinthians 2:14).

What the Apostle Paul has alluded to is the natural man is the unbeliever or atheist; they lack the capacity for spiritual thoughts and words that sums up the knowledge of God. "He that hath the Son hath life; and he that hath **not the Son of God hath not life**. These things have I written unto you that believe on the name of the Son of God; that ye may know that ye have eternal life, and that ye many believe on the name of the Son of God" (1 John 5:12-13, emphasis added). "For Christ is the end of the law for righteousness to every one that believeth" (Romans 10:4). What this means is that those whom have not received Christ as Lord and Savior will pay for their sin debt, whereas, those of us whom received Christ as Lord over all things and accept that HE paid our sin debt on the Cross at Calvary. One must confess it, believe it, and receive it. (See Romans 10:9-10).

Universalism is contrary to the Christian orthodoxy that surrounds God's love, justice, and redemptive plan; which states, "the Lord knoweth how to deliver the **godly** out of temptation, and to reserve the **unjust** unto the day of judgment **to be punished**" (2 Peter 2:9, emphasis added). At this point, a distinction is made between anyone declared godly from those deemed as being unjust. It is no question whether both incumbents will receive recompense according to their works. For one, the godly will not suffer the penalty of God's judgment, because they are delivered through the Rapture. Meanwhile, the ungodly has a one-way ticket to the Tribulation, Hell, and the Lake of Fire.

The Apostle Paul agrees, and said: "But I say, that the things which the Gentiles sacrifice, they sacrifice **to devils**, and **not to God**: and I would not that ye should have fellowship with devils. (Apostle Paul related details pertaining to the prohibition on pagan customs and rituals under the crosshairs of God's justice) Ye cannot drink the cup of the Lord, and the cup of devils: ye cannot be partakers of the Lord 's Table, and of the table of devils" (1 Corinthians 10:20-21, emphasis added). In other words, the unrighteous cannot sit at the Table of God, as it is reserved for holy people.

Let's explore this further, God does not force anyone to walk in His precepts. If it were so, love (GK. *agape*) would no longer exist, but would instead be abuse. That is why the Gospel of John teaches, "But these are written, that ye might believe that Jesus is the Christ, the Son of God; and that believing ye might have life through his name" (John 20:31). One of the early Church fathers refused to accept the Universalist theology based on its poison; Justin Martyr (AD 100 – AD 165) asserts:

For among us the prince of the wicked spirits is called the serpent, and Satan, and the devil, as you can learn by looking into our writings. And that he would be sent into the fire with his host, and the men who follow him, and would be punished for an endless duration, Christ foretold.[26]

In Mike Gendron's, "Pontif Proclaims All Go To Heaven," he claims that all unbelievers, until they receive Christ as Lord and Savior, are children of the devil.[27] I agree. Dr. R.A. Torrey, once said, "The reason that men do not believe is that they are not living up to what they do believe, or they have not surrendered their wills to God, or they do not study the evidence that is calculated to produce belief."[28] However, Satan has blinded the Pope, allowing him to speak lies, thus binding the lost to a twisted ideology that codifies evil as good. In May 2013, in the *Religion News Service,* there was printed evidence that proved Pope Francis held to the doctrine of demons, claiming, "The Lord has redeemed all of us, all of us, with the Blood of Christ: all of us, not just Catholics. Everyone… even the atheists. Everyone! The Blood of Christ has redeemed us all!"[29]

In September 2021, the Pope had a discussion on the controversy prohibiting abortion supporters from receiving communion; albeit, the Pope had encouraged priests to disregard the Catholic doctrine, which forbids communion to the unrepentant and advocates for abortion. Nevertheless, one would think doctrinal integrity would be upheld as the right course of action; however, Pope Francis said, "Whenever the church, in order to defend a principle, didn't do it pastorally, it has taken political sides. If a pastor leaves the pastorality of the church, he immediately becomes a politician."

Indeed, the Pope has joined with forty other religious leaders to create "Faith in Science," which calls for a Green Sabbath or Climate Sunday, requiring a shut-down of industries for one day a week to reduce emissions.

False Prophet: A Hyper-spiritual Mess

And if thou say in thine heart, How shall we know the word which the Lord hath not spoken? When a prophet speaketh in the name of the Lord, if the thing follow or not, nor come to pass, that is the thing which the Lord hath not spoken, but the prophet hath spoken it presumptuously: thou shalt not be afraid of him.

-Deuteronomy 18:21-22

The *St. Louis Post-Dispatch* did an editorial about a radio show that was aired on June 25, 2021, by Jan Markell, the founder of Olive Tree Ministries, during her weekend Christian radio program called *Understanding the Times*. The episode was titled: "Why Were Most of the Prophets Wrong When It Came to Predicting the Outcome of the 2020 Election?" Several well-known Pentecostal and Charismatic preachers had boldly claimed that God told them that President Trump would be reelected in 2020. In one instance, Ms. Markell played a clip of an alleged prophet, Kat Kerr, prophesying that, "Trump will win. ... He will sit in that office for four more years, and God will have his way in this country."[30]

Evangelical and Pentecostal leaders are urging preachers to be more responsible and not speak things that will draw confusion and bring reproach to the Kingdom of God. It is necessary to remind everyone who functions in the ministry of exhortation or any spiritual gift, how God will hold these workers to a higher standard, especially when claiming God said something that doesn't happen. For instance, in Jeremiah, Hananiah had falsely predicted that the Babylonian exile would last for two years, but according to God, the exile will last seventy years (Jeremiah 28:5-17). Interestingly, in verse 9, Jeremiah stood in the presence of the priests and people, saying, "The prophet which prophesieth of peace, when the word of the prophet be known, that the Lord hath truly sent him."

Another false account regarding a "Pickneyville, Illinois preacher, who claims followers across North and South America, posted a YouTube 'prophecy' in May [2021] declaring Trump would be reinstalled in the White House on July 4. It was, of course, nonsense."[31] There is a website that is actively pursuing preachers to alter their behavior by encouraging them to sign a statement of accountability on the website *propheticstandards.com* to combat manipulation:

> We recognize the unique challenges posed by the internet and social media, as anyone claiming to be a prophet can release a word to the general public without any accountability or even responsibility... the spiritual manipulation of the prophetic gift for the personal benefit of the prophet or of his or her ministry, whether to garner favor, power, or financial gain. And under no circumstances can a prophet charge money to deliver a prophetic word. This is spiritual abuse of the worst kind and is detestable in God's sight.[32]

WARNING: False Teachings

Recently, there is a resurrection of destructive false teachings that date back to the early 20th century. Daniel said it plainly, "the wicked shall do wickedly; and none of the wicked shall understand; but the wise shall understand" (Daniel 12:10). The towering philosophies and doctrines that are heard in many churches are more times likely to be accepted by the younger generation (i.e., Millennials). A weak Christian worldview translates to a person more likely to receive a false doctrine than an authentic doctrine. Satan's best practice is to confuse people by tossing in doctrinal mischaracterizations to sow into them a non-biblical worldview. There are several views that need exploration, so that you will not be deceived by them. As a watchman, the Holy Spirit will lead you to a specific area to expose. In previous chapters, we explored the worldview of Marxism, but now let's examine other competing ideas such as: secularism, post-modernism, and New Age spirituality. In general, understanding is beneficial for identification purposes.

Secularism

Whenever people hear the term secularism, the first thing that comes to mind is atheism or some type of paganism. Did you even wonder about its origin? Secularism, according to the Barna Group, is an unbiblical worldview that "prioritizes the scientific method as an explanatory framework for life and advances rational and materialistic view of the world."[33] People who are stewards of this view consider science as THE overall standard to prove authenticity in all human-centered spectrums. Matter makes up the mind, production, food, religion, technology, theories and so forth.

According to the Barna Group, just 10% of Christians hold that "a belief must be proved by science to know it is true."[34] We are now witnessing a rapid resurgence of science as a superior vehicle being used to overshadow traditional Biblical perspectives. For example, COVID has been the centerpiece to this theme, thus insulating adherents with theories that debase assembled facts. In this case, they like to use data regarding the impact of vaccine inoculations rather than less intrusive prophylactics, such as hydroxychloroquine with zinc, and the effectiveness of mask mandates. As I've indicated in previous chapters, politicians and technocrats are motivated to conjoin their intellectual revolution out of the materialist playbook.

Materialism, according to Richard Rorty, a professor at Princeton University, explains how this view has two major components: "1) all thinking, including scientific reasoning and moral deliberation, is a mechanical process, 2) new ideas can, in principle, be predicted before they occur."[35] Materialism plays a factor to what is being taught in schools, embodying toxic humanist philosophies distilled in a "common core" study of humanities.[35] Chiefly, Rorty establishes materialism developed the concept of Artificial Intelligence (AI) which claims "human though [is] a mechanical process to construct[ed] machines that seem to reason and deliberate...[for] there is nothing more to human thought than the processing of information, which probably proceeds in much the same way as it does in computers."[36] Essentially, those who hold this perspective view human beings as little more than organic computers, denying our need for God.

There is evidence that suggests Klaus Schwab's philosophy is a cocktail of secularism, materialism, and scientific humanism, and in keeping with

Geisler, is an "aim to supplant religion and make scientific knowledge the instrument of freeing man and enhancing his life."[37] He further explained that "to this end science and technology must be humanized and socialized, and man educated to respond positively to rapid change."[38] This sounds extremely familiar. In fact, Dr. Schwab has crafted his writings to reflect the prominence of scientific humanism, which is central to the DNA of the Great Reset.

The premise of his book, *The Fourth Industrial Revolution* (4IR), is to highlight the methods of achieving harmony between society and tech. He mentions the essence to the 4IR design is "empowerment" and "human-centered" cohesion.[39] finally, as far as human nature is concerned, the spirit of scientific humanism, in comparison to the Great Reset, is "secular, liberal and tolerant," said Geisler.[40]

How Can You Identify a Secularist?

People who follow secularism demonstrate universal traits uncommon to our Christian Lifestyle. Such individuals may attend Sunday services, but after departing church at 11:00, live like Jesus doesn't exist in their life. Do not be surprised to witness cursing, smoking, womanizing, acceptance of abortion as a part of women's healthcare, as one may hold science in greater regard rather than a more Biblical worldview.

The Barna Group mentions there is a growing population who perceive the materialist world as the standard for their lives. Just over 20% of Christians believe their "meaning and purpose comes from working hard to earn as much as possible so you can make the most of life"[41] Catholics and Millennials share the highest level of conformity to this worldview compared to other denominations and generations, respectively.[42]

Post-Modernism

In 2021, the California Court of Appeals struck down the 2017 bill, SB 219, referred to as the "Lesbian, Gay, Bisexual and Transgender (LGBT) Long-term Care Facility Residents' Bill of Rights," which made it illegal for staff to deliberately refuse to address the residents by their preferred "name or pronoun."[43] Situations like this California bill are increasingly becoming more of a trend in this "woke" culture. Wikipedia defines "woke" psychology, which appeared in late 2010, as an "awareness about racial prejudice and discrimination and other social inequality… used as a general term for left-wing political movements and perspectives which emphasize the identity politics of people of color, LGBT people, and women."[44] Post-modernism is a "woke" ideology that says an absolute reality is subjective, that it conforms to an individual understanding, while simultaneously relegating unbiased facts, which prove objective truth, to the wayside. For instance, if one would ask most reasonable people, "what does two plus two equal?", they would say four. This is known as objective truth. However, post-modernists would argue that two plus two equals six, regardless of truth. Furthermore, objective truth says that Jesus was born of a virgin, lived a sinless life, died on the Cross bearing our sins, rose from the dead, ascended into Heaven, is sitting at the Father's right hand, and will return to establish His everlasting Kingdom on earth. This Biblical worldview is antithetical to the post-modern view. They cannot accept either all or a partial view of orthodox Christianity. We can witness this perspective as it spreads in every spectrum of society, substituting good for evil, and evil being celebrated as good. Another term for this is called "gaslighting," which refers to persuading people to believe something absurd or false to be accepted as actually true. For instance, all of these emphatic expressions that boys can be girls. We would say those who are pushing this narrative are "gaslighting" us.

Another post-modern example, Virginia Public Schools has considered eliminating core math courses in districts' curriculum as part of an equity push. Yet in doing so, this implies that minority students are inferior, lacking the intellectual fortitude to satisfy academic requirements. Overall, these thinkers believe dummying-down children will compensate for their leadership failures to educate underserved demographics. Think in twenty years, Virginia will produce adults not knowing simple mathematics, thus leaving them incapable of budgeting their personal finances.

One of the most prevalent places for this worldview is within the LGBTQ+ community, where they believe God has erred regarding an individual's gender. You should not be surprised at the number of mainline denominations which are jumping on the bandwagon in support of a post-modern view, while neglecting the evidentiary facts of the Bible. This is why 23% of practicing Christians are conceding to this view. "What is morally right or wrong depends on what an individual believes," said the Barna Group.[45] In May 8, 2021, the Evangelical Lutheran Church in America (ELCA) elected Megan Rohrer, as the first "transgender" bishop. What is so egregious about this offense is that he will supervise the ELCA's Sierra Pacific Synod under California's jurisdiction. In 2009, ELCA lost large numbers of members after voting to ordain homosexual clergy.

New Age Spirituality Worldview

Exodus gives us the first accounts of the ancient Egyptians use of spiritualist ritual within their religion when Pharaoh summons his priests to emulate the signs shown by Moses and Aaron. In Daniel 1:20, King Nebuchadnezzar had among his staff "counselors," whom were magicians (which means "engraver") and astrologers (which means "conjurer") whom practiced incantations to interact with the spiritual realm. New Age Spiritualism is nothing new, a fresh coat of paint on an old, run-down car. Alas, the only significant difference is its infiltration within the twenty-first century Christian community. What, then, is spiritualism, and how is it heresy? The National Spiritualist Association, in 1919, defined it as some:

> Science, Philosophy and Religion of continual life, based upon the demonstrated fact of communication, by means of mediumship, with those who live in the Spirit world... a Spiritualist is one who believes, as the basis of his or her religion, in the communication between this and the spirit world by means of mediumship, and who endeavors to mold his or her character and conduct in accordance with the highest teachings derived from such communion.[46]

Conversely, it is a love affair with the supernatural that aligns closely with Charismatic-Pentecostal doctrines that is very appealing to these congregations. In fact, 61% of Christians practice spiritualism, per a study from the Barna Group.[47] What this entails, for one, is that 28% of Christians believe every faith group prays to the same God of the Bible; which is emphatically far from the truth.[48] I want to point out how Tarot cards are dipped in "Christian-sauce," and passed off as Christian "destiny" cards. If you put lipstick on a hog, it is still a nasty, stinky hog. Since 2019, several churches, such as Bethel Church in Redding, California, have been a source of controversy, after being accused of spiritualist practices, such as grave sucking, resurrecting a two-year-old, and other divination practices.[49] Ryan Pitterson provides historical detail about the origin of the "destiny card," and writes:

> Some churches have drawn controversy in early 2019 for using "destiny cards," a set of cards with imagery and symbols used to "divine" someone's future and give them a "reading." Christalignment, the company that makes the cards, states this about their spiritual services: All Christalignment team members operate only out of the third heaven realm. That means we are all hearing from Christ spirit. This ensures safety for you and a way higher level of accuracy…We have developed 7 sets in total of destiny cards which are so accurate, that even if your life circumstances change dramatically, on your return to do them again years later, you will find the results identical, such is their accuracy. They are able to give profound insight into relationships, career, and your spiritual life.[50]

The problem here is Christalignment's language when explaining their heathen product, as it dabbles with familiar spirits. Instead of identifying Heaven as the place where Christ abides, they use the New Age terms "third heaven" and "Christ spirit." Another red flag is the fact they felt obligated to mention they are ensuring your safety in using their product. Such statement implies that those who use these items are being subjected to some form of danger. Does seeking our Heavenly Father bring danger to those who seek Him? Absolutely not! If anything, this affirms the cards are a product of Satan. We will never be in danger from the Lord. The Bible tells us, "the name of the Lord is a strong tower: the righteous runneth into it, and is **safe**" (Proverbs 18:10, emphasis added). "For thou hast been a **shelter** for me, and a strong tower from the enemy" (Psalm 61:3, emphasis added). If you neglect the warning, just prepare yourself for the worst-case scenario, because you are tampering with familiar spirits. Consider 1 Samuel 28. Samuel was dead, and Saul had outlawed Spiritism (wizards and witches) in the land. Saul was worried about the Philistines. At first, Saul inquired of the Lord, but "the Lord answered him not, neither by dreams, nor by Urim, nor prophets" (1 Samuel 28:6). Saul knew he was in trouble, and desperation consumed him, regarding possible war with the Philistines. Unsure of what to do, he summoned one of his servants to find a medium, and one was found in Endor. Saul goes to this woman, and asks her to conjure Samuel. She does, and note that she is surprised she actually gets Samuel. The response from Samuel is horrifying news. First, Samuel confirms God's silence towards Saul means he is separated from God. Secondly, Samuel announces that Saul's kingdom will be confiscated and given to David, and that Saul's disobedience for not destroying the Amalekites will become his downfall (See 1 Samuel 15:3). Lastly, Samuel pronounces that God has rendered Saul and his household a death sentence.

Consider Jesus' warning to us, when He said:

Not every one that saith unto me, Lord, Lord, shall enter the kingdom of heaven; but he that doeth the will of my Father which is in heaven. Many will say to me in that day, Lord, Lord, have we not prophesied in thy name? and in thy name have cast out devils? And in thy name done many wonderful works? And then will I profess unto them, I never knew you: depart from me, ye that work iniquity (Matthew 7:21-23).

Indeed, Jesus is referring to spiritualism. This included "Christian-themed" spiritual gifts. Just because you added Christ to something doesn't make it "good."

In conclusion, the Apostle Paul had warned the Corinthian Church to "be not deceived: evil communication corrupt good manners. Awake to righteousness, and sin not; for some have not the knowledge of God: I speak this to your shame" (1 Corinthians 15:33-34). In the King James Version, "bad communication" refers to the Greek word, *onilai*, describing people of whom one associates with and talks to on a regular basis. Paul is saying, come to your senses and stop living like Jesus does not exist in your life, simply because it is inconvenient to your "modern" friends. Stop acting foolish and repent! There are many people in the world who do not know what you know, and this knowledge will be accounted against you.

Selah! Think about it.

CHAPTER 8

WARS AND RUMORS OF WARS: UNRESTRICTED WARFARE

After serving in the military, in the capacity of a Commissioned Officer and God's grace, I have gained valuable experience, to what I call, **flexibility of significance** – to understand and articulate developing threats to nations, which at one time, were close allies. It is from my experience and being immersed in eschatology, I find it necessary to share relative evidence to align current events with Matthew 24; Revelation 6, and Ezekiel 38.

When was the last time you heard a pastor preach a message on Tribulation events? Recently, many pastors are delighted to see Sunday morning attendance increase, but people have concerns about the condition of America. People, both young and old, churched and unchurched, are seeking answers at the place where the Bible intersects with this present-day chaos.

Did you know, according to LifeWay Research, one in ten pastors (11%) discuss end-times prophecy with their congregation at least once a year, while three in five pastors (60%) say, "it is important to preach on end-times prophecies in the book of Revelation."[1] Beloved, do you see these numbers are a serious problem? Consider this: there is a major disconnect when pastors believe it is important to preach on Bible prophecy, but choose not to teach on it. Scott McConnell of LifeWay Research asserts, "The current global pandemic will create interest among churchgoers and nonreligious people about what the Bible says about plagues, disasters, and the end times. The urgency pastors feel is less about stockpiling toilet paper and more about helping people be ready for Christ's return."[2]

No wonder people are starving to understand the times we are living in, if pastors are suffering from "tight-lip" syndrome. It is detrimental to a believer's spiritual growth to remain silent about Jesus' redemptive plan for Israel. Period. It is imperative to read how serious our Lord is in His desire to save those who refuse to repent, as in Revelation 9, or regarding His plans to rapture the Church to meet Him in the clouds, and give us glorified bodies at the Bema Seat. Also, it is important to understand war is necessary as a part of God's redemptive plan, a divine judgment set against Israel's enemies bringing His people into greater glory than ever before.

A Quiet Storm: The Invasion of Israel

In Revelation 6, the Apostle John was invited to take a little trip into Heaven for a sneak-peak inside the Throne Room. To no one's surprise, sitting on the throne was Jesus Christ, ready to begin the Seven Seals Judgment. According to John's account, as Jesus opened the first seal, he heard a loud bang – something like the sound of thunder – then one of the mighty angels, said to the apostle, "Come and See." Without delay, Jesus opened the second seal, and John heard his chaperone-angel once again say, "Come and See."

Imagine, in that moment, the Second Seal is in Jesus' hands, and He breaks the seal in half. Immediately, the Bible says, John witnessed a red horse, and "to him who say thereon," named the False Prophet, was granted "power to take peace from the earth, and that they should kill one another: and there was given unto him a great sword" (Revelation 6:4).

I'd like to put the kick-stand down here for a moment to say that John's prophetic experience transitions back to Ezekiel 38:1-4, with this scene focusing on the judgment of Gog and Magog, which will be known as the battle of Armageddon. In Ezekiel 38:2-4, he proclaims a word from the Lord:

> Son of man, set thy face against Gog, the land of Magog, the chief prince of Meschech and Tubal, and prophecy against him, And say, Thus saith the Lord God; Behold, I am against thee, O Gog, the chief prince of Meshech and Tubal: And I will turn thee back, and put hooks into thy jaws, and I will bring thee forth, and all thine army, horses and horsemen, all of them clothed with all sorts of armour, even a great company with bucklers and shields, all of them handling swords.

As you read this text, a variety of questions might have come to mind, like "what does this passage mean?" or "how does this passage absorb relevance with today?" To navigate through this prophecy, I want to address three tiers that are crucial points within this text: (1) a composition of the demonic alliance against Israel; (2) an evil plot and God's wrath; and (3) how the Lamb of God refers to the conflicts that occur within the 21st century.

Nevertheless, it is necessary to address the shadow that the Tribulation casts back in time. Just like birth pains tend to intensify closer to birth, these conflicts and wars will intensify as the Tribulation and the Antichrist draw closer. However, there is a problem: people are blinded by the disinformation and media blackouts that hinder one's ability to adequately identify the countries forming the alliance mentioned in Ezekiel 38.

Identification of the Demonic Alliance

During the season when Israel will be in a state of peace and security, other nations will be swirling recklessly in a state of geopolitical contention. In that day, she will prosper economically and bless the world with her spoils, which without a doubt will draw greedy dictators' attention. Importantly, this alliance will be a colorful combination of powerful nations hand-picked by God. No matter what, these nations will have no choice but to wage war against God's chosen people, for God will "put hooks into thy jaws, and I will bring thee forth" (Ezekiel 38:4). Needless to say, none of these nations are capable of shying away from their ambition to become the world's leader, hoping to replace a weakened United States. To successfully accomplish this endeavor, it will require someone to dominate the Middle East and secure its rare mineral deposits.

Plainly stated, the alliance proliferation has already begun. There are countries making their attempt to cordially negotiate business deals with Israel, thus appearing to jockey for her rare fruit (natural resources) as prize. In time, this greed will inevitable evolve into hate, and hate will escalate into violence. Of course, Israel will reject every offer because she has everything to lose, while the adversary has much to gain. In essence, Israel recognizes that to give a little now will mean, in the long-term, losing everything.

In Ezekiel 38:10 & 12, the Bible provides details into the psychology of this coalition, which possibly could exploit Israel's rejections of their deceptive business practices, as that rejection being the reason to attempt to strip Israel's sovereignty.

Ezekiel declares:

> Thus saith the Lord God; It shall also come to pass, that at the same time shall things come into thy mind, and thou shalt **think and evil thought**... To take a spoil, and to take prey; to turn thine hand upon the desolate places that are now inhabited, and upon the people that are gathered out of the nations, which have gotten cattle, and goods, that dwell in the midst of the land (emphasis added).

What is most shocking about this alliance is that God chose these wicked nations over 3,000 years ago. Today, we can view the character of these nations by their consistent threats against other nations and the evil deed perpetrated against their own people. Then, who are these nations charged to commit these wicked acts? According to the Scripture and historical data, the countries of Gog, Magog, Gomer, Togarmah, Cush, Persia, Rosh, Meshech, Tubal are the biblical actors featured in God's plan.

Actor Number One: Gog and Magog

There are three places where we can find Gog in the Bible: Ezekiel 38, Revelation 19, and Revelation 20:7-9. Under the Revelation account, Gog represents Satan, with the Antichrist being the keynote oppressor toward the nations of Israel, the two witnesses, and the Tribulation saints. It is likely, though, that this person is empowered by Satan as an agent, able to do his bidding. According to Ezekiel 38:16, the time frame for this invasion on Israel "shall be in the latter days."

Did you know Russia is described in the Bible? Gog, in Ezekiel, refers to a leader or a ruler of an empire north of Israel, in the south Russian Steppe, just northeast of the Caucasus region, the Caspian and Black Seas. God said, "and thou shalt come from thy place out of the **North parts**, thou, and many people with thee, all of them riding horses, a great company, and a mighty army" (Ezekiel 38:15, emphasis added).

Evidence suggests that Gog, Rosh, and Magog represents Russia and the former Soviet nations that end with "-stan;" for example, Kyrgyzstan, Afghanistan, and Kazakhstan, to name a few. Also, China should be considered part of this invasion plan. The mighty CCP, with over three million people in their military, sits just adjacent to Russia and the "-stan" nations. In fact, China has the world's largest military, with a two million ready personnel force. In addition, they have 1.7 million para-military police, known as the People's Armed Police, whose mission it is to perform custody and control of occupied countries. Ezekiel asserted the coalition will have many people with them, which may include 3.7 million Chinese troops.

"Magog" is defined as "Gog's region," which is inherent to the Scythian people.[3] Scythian means "fierce-looking,' thus earning them the reputation for being an exceedingly vicious, nomadic nation in the South Russian Steppe.[4] During my deployment to Afghanistan, we stopped for several days in Manas, Kyrgyzstan, and I realized the local nationals who were authorized to work inside the dining facility, looked strange to me. The best way to describe their appearance was as a mixture of Mongolian and Russian features. They were also identified in Colossians 3:11, referring to an abolishment of the old racial order, which discriminated against them and tried to separate these peculiar people from any fellowship with believers.

Amir Tsarfati mentions the reason why the Chinese placed great effort into constructing the enormous "Great Wall of China," so to erect a sufficient, defensive structure to discourage a potential slaughter perpetrated by Gog and Magog, the modern-day Russia and Balkans region.[5] No wonder it is impossible for the West to maintain peace with Russia because of this historical character flaw. Tsarfati explains, "In old Arabic, the Great Wall of China was called the wall of Al Magog. Other ancient writers referred to the walls as *"SudYagog et Magog*, that is, the mud, or rampart of Gog and Magog."[6]

Most alarming, what we do know now is that Russian President Vladimir Putin has made laws that would allow for him to remain as president in perpetuity. However, anything can happen, particularly if Putin is deposed, dies, quits, and someone else assumes the mantle of leadership against Israel.

Finally, I remember Putin deployed large numbers of military hardware and troops to several Syrian bases as a deterrent to NATO. Once I heard about this movement, the picture of Ezekiel's prophecy came to life with every news report. And now, people wonder if Russia will declare an all out war against Ukraine; even after destroying the nation and murdering thousands of innocent civilians.

Gomer, Togarmah, Meshech, and Tubal

Turkey is the nation that represents these four names in Ezekiel, although it is a NATO member and home of Incirlik Air Base, an American military post. Ezekiel 38:6, says: "Gomer, and all his bands; the house of Togarmah of the north quarters, and all his bands: and many people with thee." This country will play a major role in the invasion, possibly developing an Islamic coalition that will consist of Egypt, Lebanon, Libya, Yemen and other Middle Eastern countries.

Since being a NATO member, Turkey has enjoyed the tactical training and innovation provided by the United States. Well-trained and equipped, the Turkish Air Force is capable of major airstrikes deep into Israel, and have one million troops for a ground assault. However, Israel has an advantage over Turkey, due to their purchase of our most advanced aircraft, the F35 stealth fighter. In 2020, Israel used the stealth technology to bomb targets deep inside Syria and Iran undetected. However, Turkish President Recep Tayyip Erdogan, had to apologize when his American-made F16s fighters shot down a Russian fighter jet. An international incident nearly sparked a major conflict.

Did you know the Ottoman Empire had ruled much of the Middle East, even parts known as Palestine (Israel today) and Jordan for many years? Perhaps, Erdogan is flirting with the idea of the Ottoman Empire legacy. Considering a weakened NATO alliance, and an impending American conversion to Communism, perhaps, in due season, Turkey may abandon the West and align with Russia and CCP. The writing is on the wall; it's only a matter of time.

Persia

Iran is the nation that has historically been the Persian Empire, it is reasonable to say, the Iranian leadership is on a crusade to reinvigorate itself to its Persian glory. Nevertheless, it will be unlikely for a couple reasons. First, the country is suffering a severe water insecurity, due to drought. Notable, Israel offered Iran new technology to make water from air moisture. Unfortunately, the innovation was not considered essential, and Iran wasted no time rejecting the lifesaving technology.

Lastly, America has imposed sanctions on Iran, crippling the nation's economy. In previous years, Iran has perpetually promised to pulverize Israel with weapons of mass destruction. Both Russia and China have sold advanced technology to Iran in order to improve their tactical capabilities. Emboldened, Iran instigated attacks against Israel by supplying Palestinians (Hamas terrorists) with missiles to overwhelm the U.S. Military's Iron Dome defense platform. These birth pangs are going to increase as the world drifts closer to the Tribulation.

Cush and Put

Persia, Ethiopia, and Libya with them; all of them with shield and helmet... Thou shalt ascend and come like a storm, thou shalt by like a cloud to cover the land, thou, and all thy bands, and many people with thee" (Ezekiel 38:5, 9). In the Bible, Cush translates to Ethiopia or modern day Sudan. There is a uniqueness about this nation, as it was split into two separate countries for political reasons. A large chunk of the nation is an Islamic state steeped in radical ideology. Not so long ago, Israel conducted air strikes to punish Sudan for a secret Iranian partnership to harm the Promise Land.

I have often wondered how and where Sudan's role will play out. Perhaps Russia, Iran, or China will establish bases there, stationing it with bombers and fighter aircraft. It is possible these bases could launch air strikes destroying tactical sites. What is most interesting is that this force is now in the planning and building of platforms that can be utilized to position military assets within Gog's theater of operations. Lastly, Libya (Put) is another nation that will partake in the invasion. However, it is unclear as to what their role will be. The country may be used as a staging ground, because of its proximity to Israel.

Sheba, Dedan, and Merchants of Tarshish: The Young Lions

Ezekiel 38:13, reads, "Sheba, and Dedan, and the merchants of Tarshish, with all the young lions thereof, shall say unto thee, Art though come to take a spoil? Hast thou gathered thy company to take a prey? To carry away silver and gold, to take away cattle and goods, to take a great spoil?" In this passage, the nations listed are countries that have nothing to do with the Gog alliance, but instead passively denounce the motive and actions of the war. Who are they, and why did these countries not assist Israel? "Sheba" is modern day Yemen. In Ezekiel 27, it is described as an illustrious, rich nation distinguished in commerce. Today, Yemen is under the state of war, famine, and seen as a terrorist stronghold.

Saudi Arabia is "Dedan," and is one of the wealthier Middle Eastern nations to have designated Iran as its regional foe. With this thread of enmity, they share a common goal with Israel to prevent Iran from dominating the region. This is the motivation that affix the Saudis in an alliance with Israel to balance out the region from the Iranian terrorist aggression. It is my bold opinion that the Saudi government clearly understands that America will stand shoulder-to-shoulder with Israel against her enemies. Therefore, knowing this, it would be advantageous for Saudi Arabia to befriend Israel, as to fall under the umbrella of American protection. I'm not a prophet, so anything is possible, particularly when dealing with a nation that is as unpredictable as America. It is likely Saudi Arabia will eschew any aggression towards the nation of Israel.

Conversely, Tarshish is none other than present day Spain (Jeremiah 10:9), yet it is believed the "Merchants of Tarshish" refers to the European Union (EU), with over twenty member nations that constitute the "young lions." Over the decades, many people have wondered where America fits in Ezekiel's prophecy. This is a great question, but first let's explore the dynamics of America historically.

Since the early 20th century, America has been a "melting pot" of society, composed of different ethnic groups and cultures from every nation around the world. In fact, our flag and national anthem are carbon copies of the British anthem and flag, to include some cultural observances being practiced today, with their origin from other Europeans nations (i.e. Christmas and Easter). Therefore, it is safe to say that America may be one of the "young lions" in Ezekiel 38. Here is why: since the 2020 election, there has been a growing movement to isolate Israel by blaming her for the death of Palestinians who attacked Israel. Biden has made plans to send millions of American taxpayers' money to fund the Palestinian terrorists' operations against Israel. Someone might ask, "How is this isolating Israel?" Simple, the act of funding the Palestinians, gives the implication that the United States supports Palestine, regardless of terrorists launching hundreds of rockets into Israel, provoking a response from Israel that leads to the destruction of infrastructure and the killing of innocent civilians.

During President Trump's four-year term, Israel lived in safety and security. They were sold America's most advanced military assets and enjoyed the move of the American embassy to Jerusalem. Once President Biden assumed the role as Commander-in-Chief, things went downhill, fast. We witnessed the flawed withdrawal from Afghanistan with the abandonment of thousands of Americans and billions of dollars' worth of equipment left in the Taliban's possession. We lost thirteen brave service members at the Kabul Airport which could have been avoided, had Biden listened to his generals. What a fiasco!

Now, Israel is in a do-it-alone posture, because this passive, charlatan administration has proven it is more interested in imputing social experiments and communism, instead of reassuring our allies, "America's got your back." Unfortunately, that is not the case, and now, General Mark Milley, the Joint Chief of Staff, reassures our enemies (CCP) during a telephone conversation with his communist counterpart and said, "If we attack China, I will give you a heads-up." Treasonous! Who, in their right mind, will trust a nation that sleeps with their enemy? And I assure you; once China takes Taiwan, the American alliance will no longer exist. Such allies as Japan will consider building their forces for future conflict with China. Trust is a factor that has been written on a block of ice, placed outside in the sun.

The Tribulation: The Second Seal Judgment

Please understand all of the wars and conflicts throughout history combined will not measure to the horror the Lord will send in the Tribulation. In Revelations 6:3 & 4, Apostle John writes, "And when he had opened the second seal, I heard the second beast say, Come and see. And there went out another horse that was red: and power was given to him that sat thereon to take peace from the earth, and that they should kill one another: and there was given unto him a great sword." In this text, it identifies God's unveiling His wrath upon the earth by allowing Satan to cause havoc on the world. Violence will elevate to unimaginable heights. All the chaos seen since February 2020 is but a shadow before the storm clouds cover this world. Metaphorically speaking, you think all the riots are out of control now? Riots will become common occurrences, like Saturdays are to a weekend.

The end-times gear is in full speed, as it is safe to say, powered by this Great Reset. I believe the most important statements that, perhaps, can be aligned with Revelation 13 is this: globalists are the world's number one threat, followed closely by the CCP. Period. These two are working hand-in-hand to strip the world of its sovereignty. Any live-action conflict between China and America is inevitable, no matter how you squeeze the geopolitical fruit. It is not a matter of "if" a war will occur, but whether it's when this destruction will manifest. It is even possible that a nuclear weapon or even an Electromagnetic Pulse (EMP) will be used to cripple the world's economy and kill millions of people.

One October 16, 2020, the CCP informed their soldiers to prepare for war. Although the CCP did not specifically indicate the United States, this call came after President Trump had mentioned America may need to de-couple from China for their repulsive behavior towards our nation.

It was reported the January 6, 2021 Protest in Washington, D.C., made the CCP extremely nervous, because of the rumor that Trump was going to start a war to stay in office. Consequently, the CCP bought into this fake news and almost started a war out of fear. All it will take is for a misunderstanding to become a miscalculation, sparking a nasty conflict.

It appears we have passed the one-mile marker to arrive at the Scriptures which warns us to look up for the blessed Hope.

Now, looking back to 2019, it is clear as to why President Trump was announcing his desire to de-couple America from the pockets of the CCP, similar to what Japan had done years prior. The intent was to save this republic by preserving the leadership blessed by God and loved by most nations. Now every nation feels the same about America, whereas China has proven over and over again that its intentions are diabolic and destructive. According to Scripture, everything points back to Israel. More than likely, the CCP will be the primary opposing force against Israel during the Tribulation. Keeping this in mind, I challenge you to observe how their aggressiveness intensifies. On October 22, 2020, Fox News reported China and Russia were considering forming a joint alliance. It is obvious who this alliance will contend, since NATO is a deterrent to any evil aggression from these two nations. In essence, this alliance may become part of the Ezekiel 38 alliance against Israel. We will see if Turkey cedes from NATO and sides with this alliance, along with other Middle Eastern nations.

In 2020, *The Epoch Times* published a piece examining CCP methodology to defeating America. One thing that stood out was that the CCP believe they are currently at war with the United States under a passive-aggressive strategy that includes using non-lethal blows to weaken their adversary. With our current leadership structure in Washington, China would defeat America. As far back as 1999, the CCP published a military strategy called Unrestricted Warfare, which is designed with the intent to engage their enemies in a covert war, "without engaging in troop-to-troop combat, against the United States."[7] It is understood that in any plan to defeat America, the CCP must use four strategies to win: 1) demoralize, 2) destabilize, 3) conflict, and 4) intervention.[8]

Demoralize

This strategy consists of a variety of tactics, such as misinformation (spreading false information to invoke confusion), culture warfare (using money to finance Hollywood films, allowing them to direct the narrative and manipulate society through popular culture), and memetic warfare (devise and disseminate fictitious narratives within targeted demographics).[9] Indeed, the CCP is very active in culture warfare, funding many

Hollywood films that are obviously China-friendly. They are ensuring we cannot to likewise, such as in the 1980s and 1990s, when movies depicted our military fighting and defeating Russia, back when it was a Communist country, similar to *Top Gun* and other patriotic movies. The media played a vital role in defeating President Trump with the relentless negative press which altered society's perceptions. We know China played a role in this propaganda with the *Washington Post*, the *Wall Street Journal*, and *The New York Times*. In June 2020, the U.S. Department of Justice filed a complaint against the *China Daily* for paying millions of dollars to both the *Wall Street Journal* and the *Washington Post* for them to maliciously publish propaganda in the form of disinformation.[10] China has been quite aggressive in this form of warfare.

Destabilize

These efforts are designed to paralyze America's financial, geopolitical, and social foundations in many subtle creative apparatus models.[11] Back in March 2020, the world watched as China's "subversions warfare" tactic was executed to exploit George Floyd's death with growing social and geopolitical provocations in Oregon with riots.

A pro-communist group called Freedom Road Socialist Organization (FRSO) claimed responsibility for the Minneapolis and Portland riots. It was reported their mission was performed under the spirit of Maoist revolution, which is to "carry forward the best aspects of the new communist movement."[12] What we are witnessing is only the beginning to a demonic blitz by evil people whose hearts are hardened against any truth.

As previously stated, these models are fluid and graduate to a more sophisticated operation within the political arena. For instance, they use political infiltration (the CCP will engage political circles that are lynchpinned to business entities and circle back to politicians) and diplomatic warfare (the CCP will deploy "wolf warriors," a group of diplomats trained to humiliate any nation's delegates who chastises Beijing for any mishaps). In March 2021, at the first meeting between the CCP and Biden Administration, officials did meet with Wolf Warriors. Frank Fang and Cathy He, from *the Epoch Times* observes, "the Chinese display of an aggressive [diplomacy] style dubbed 'wolf warrior' was on display during the 'first face-to-face meeting."[13] Notably, the wolf warrior descriptor, according to Fang and He, is named after to hit jingoistic Chinese movies of the "Wolf Warrior" franchise, released in 2015 and 2017. The movies are centered around a Chinese Special Forces soldier fighting foreign mercenaries at China's southern border and Africa.[14]

Conflict

This strategy uses controlled opposition warfare, which establishes groups that infiltrate a movement using deception to support an enemy point of interest, but actually are double agents.[15] In 2019, New York City Police Department had a Chinese agent who provided the CCP with intelligence on the Falun Gong community in the city. Fortunately, the spy was caught and will suffer the consequences for his actions.

Intervention

Jonathan Watts, a contributor for *The Guardian*, wrote about a Chinese General boasting about a preemptive strike against the United States. In 2005, Zhu Chenghu, a Major General in the People Liberation Army, said in a threat, "if the United States intervened in a war in the Taiwan Strait, China would preemptively use nuclear weapons to raze hundreds of cities in the United States, even if all of China to the east of Xi'an (a city located at the western edge of China's traditional boundaries) were destroyed as a consequence."[16] Does this General sound friendly, or like a "competitor" as President Biden claims? Absolutely not. China is willing to risk losing millions of their citizens just to hit hundreds of American cities, likely on the West coast. Like I said before, they do not think like Westerners think, but are willing to sacrifice their sons and daughters to murder Americans.

Beloved, you have not seen nor heard anything yet. As I mentioned previously, one weapon being talked about is the Electromagnetic Pulse (EMP). This weapon system can take America back 150 years, destroying the "electricity grid and most electronics for thousands of miles."[17] In his article for *The Epoch Times*, Andrew Thornebrooke contends:

Development of these capabilities...2007, when the CCP successfully exploded a satellite with a missile in low-earth orbit. And earlier this year, the Chief of Operations for the U.S. Space Force testified that both Russia and China were continuing the development of electric warfare packages, signal jammers, and directed energy weapons…CCP has continued (ASAT) Anti-Satellite Weapons. Inspector Satellites capable of grabbing other objects in space; and "nesting doll" systems consisting of seemingly harmless satellites that then release other, smaller satellites of unknown capabilities.[18]

Lastly, there are additional weapons packages China could deploy in "biochemical warfare," which is a conflict where nations are "deploying chemical weapons and biological agents to create disease and chaos or to wipe out population centers."[19] In 2015, one CCP scientist discussed plans to "unleash a bioengineered SARS coronavirus" to destabilize America and "advance the communist regimes global political ambitions," according to *The Epoch Times*.[20] Major news outlets reported in April 2020 that the CCP Foreign Minister confidently suggested to his leadership, "we need to prepare for war with the United States due to an increase in anti-China sentiment." How many warnings does the United States government need to understand China is a foe and not a developing country? Again, it's not about "if" a war will occur between our two countries, but WHEN will it happen? Why hasn't the government warned the American people of the danger of China's threats? Perhaps, there are some who know that once the American people are made aware, the globalist agenda will be compromised in short order.

COVID-19: What Is Really Going On?

Fast-forward to 2021: the Intelligence Community (IC) provided a report to President Biden in September on the COVID-19 origins. Jeff Carlson and Hans Mahncke, journalists, purported that Dr. Anthony Fauci, the Director of the National Institute of Allergy and Infectious Diseases (NIAID), had awarded two grants to Peter Daszak, the head of Eco-Health Alliance. The first was $3.7 million, and the last, which was cancelled by President Trump, was $7.5 million. According to Carlson and Mahncke, "some of the grant funds went to Wuhan."[21] Carlson and Mahncke identified the latest IC report as grossly incomplete, saying:

The IC report also fails to address a February 1, 202, teleconference that was hastily organized by Fauci and Dr. Jeremy Harrar, director of the *British Wellcome Trust*. The teleconference took place after the previous night's public reporting of a potential connection between COVID-19 and [Wuhan Institute of Virology] WIV. Fauci and Farrar were connected about previous U.S. involvement with the lab, and that they had knowledge of public statements made by the Wuhan lab's director about U.S. funding being used for controversial gain-of-function research conducted there.[22]

At the conclusion of Dr. Fauci's teleconference, the media, the World Health Organization, and other government entities immediately collaborated an aggressive disinformation campaign to discredit leaks, spurring public discussion.[23] The corrupt nature of this cover up required that the "teleconference participants," according to Carlson and Mahncke, "were also instrumental in publishing two influential articles that were used extensively by media organizations to push the natural origins theory. Simultaneously, alternative theories- including that of a possible lab leak – were widely discredited as conspiracy theories."[24] As time goes on it appears more evidence is unearthed, supporting the "lab leak" theory.

The CCP Collects America's DNA

On June 30, 2021, Tony Perkins, the host of *Washington Watch*, discussed how the CCP is stealing Americans' DNA data. It is purported the CCP is motivated to use this data to develop biological weapons to eliminate specific racial groups or any race other than Chinese. My question is which racial group is being targeted for elimination? For this plan to be successful, though, Chinese will have to develop a virus that is nonlethal to their citizens. Equally important, China does not shy away from voicing their intentions to cause destruction to nations. They had announced World War III will consist of biological warfare. What if the CCP was planning to harvest the DNA of every America in order to construct a biological weapon that is demonic partisan, allowing it to eliminate those of a specific genetic type? For them to accomplish this task, they must steal massive amounts of healthcare and genomic data. Here is how China has already successfully done it.

Cyber Attacks

In 2014, CCP hackers infiltrated and stole the personal data of 78 million Americans, easily by-passing the cyber-security of the health insurer, Anthem. This allowed them to obtain names, birth dates, addresses, social security numbers, and health identifications numbers of millions of Americans.[25] That same year, CCP hackers also pilfered the records of 21.5 million Federal employees (19.7 million) and families (1.8 million) from the Office of Personnel Management (OPM).[26]

Data Collection

Remember, the serpent in the garden was quite sophisticated in its ability to deceive Eve. In China, everything goes through the CCP. This includes the Chinese companies which are heavily investing in American corporations that "handle sensitive health care and personal data."[27] Therefore, the Chinese strategy is to gain access to the market, which will allow for them to handle the data. Once this effort is accomplished, the data is transferred back to China. Here are a few key pieces of evidences of this:

In 2010, the Chinese company, FDI, enters the pharmaceutical market.[28]

In 2015, the Chinese investment firm, Wuxi Healthcare Ventures, invested in the genetic testing company, 23andMe, and gained access to their DNA (genomic) database.[29]

In 2019, a report was published that indicated that fifteen Chinese firms had obtained the necessary credentials to conduct genetic testing on American citizens.[30]

Since the COVID crisis, cyber-attacks on our infrastructure have occurred, amid an alleged "scorched earth" accusation against former President Trump, which was made by General Mark Milley, the Joint Chief of Staff, to his communist counterpart, General Li Zuocheng of the People's Liberation Army.

Once war erupts between our two nations, success will be determined by the sustainment of logistics platforms and ability to retain the momentum of the fight. Overall, one thing is certain: the CCP will waste no time in exploiting America's weaknesses through the deployment of biological weapons, which are extremely deadly (think of COVID-19 on steroids). One of their first acts will be to poison water sources, even manipulate or destroy major dams that protect communities from flooding. With just this action alone, millions of people and livestock will succumb to either water contamination or disease.

The electric grids and cell phone towers will suffer disruption from EMPs. Imagine the hysteria when people are unable to contact loved ones; first responders are unable to perform their duties, and hospitals are deemed useless. In three days, society will break down, people will have no heat, leaving them at the mercy of the elements.

The things you do not know can hurt you, especially not knowing these hostile threats exist. While looking back to the Cold War era, what made America strong was our preparedness and our understanding that threats against our nation do not come from our allies. Our country was stronger, while people joined the military to become protectors of liberty, something that America has always stood for.

Aware of these facts, I struggle to understand why Washington D.C. continues to act as if everything is copacetic? President Trump began to expose the malevolence of the CCP and the EU, while politicians made great strides to contradict him, claiming that Russia is the real threat, not China.

It is disheartening that, even today, people are misinformed about current events because of mainstream media blackouts. Likewise, churches are not using these events as opportunities to teach their congregation about the correlation between this wholesale chaos and eschatology. The Church has become like the children of Ephraim in Psalms 78:9-11, which says, "The children of Ephraim, being armed, and carrying bows, turned back in the day of battle. They kept not the covenant of God, and refused to walk in his law; And forgot his works, and his wonders that he had shewed them." We are in a point of no return, where societal unrest is paramount, and it is important to hold to Christ and share the Gospel message with those who are still lost. These events are real, and people need to know what is coming can be avoided, if they receive Christ as Lord and Savior.

CHAPTER 9

THE GREAT BETRAYAL

"For nations shall rise against nation, and kingdom against kingdom; and there shall be famines, and pestilences and earthquakes, in diverse places."

-Matthew 24:7

In this day and age, do you find it hard to stay motivated in the faith? After witnessing the gradual dismantling of our nation one thread at a time, does it appear our nation has embraced an "us-verses-them" mentality? Does it appear the government has taken a position to lord over the American people, when the power is supposed to rest with the people? These pains we are feeling today are the beginning of sorrows. Whenever trouble births sorrow, according to the Apostle Paul, "let us not sleep, as do others; but let us watch and be sober" (1 Thessalonians 5:6). Here, "sober" is meant for us to remain aware that these challenges are like the stones of the temple, which will be thrown down, as Jesus said. In the end-times, there will be a certain group of people who must be thrown down. In Matthew 24:2, when Jesus explained to His disciples to not get stuck on how wonderful things may appear now, because these things are about to be thrown down.

A lot goes through my mind when I think about Matthew 24:7. Over the past decade, I have been glued to global affairs, particularly in America. After COVID-19 was introduced, we saw riots and violence increase in the name of social justice. Everything on the news was processed through a filter of hate. One particular party, however, became a pyromaniac, lighting all the matches in the box of "racial politics," setting the Black community on fire.

After George Floyd's death, cities burned, compounding the excessive violence. Chicago, Philadelphia, and St. Louis all burned in the name of social justice. However, I like to call this salvo of lawlessness "demonic justice." We witnesses politicians disparage sitting presidents, while presidents reviled other national leaders. How do all of these difficulties correlate to Matthew 24:7? Jesus' message is a warning to the world that nations will rise against nations, foreshadowing future events, but who are these nations?

One Nation

The word "nation" comes from the Greek word, *ethnos*, referring to a race of people; in the English language, we derive the word, "ethnic." The *Oxford Dictionary* defines "ethnic" as "having a common culture tradition," or "relating to race."[1] It occurs 162 times in the Bible, while only appearing 97 times in the New Testament.[2] In Scripture, one can find in fourteen places where the Jewish people are referred to as *ethnos*. Likewise, Christians are referred to as *ethnos* in 100 instances.[3] We can agree that people are the composition of nations, much as Blacks, Whites, Asians, and Latinos make up America. No country can exist without people, and no man can govern without people. When Jesus told the disciples, "There shall not be left here one stone upon another than shall not be thrown down," I apply this to race relations in America being torn down (Matthew 24:2). Just think of the major feat accomplished by the Civil Rights Movement in the 1950s and '60s being torn down in a matter of one year.

A Man That Does Not Know the Past Will Repeat It

In chapter four, I mentioned that America is not a totally racist nation, as it had once struggled to shed the loose skin of racial hate. I really mean it. However, some forms of racism still exist. In today's society, whenever a person (typically White) is accused of racism, I have to stop, listen to the charge, and ask myself, "who is the accuser?" Then, I analyze whether the charge meets the scope of "racism" by comparing the alleged claim against racism of the past. For this very reason, my spirit is troubled by how easy it is for agitators, such as the Democratic Party, to accuse someone of being a racist. It is often used against spirited individuals whom find themselves in the Democrats' web of confusion, contending against the party's logic. I want to be clear: not everyone in the Democratic Party are bad people. For the sake of this topic, most of my family consider themselves as a Democrat. There are godly people who align with many hardline, liberal views, and this does not make them a terrible or an ungodly person. However, to slander someone with the racist moniker, without researching the asserted claim, is evil. Remember, the Apostle Paul warned us that "in the last days perilous times shall come," and in those times, people will be "false accusers" (slanderers) of men (2 Timothy 3:1 & 3). Solomon insists, "He that hideth hatred with lying lips, and he that uttereth slander, is a fool" (Proverbs 10:18). There you have it. A person who twists and distorts another person's words is a "fool."

Since the 2020 election, there have been leftists whom deliberately mischaracterize people's statements with the intentions to communicate a position contrary to the actual context of the statement. What is happening today is a form of racism being perpetrated by people who have hijacked sensitive elements from the Civil Rights era and are corrupting the freedoms gained by the blood, sweat, and tears of laborers, whom diligently fought for the principle to secure Black people a system of unalienable rights, a thing firmly provided by the United States Constitution.

People need to know exactly how racism really materializes, contrary to what has been furnished by politicians and mainstream media. It is necessary to calibrate one's understanding in order to decode racism in the 21st century. For this to happen, people need to have discussions about "true" racist events towards Blacks that have gone unrecognized far too long. Therefore, I would like to address various historical and current racial struggles of African-Americans. In 2021, many lawmakers mentioned reparations for descendants of former slaves. What comes to mind is the age old saying, "I want my 40 acres and a mule."

40 acres and a Mule

It was January 12, 1865. Out of curiosity, General Sherman and Edwin Staton, the Secretary of War, had conferred with twenty prominent Black ministers to inquire about the welfare of 4 million newly freed slaves to plan for survival on their own. Out of all the preachers, only one stood out, Garrison Frazier. According to Natalie Basile, an expert in African-American History, Frazier's amazing response was the key that opened the door to what is known as "40 acres and a mule." Frazier explained to the two dignitaries, "The best way we can take care of ourselves is to have land. We want to be placed on land until we are able to buy it and make it our own."[4] General Sherman was so moved by this account, he gave an order known as Special Field Order 15, and ordered for all Confederate Army land, estimated over 350,000 acres of land, to be given to the freed men.[5] You can imagine the praise and worship made to God for supplying these former slaves 40 acres and a mule to build a life on the very land some of them once picked tobacco. Here was an opportunity to provide an inheritance to their children's children. However, this prize did not last long, because Abraham Lincoln's death became the excuse for a revocation of Special Field Order 15, thus decreed by the newly-installed President Andrew Johnson. He knew that recoupling the land from the freemen, and returning it into the hands of the "confederate planters," would ease tensions and win favor with the Confederates.[6]

History has taught us that evil men will attempt to "white-out" noble, godly and successful men in the name of their iniquitous purposes. A terrible example occurred in Tulsa, Oklahoma in 1921 in the prosperous Greenwood section of the city called "Black Wall Street," which was co-founded by a Black millionaire named O.W. Gurley. This was not the "Wall Street" as known in New York City, but an illustrious middle-class community that had beautiful homes, banks, pharmacy, library, great schools, and more than one movie theater. Paul Davidson, a contributor for *USA Today*, had done a piece about a false allegation made by a White woman against a Black man, and this became the excuse to conduct the

Tulsa Massacre. According to Davidson, the purpose for the 1921 race massacre in Tulsa was deeper than the general "white woman's false allegation against a black man." It was instigated by jealousy being born from the object of hate.[7] Indeed, these malicious acts were perpetrated by "less fortunate Whites" who held the belief that the Blacks were "out of line" for exceeding the wealth of local Whites and building an illustrious "community."[8] Black Wall Street's success was impractical for Whites to accept. So, White mobs conducted raids on this community, shooting people on sight and burning almost every structure in sight. In the end, the number of lives claimed through violence is debatable. It is estimated that over 300 people were murdered and damage "exceeded $2 million," which today would be estimated over "$100 million."[9] Notable, one piece of history that is often omitted is the use of airplanes during the violence. The dispirited story of America's darkest days testified to other Black Wall Streets, where African-Americans built prosperous communities, and jealous White mobs murdered and destroyed these communities (i.e. East St. Louis, Ill). Thomas Sowell, a renowned economist and Senior Fellow at Stanford University, explains how Black economic have gone unnoticed, but not forgotten. Did you know through the 1940s and 1960s, according to Sowell, "the Black community led our country in the growth of the middle class and led our country in men matriculated from college."[10] People are not taught that nearly half of African-Americans (40%) had created their own businesses during Segregation.[11] Equally important, Blacks had the lowest unemployment compared to Whites in the 1930s, according to Sowell.[12]

Many people have not heard of Annie Malone, a Black millionaire in the early 20th century, celebrated to this day in St. Louis as an inventor and philanthropist. Malone had developed a chemical product that was used to relax real coarse hair. This success afforded her the capacity to finance the St. Louis Colored Orphans Home (STLCOH), eventually joining the organization as its President of the Board of Directors.

What Happened to Black Economics?

On February 22, 2021, the Brookings Institute published details recognizing how Black Americans are still attempting to climb that disparity mountain of wealth. Much of the disparity comes from the Jim Crow laws of the South, which were blueprints to restrict Blacks from gaining wealth. Brookings suggested, "much of the racial wealth dispari- ties are the product of a long historical process of Black exclusion."[13] Historically, Whites have enjoyed the American wealth "via homesteads," and homeowner programs," while Whites purposely barred African- Americans from the wealth building platform.[14] There are still problems in this area, spanning from obtaining loans for farmlands to simply improving one's credit score.

Still, conversations need to be had to improve a system that uproots the racial barriers that routinely discriminate against people of color. Listed below are some problems needing attention:

Discussion #1: Freedmen and Native Americans

There are descendants of Black slaves, known as Freemen, whom are seeking acceptance of the Native American tribes that once enslaved their forefathers. The Associated Press reported some of the Indian na- tions, called the "five Tribes" – Cherokee, Chicasaw, Choctaw, Muscogee (Creek) and Seminole – owned slaves.[15]

Today, some Native American tribal nations that once owned slaves are dealing with their mistreatment of blacks today. When Native Amer- ican tribes were forced off their ancestral homelands in the southeast- ern United States in the 1800s (an event known as the Trail of Tears), thousands of Black slaves who were owned by tribal members were also removed and forced to provide manual labor along the way. Once in Oklahoma, these slaves often toiled on plantation-style farms and were servants in the tribe members' homes.[16] Why is it so hard to recognize people who share the same history as the tribal nations for over 200 years, yet refuse to recognize the children of their ancestral slaves? A Black woman (Freeman) had made an attempt to seek medical attention from their Indian Health Services; however, she was denied the same treatment afforded to other "tribal citizens."[17] Therefore, the Indian na- tions that enforce this prohibition are practitioners of textbook racism. Why aren't these legitimate issues being examined by Washington's hard- line liberals? Does the mainstream media ignore these prohibitions, be- cause it does not align with their narrative?

Discussion #2: Overcome Racial Barriers for Black Bull Riders

In professional bull riding, Blacks are struggling to overcome racial strongholds in a predominately Caucasian sport. The *Washington Post* reports after the cessation of "the Civil War," roughly "25% of cowboys" were African-American. While jobs were difficult for Blacks to find in rural areas, many found employment gathering cattle on "ranches."[18] During the 1950s and 1960s, at the height of the Jim Crow era, Blacks were precluded from competing in rodeos against Whites. You would think all of these obstacles would outweigh their ambition to assimilate, but no, these cowboys were not dissuaded by their adversaries' malicious intent. Instead, Blacks were motivated to create their own network of rodeo competitions.[19] Roman Star, a journalist with the *Washington Post*, said, "pro rodeo remains a predominant White sport, and reported estimates are that roughly 75% of the Pro Bull Riders' viewers are Whites."[20]

One particular family came from a long line of "horse trainers" and "sharecroppers," and conveyed the hardships their family endured some decades ago. In one historical account, a family member who trained horses asked the owner of the farm to "ride the same horses that the farm owners' children rode for leisure;" Star continued, "The owner would say: 'No, those aren't for you. You work with the mule.'"[21] To this day, Blacks are slowly being accepted in a sport that pays its top riders nearly a half-million dollars a year. Perhaps, once the red tape of discrimination is removed by developing an inner-city recruiting or a scholarship program to tap into the raw talent of young Black men, the conversation will change the culture. It is always a "culture" which keeps people tangled in the past.

Discussion #3: 75% of Abortion Clinics Are Hubs in Black Communities

On September 1, 2021, the Texas Heartbeat Bill is the new state abortion law being enforced after the United States Supreme Court struck down a request to delay the law. This law targets certain forms of abortion procedures after six weeks of gestation. This fight is gaining momentum over the practice of infanticide. Most liberal groups, including the Satanic Temple, have challenged the Texas law by disputing a religious freedom violation, i.e. their Constitutional right to perform Satanic abortion rituals are impeded by this state directive. The idea here is mined-boggling.

The purpose for this section is not to argue abortion legality. It is to briefly explore a generational breakdown gripped by a universal satanic sacrament to destroy innocent lives. Just think, abortion is used to eliminate a certain demographics of people. Dean Nelson of the Human Coalition, suggests that "36% of abortions" equals heartbreaking "22 million Black children were slayed to abortion since Roe V. Wade."[22] There would be no need to accept millions of illegals from South America to compensate for infanticide's impact on America's birth rate. Did you know that Hilter's Third Reich used abortion methods to exterminate an undesired race? Many people are clueless about who Margaret Sanger was or her secret eugenics "Negro Project," which used alternative techniques to eliminate African-Americans, one child at a time? Most people do not know Planned Parenthood exists because of Margaret Sanger's racist love affair with negative eugenics. Sanger wanted to use Black pastors to persuade their congregations to use artificial means to control unwanted pregnancy in their community. In her mind, the more Blacks exterminated, the better society would be. What can you expect from someone with ties to the Ku Klux Klan, but hate for Black people and adoration for eugenics? I challenge you to google Margaret Sanger to learn more about her ambition for Blacks and Planned Parenthood. In essence, one cannot have a conversation about racism without discussing the topic of eugenics (GK. *eugenes* meaning 'well-born'), the defining and selecting of deleterious genetic traits. It is in the process of reducing the conception of individuals, who were plainly considered inferior. In the early 20th century, eugenicists became concerned about human reproduction within certain racial groups involving intelligence, disease, and gene modification. In fact, many eugenists, like Bill Gates, believe genetic improvement can be done through sterilization. You might ask; "What relation does sterilization have with genetic improvement?" Sterilization improves the gene pool by removing a person's ability to reproduce and thereby eliminates their unwanted genes from the "pool" of humanity. As some may note, there are two forms of eugenics: positive and negative eugenics.

Positive eugenics supports family development. For instance, some European countries have provided tax deductions and other incentives for couples to have four or more children. In China, national laws were modified to make it legal for couples to have more than one child. Artificial insemination is another method that has allowed for couples to test and select genetic qualities, setting the stage for gene modification after the discovery of some genetic defect. If you want a child with a certain hair type or eye color, this is positive eugenics.

Negative eugenics has been practiced for decades. In African countries, and more recently India, thousands of women were sterilized by vaccines tied to Bill Gates. Even in America, people have been subject to negative eugenics through an implantation of contraceptives in genetic modified foods (GMO). However, abortion is the most common form of eugenics as a measure to control and to eliminate an undesirable population.

The Great Reset Affliction

Then shall they deliver you up to be afflicted, and shall kill you: And ye shall be hated of all nations for my name's sake.

- Matthew 24:9

The first thing that must be asked is who are these people, according to Jesus, who will suffer affliction for His name's sake? This message pertains to all who believe in Jesus as Lord, especially during the Tribulation when many Jews will receive Christ as Savior. Not all of the Jews will suffer for the sake of Christ, because many will receive the Mark of the Beast. Systematically, the Antichrist will allow the Jews to worship in their synagogues and the Temple, then reverse his promise. I once heard a quote that best reflects this forthcoming tribulation: "First is the Saturday people, then come the Sunday people." In context, it means those who hate Christ will viciously seek to kill the Jewish people, and then pursue the Church. I imagine it will be a period of terror, when believers all over the world are hunted like wild game. There will be monetary rewards provided to anyone who reports on Christians' activities. Pastors will experience harassment, and some will be jailed for preaching the Gospel. Churches will be ambushed by "morality police," subject to rapes and beatings, or placed in reform camps, likely even killing them.

Secular Democrats of America (SDA) is a PAC that submitted a 28-page document to then President-elect Joe Biden with the objective to influence policy change. They are asking the Biden administration to rescind the religious protections imposed by the Trump administration. One news agency reported,

> Those recommendations included dismantling the HHS Conscience and Religious Division; defunding any government aid to private religious schools, crisis pregnancy centers and abstinence-only education programs; and enforcing the Johnson Amendment, which would threaten the tax-exempt status of nonprofit organizations that endorse political candidates.[23]

This, in effect, would remove our ability, as Christians, to positively influence our society. The liberals understand, to remove the churches ability to influence their communities, ultimately will allow for the employment of socialist and communist culture. Here is how it is done, socialism is implemented by non-violent means but through strict legislation and draconian methods (i.e., people's property and freedoms are being seized in Australia); while communism is implemented through horrific violence.

Global Christian Affliction

The Epoch Times published several articles describing similar persecution in atheist, communist China, where over 100 million believers seek to worship underground. For one, it is illegal for Christians "to read, print," or distribute Bibles and evangelism material. Doing so will result in confinement or placement in hard labor camps.[24] Did you know the Chinese constitution preserves citizens' rights to religious freedom? You would think the contrary when the media depicts China as an inoffensive, Constitutional nation. When it comes to Christians in China, "at least 250 state-sanctioned churches had their crosses removed between January and April 2020," according to *The Epoch times*, "often on the pretext of 'being too tall, too large, too wide, or too eye catching.'"[25]

Frank Fang wrote in an article, about Trinity Gospel Harvest Church in Shenzhen City, China, which had several worshipers in this small congregation arrested, because one of its members had chatted with an employee from the U.S. State Department. Fang asserts, "10 people – two pastors, a clergyman, and seven churchgoers – were arrested and taken to a local police station therein this city."[26] In another instance, Frank Yue explains that in the Guizhou Province, Southwest China, house churches were being subject to raids and members were subject to "15 days of illegal administrative detention [, and] repeated summons and harassment."[27] Shockingly, Yue says, a "pastor's wife was illegally held in handcuffs and shackles for 24 hours."[28]

Through all of this, our Chinese brothers and sisters in Christ are pressing forward, despite the repressive tactics used by the enemy. Anugrah Kumar, from *Christianpost.com,* published an article about how Hundu Nationalist Bharatiya Janata Party (BJP) leaders in eastern India proclaimed conversion-free zones during a pro-Hindu rally. Amit Sahu, president of the State unit of BJP, exclaimed, "Let us drag people from the church and stop conversions at any cost."[29] Another BJP leader, Roop Singh Mandavi, said, "We will frighten Christians who are involved in conversion work in the region… We will not allow the missionary work to be carried on in Bastar and will protect the Hindu religion by stopping the conversion."[30] These men will stop at nothing to rid themselves of Christians.

Anti-Christian repression is expanding incrementally worldwide, particularly in Nigeria. They are experiencing a burst of violence instigated by radical Islamic terrorists throughout the northern and central regions by Boko Haram, whose name translates as "Western education is forbidden." History ascribes Boko Haram's terror beginning in the state capital, Maiduguri, targeting several military and government institutions. After experiencing defeat in this arena, the jihadists altered their strategy to specify violence towards Christian communities, such as in Gwoza, a city with a larger Christian population. Wickedly determined, Boko Haram has razed small villages and farms, killing residents on a common basis.

In the first half of 2021, close to 1,500 Christians we killed, with over 2,200 people abducted in Nigeria, and the majority of murders were perpetrated by another radical Islamic terror group called the Fulani Herdsmen.[31]

In Cabo Delgado, Mozambique, radical Islamic extremists have beheaded over 3,000 children, younger than thirteen years old. Emily Wood of *Christianpost.com*, said:

Conditions in Cabo Delgado, Mozambique, have "seriously deteriorated" over the past year, affecting children "disproportionately" as nearly 3,000 people have been killed and over 800,000 displaced since the violent insurgency that began in October 2017, according to report. Violent attacks by Islamic rebels in the Cabo Delgado province have led to deaths of more than 2,838 people, including over 1,400 civilians.[32]

Across the world, Christians are losing their lives for simply being who they are.

Then Shall Many Be Offended and Hated

In Matthew 24:10 & 12, Jesus explains, "then shall many be offended, and shall betray one another, and shall hate one another. And because iniquity shall abound, the love of many shall wax cold." America has become a cesspool that is beginning to resemble the descriptions in this chapter. These incidents are examples for us to be reminded of the gospel message regarding the intense hate the ungodly harbor towards Christians. One thing is for certain, people will become more easily offended because of our faith and will try everything in their power to discourage evangelism of Christ's message. For instance, the American Atheists and the Mississippi Humanist Association were offended and filed a lawsuit against the state of Mississippi over its license plates, which read "In God We Trust."

MSNBC host Joy Reid is not short of disparaging words, when it comes to Christians. Ryan Foley wrote, "MSNBC Joy Reid, the host of *ReidOut*, has frequently likened the Christian Right in the United States to the Taliban as the terrorist group [gains] control of Afghanistan."[33] Our message has become as offensive as murder to these people.

Many mainline denominations have waxed cold, resulting in a split over clergy acceptances of Queer theology. Proponents for confuse doctrinal examination as a threat against Queer Theology. Those who resist this apostate doctrine are labeled as evil, bigots, or supremacists. This is why it is necessary for you and I to keep watch over the activities in the media and in your community, connecting the dots and using these signs to minister the Gospel to those who are lost. You will be surprised at the number of people who are willing to lend an ear to hear about these days, and their relevance to Scriptures. However, this requires extensive research and prayer on your part.

Church! Take Heed of Antifa

More recent events occurred when Antifa members converged on a church prayer event held outdoors on August 7, 2021, in Portland, Oregon. These domestic terrorists were wearing their signature full-black outfits armed with shields (some having guns), mocking and physically assaulting Christian attendees and children. Unthinkable, Antifa sprayed the church attendees with bear spray and threw flash-bang grenades in the vicinity of children. It was reported that Portland police refused to intervene while Antifa terrorized the church event. As I said previously, it is only a matter of time before Antifa and other radical leftists groups perpetrate violent assaults on churches, and these events become the norm.

Bottom-line up front: in no way am I advocating violence. Like many who believe, there is a time and place to defend your family and our church flock. Nehemiah comes to mind, when the walls and gates in Jerusalem needed repair to keep their adversaries out. Nehemiah organized with his congregation this major engineering project, and all of sudden, their enemies (Sanballant, Tobiah, Arabians, Ammonites, and the Ashdodites) became angry after hearing about the walls of Jerusalem "were made up, and that the breaches began to be stopped, then they were very wroth, and conspired all of them together to come and to fight against Jerusalem, and to hinder it" (Nehemiah 4: 7-8). Does this not sound like these five men display an Antifa-like spirit? In the ancient world, there were no Facebook or Twitter. News spread by word of mouth. I imagine Nehemiah's feat was the biggest news in the surrounding area in a long time. People love to talk.

In Portland, the prayer event was big news to the anarchists, as they felt it was necessary to engender fear among the women and children, because this scheduled worship meeting was for committing prayers to God to fix breaches within their community. Nehemiah describes, in verses 9 and 10, similar conditions asserting, "we made our prayer unto our God, and set a watch against them day and night, because of them. And Judah said, 'The strength of the **bearers** of burdens is decayed, and there is much rubbish; so that we not be able to build the wall'" (emphasis added). The people in Jerusalem had prayed to the Lord for their hostility to the end, but discouragement had sapped their morale and courage, until it failed them. Before the incident, every piece of rubbish was valuable; then the threats came, and each person's courage began to view every little piece of rubbish as a weakness. Labor became overwhelming, because they viewed the rubbish around them through the lens of their fear and suffering. It was no longer about building, but surviving. Likewise, I can imagine many at the Portland church felt weak and helpless at some point in their ordeal.

People find themselves most challenged when standing toe-to-toe with clear and present danger. Have you ever experienced those ruminating "should have, would have, could have" thoughts? It is easy for one to sink into a pity party, allowing fear to frustrate one's purpose.

In Nehemiah 4:12, the people had to deal with something similar, saying: "And it came to pass, that when the Jews which dealt by them came, **they said unto us ten times**, from all places whence ye shall return unto us they will be upon you" (emphasis added). Most likely, the Jews who lived in nearby villages were pressuring the builders to stop the building before the assault ensued.

Beloved, you may face situations that will force you to be vigilant of the people allowed into your sphere of impact. I'm referring to those people who can encourage or dissuade you. A failure to watch and wait could lead to a life-altering outcome from a short-sighted decision. Fearful people tend to make short-sighted decisions out of haste, influence by those who perceive themselves as a helper to the person. In other words, if the "bearers" in Nehemiah had departed, their adversaries would have stolen their testimony, celebrating their downfall, instead of cheering for their success. When people repeatedly perceive things as impossible, this way of thinking will eventually influence their reality. No good result can be harvested from a defeated attitude, because no defeated attitude will ever nourish the faith and hope required to make the impossible possible. To walk out of a bad condition requires you to ignore the current situation.

I believe Nehemiah 4:14, 16-17 is the place that changed the trajectory of the entire event. The man of God made a decision to protect the people, while at the same time empowering them to continue to rebuild the walls. It is through Jerusalem's experience that we can find valuable lessons for any pastor. It might be wise to establish a security ministry team (watch-dog ministry) to cover the most vulnerable areas. Perhaps, pastors should consider hiring a security consultant, although this can be expensive. Churches could train volunteers in non-lethal tactics or as armed security, if necessary. In the ancient world, shepherds carried a staff with a pointed end, and it was definitely not for drawing pictures in the dirt. It was a defensive tool, in case he needed to defend the sheep from wild dogs, wolves, or thieves. Antifa is the evil wolf, and in the case of the Portland incident, a true shepherd needed to protect and defend his flock. Even Jesus suggested to the apostles to physically protect themselves asserting: "he that hath no sword, let him sell his garment, and buy one" (Luke 22:36-38).

Family Will Betray One Another

Jesus said in Mark 13:12, "Now the brother shall betray the brother to death, and the father the son; and children shall rise up against their parents, and shall cause them to be put to death." Families are becoming more estranged since the 2020 election. I have heard of couples divorcing, simply because one spouse stood for values associated with the Republican Party (conservative, Christian, and patriotic) while the other inclined towards the Democratic Party (pro-abortion, secularism, and socialism). The same hate that radiates between each party leaves a marriage emotionally bankrupt. It has been not only the dissolution of marriages that we see, but friendships have suffered, because of the intolerance of another's political views.

It is through these challenges that our society has transmigrated to what I call the "Coronavirus Divide," which has created a wedge between families. Just by observing the social climate in America, we can expect controversies to progressively worsen as the Rapture and Tribulation draw closer. There will be more hostilities among families to the point of violence. Satan has set out to destroy the family, the very unit God created among man to experience a representation of His divine unity. The devil has aimed his efforts to divide the family through corruption generated by strife. It was strife that broke the divine harmony between Cain and Abel. It was strife that, at one time, broke the relationship between Abraham and Lot, and it was strife that broke the harmony between David and his son, Absalom. It does not matter if the problem is fueled by the faith or politics. All these divides develop as a small matter, and eventually snowball into an avalanche.

In September 2021, a Muslim father bound and killed his twenty-year-old son for refusing to denounce his Christian faith in Uganda. Such flagrant abuse is becoming more and more common, leading up to the Tribulation. It is important to note that families are more important than current events. A strong family is not without conflict, but it is through the heat of family conflicts that a family can strengthen their bonds, as long as Christ remains the blacksmith.

The Government Instigates Betrayal

The FBI is planting seeds of discord by encouraging colleagues and family members to snitch on one another. *The Epoch Times* describes how the "FBI posted a tweet that suggests Americans should monitor family members and peers 'for signs of mobilization to violence' and report 'suspicious behavior' in an effort to prevent extremist activities."[34] What needs to be noted is their interpretations of extremist does not carry the same meaning as it did ten years ago. This new meaning includes a "new" category for conservatives, advocates of the Second Amendment, military members, patriotic fellows, and Christians.

What is bizarre about this account is that there are quasi-Americans who are proactive in seizing crayons from their colorful box of Communism, and coloring between the lines, using fifty-year-old manipulative tactics. I would ask you to walk back with me through history during the Culture Revolution, under Mao's Communist government, which purposely instigated schisms among families. Alex Newman describes Mao's psychological battles would shame young family members to a point where one "would do anything to escape the shame and association, including reporting their own relatives to the CCP... ten million died amid the Culture Revoltuion."[35] What happened in China was a result of identity politics being used as a gateway to have relatives report one another, leading to a divide in society, which included the aid of indoctrination centers for children disguised as secondary education.

Let us explore the path America is traveling, so we can sound an alarm for voters to depose those who are readying to light political matches to torch our freedom. Newman states Mao's regime's mission was to destroy the customs and culture by dividing the citizens into ten classes: five red and five black. This scheme of things is fairly interesting, as "the red classes included the poor and lower-middle peasants, workers, etc.; and the black class consisted of landlords, rich farmers, counter-revolution-aries, bad influencers, and rightists."[36] A person was labeled "born black," if one had any relatives within the black class.[37]

Mao "urged Red Guards to publicly shame the black classes by raising their fists, making them do self-criticism, confess and denounce themselves, or they would get beat up, locked up in a room," Newman furthers, "to write about their 'blackness,' apologize for their families or themselves, and be sent to re-education camps to do hard labor."[38] In George Orwell's novel, *1984*, he described children reporting their parents, while citizens would report their neighbors to the Thought Police over mere suspicion. If a person looked at someone wrong, this was considered grounds to report them to the authorities. When someone misspeaks, someone disappears. The same thing happened during the Culture Revolution, where "teens were encouraged by communist officials to beat their parents and teachers; thousands of teachers were beaten to death."[39] These were the same children were conditioned to cast about people's homes and demolish any property that was reminiscent to traditional Asian culture. It took communist countries twenty-five years to develop this wolf cub generation that was indoctrinated to invoke violence and despise Western values and culture.

Critical Race Theory (CRT): A Sudden Four-alarm Fire

Critical Race Theory is the corrupted fruit of Marxism that condemn the fabric of the United States and any Western culture. It was born from the Marxist *Critical Theory*, centered upon a plan to have the working class transform into a workers state. However, the Marxist intellectuals became displeased with the overall process, snubbing it as a failure. Today, the Marxists have diligently pieced together a plan since the 1950s to invade and conquer three American institutions: academia, the entertainment industry, and the media to influence society at large. Leonard Pitts wrote an article, finding that the "Nexis database finds that the term "Critical Race Theory" appeared in U.S. newspapers 3,361 times in the 21 years between January 2000 and New Year's Day 2021. It appeared 6,000 times in the six months since."[40]

CRT emphasizes that America suffers from being a racist nation, while white people are labeled as "oppressors" and non-whites are described as the "oppressed" (e.g. African-Americans), reminiscent of the distinction of the "proletariat" and the "bourgeois" in Marxism and Hitler's master race theory. CRT "educates" children that American institutions encourage white supremacy, because White males are the larger representation, perpetrating institutional racism against non-whites. However, in August, 2021, the census showed that for the first time ever, the White population actually decreased in the past decade. All of this hate brings us to doctrine of critical race theory.

Critical Race Theory (CRT) Indoctrination

Ryan Goley, a journalist for *Christianpost.com*, had interviewed Civil Rights trailblazer, Bob Woodson, who believes "America does not have a race problem, but it has a grace problem." Critical race theory is defined by *Encyclopedia Britannica* as:

[A]n intellectual movement and loosely organized framework of legal analysis that argues race is a socially constructed category "used to oppress and exploit" people of color. The reference source reports that 'critical race theorists' hold that the law and legal institutions in the United States are inherently racists insofar as they function to create and maintain social, economic and political inequalities between whites and non-whites, especially African-Americans.[41]

Parents are currently waging war against school districts' aggressive endeavors to corrupt their sons and daughters by indoctrinating them in a variety of issues: racism, anti-nationalism, gender politics, sexuality, and socialism. The scheme to influence our children is nothing new or a secret. In fact, there is a plan to incorporate communism into America through indoctrinating our children, as early as toddler age. This means that, in time, parents will lose control over their child's education, leaving this responsibility for the government to shape their child's education, leaving this responsibility for the government to shape their children worldview. Sheri Few, founder of the US Parents Involved in Education, insists, "The U.S. Department of Education has existed because it is about control and not about children."[42] It is important to educate parents about the Marxist long-term plan to steal the mind of our children, which has gone back nearly 100 years. I believe it is important to assign the "crazy" label to this CRT movement, with the sole purpose to outfit you with information to challenge local school district officials. Robert Knight declares, "One of the silver linings of the pandemic has been parent's ability to see the Marxist brainwashing occurring at many of America's public schools, prompting a record number of families to homeschool their children or place them in religious school that reject leftist educational trends."[43] History has taught Communism changes cultures through the indoctrination of children. In this case, the children at threat is your children and your grandchildren. During the Culture Revolution, Mao encouraged the youth to destroy anything that was vintage. We are encountering the very essence of a "21st-century culture revolution" packaged in sex-education, transgenderism, and racism. American cultural values and principles are being destroyed.

CRT not only teaches that America as a whole is racist, but that "White, bad; darker complexion, good," much like in George Orwell's other Communist-focused novel, *Animal Farm*. This collection of ignorance inspires Whites to apologize and regret their "whiteness." If a White person is deemed best qualified for a position, he needs to humiliate himself and submit to accepting second or third place. It is not fair for any person (Black, White or any race) to be passed over for racial gratification. Does CRT sound like a program your children need to embrace? You cannot overcome an issue you do not despise. If not, you will only become a capitulator to that very issue. Therefore, speak out and say something about this evil.

The Root

In the *Communist Manifesto*, Karl Marx was instrumental in establishing the blueprint for government control over educational system by creating standards that mirrored his ideology. In his ten planks, specifically plank number ten, he advocates for "[f]ree education for all children in government schools… Combination of education with industrial production."[44] Such doctrines later influenced John Dewey, who was an atheist, a professor at Columbia University, founder of America's school system, author of numerous literature in genres ranging from socialist theory to pedagogy, and a signer of the Humanist Manifesto. Dewey was responsible for injecting Marxist propaganda into America's classrooms. In the 1930s, Dewey and several of his cronies introduced social studies in schools curriculum, thus removing subjects that communicated our American heritage, such as Western Civilization and American History.[45]

Israel Wayne writes, "Dewey confessed that the schools were being (and should be) used as machines of propaganda, promoting a radical new Marxist worldview to children."[46] A key objective for Dewey was to deliver an alternative to the Christian doctrine that seated morality at the root of society, and within the family unit. Wayne further suggests:

> Dewey's goal was to replace Christianity with humanism as dom-inant force in American culture... Every teacher should realize he is a social servant set apart for the maintenance of the proper social order and the securing of the right social growth. In this way, the teacher is always the prophet of the true God and the usherer in of the true kingdom of heaven.[47]

He really believed humanism was a religion that would free the world. Humanism focuses on man's fundamental welfare and evolving values, stressing humanity's significance over the God of the Bible. It believes that the State is the supreme authority over man, much like Marxism. Adding this humanity "solution" to global questions is what brings us "big" government.

In his book, *Towards Soviet America*, William Z. Foster, the leader of the communist Party USA, devised a plan in 1932 to create a department of education, designed to sterilize children from patriotism and Chris-tianity, while indoctrinating children, writes Newman, in "Schools for communist and globalist views... Among the elementary measures the American Soviet government will adopt to further the culture revolution are the following: schools colleges, and universities will be coordinated and grouped under the National Department of Education and its state and local branches."[48]

What is astonishing about this next statement echoes the talking points of today. Foster continues, "the students will need to be taught on the basis of Marxian dialectical materialism, internationalism, and the general ethics of the new Socialist society."[49]

In 1979, the Department of Education was established under Pres-ident Jimmy Carter, along with support from the National Education Association (NEA), an organization which has long been tied with Com-munism. We can start with Terrel Bell, the Secretary of Education, who introduced a diet of Pavlovian behavioral conditioning in schools with "Pavlov's bell," referring to an experiment where psychologist Ivan Pavlov rang a bell while presenting a treat to dogs. Wayne explains:

> Most famous for his research on dogs, one of Pavlov's experiments involved introducing a piece of meat to a dog, simultaneously ringing a bell. He did this each day until eventually the dog was conditioned to associate the ringing the bell with receiving some meat. After a time, all Pavlov had to do was to ring the bell and the dog would begin to salivate in anticipation of a meal that may (or may not) be forthcoming. What many do not realize is that the Soviets were utilizing this king of "operant stimuli" and behavioristic conditioning, not to learn to control *people* so they would act predictable and without question, just like the experimental dogs and laboratory rats.[50]

To control and modify behavior, the American education system has incorporated numerous experiments extracted from the Marxist mental health modification. CRT is no different. The objective is to demoralize family units and reprogram society to promote the Marxist agenda that is set to overthrow this Republic. You and I may be looking at the first generation with which Marxists will accomplish their goal to radically change America into the United Socialists States of America (USSA). Tony Perkins, host of *Washington Watch*, observes:

> In Oklahoma, a teacher-turned-state-legislature was so outraged by the woke curriculum invading his state that he wrote a bill to ban it… State Representative David Bullard (R) said that of all the people who were grateful for his idea (which is now law, thanks to Republican Governor Kevin Stitt), teachers have been the most appreciative. They see these things creeping into their classrooms that have nothing to do with real learning and they're frustrated. They don't know what to do or where to go.[51]

The growing push to inject woke curriculum has spurred state legislatures to draft bills to prohibit any form of this destructive material. The Lord has exposed the liberals' ambition, and now, more states have begun to send forth similar bills banning this repulsive filth.

Does CRT Compliment Sex Education Perversion?

We are learning how many American school districts have commenced teaching elementary school age children on homosexual sex and masturbation. There is great concern about this debauchery and willingness to defile innocent children, consequently engendering mental health and spiritual issues, such as premature and pre-marital sex, teen pregnancy, abortions, STDs and STIs to name a few. In January 2021, the CDC reported "one in five Americans had a sexual transmitted infection," and "over 45% of all new STIs in 2018 were among people 15-24."[52]

Science has been used as a cover-up for child molestation under the pretense of improving sex education. Until now, we have learned this scaffold of perversion is interconnected with perverted "woke" history. In the 1940s Sexologist, Alfred C. Kinsey Ph.D, a child sex predator, focused much of his "sexuality research" known as the Kinsey reports. These theories evolved into two published books in 1948 called "Sexual Behavior in the Human Male," and in 1953 "Behavior in the Human Female," both are considered controversial to this day.[53] In the words of Leslee Unruh, Founder of *Abstinence Clearinghouse* "explains how the texture of Kinsey's work focused on "ripping down the institution of the family and pushing homosexual, pedophiliac, and bi-sexual relationships as normal, socially acceptable behavior."[54]

Kinsey's report hinges on exposing hundreds of young male and females, as young as infants to countless acts of child sex exploitation. Dr. Judith Reisman, author of *Kinsey, Sex and Fraud: The Indoctrination of A People*, affirms "while no one noted that at least 317 infants and children were sexually tortured by pedophiles for Kinsey's allegedly 'scientific' child sex data, educators repeated his pedophile conclusions – that children were sexual from birth, hence school sex education should be mandated."[55]

Alarming, though it was common practice for Kinsey to invite other morally-depraved men to indulge in these experiments, with the sole purpose to measure the duration of minutes it took for his young victims to reach an orgasm. Depraved and distorted, Kinsey's research suggested that children, not only capable of being sexual at a very young age, but wanted sex more often. In his book "Sexual Behavior in the Human Female," mentions it is advantageous for "girls younger than age 4" to have sex with men.[56] Does this have anything to do with the challenges we've seen in premarital sex and pregnancies? Joan Veon, of the *World-NetDaily*, reports Hugh Hefner inspiration to start *Playboy* evolved after reading Kinsey's depraved book on perversion.[57] Does such covert research happen today? In March 2020, in Aims, Iowa, the elementary and middle schools are teaching children, as young as first grade about gender identity. Kids are given coloring books where they can choose which gender they want to be, which sounds like a type of Kinsey research. Perkins reports that in April, 2021, Jonathan Koeppel, a Spanish teacher in Saint Tammany Parish, Louisiana, gave a sharp rebuke to the school boards and warning to the district's parents of the toxicity of CRT and wokeism. He said:

> You cannot give birth if you're a man… Don't push this ideology on children. I'm not going to work in a district that's okay with that… Parents are already pulling their kids out of public school… [their] going online is going to increase as this liberal ideology comes into our schools. This isn't a political indoctrination camp, okay? It's public education. We want to teach education, not left-wing ideas.[58]

Perkins noted that Koeppel was fired-up over the Board's attempts to sneak in teaching resources like BrainPOP, in lieu of CRT. Perkins reports, "He blasted critical race theory, the new gender radicalism, and teaching resources like BrainPOP that are infiltrating classrooms like his and promoting horrible ideas to children."[59] Koeppel's final words were a poignant indictment over the plot to corrupt their children by exclaiming: "I said I'm not going to be silent on this. This is disgusting."[60] More and more parents are finding themselves in a tug-of-war against their school districts, but really, this issue has matured over decades of "trusted neglect" that has allowed these people to grow emboldened and vicious. Just like Kinsey's 'research has influenced the acceptance of perversion into our schools and homes dating back to the 1950s.

Even the Biden Justice Department has taken a position to label these concerned parents as "domestic terrorists." One must thank God for watchmen like Tony Perkins and FRC. Thank God for raising godly politicians unafraid to employ the power of the pen and calling people out by name to hold them accountable. To corrupt innocent minds is blazing evil, but this will only progress until we return with Christ in the Second Advent.

It seems, as though, the leftists have scattered hundreds of controversial issues like land mines to purposely distract serious Americans from focusing on legitimate, controversial issues. To not lose focus on the context of this section, history has documented abominable acts that bled through our Judeo-Christian values. Charlie Butts and Billy Davis presented an article, "Public Libraries Bringing Back Drag Queen Story Hour," which argues:

> The perverse, wig-wearing queens are back in American public libraries, where they are again poisoning the minds off innocent children... Boston-based MassResistance showed up recently to protest a "story-hour" in historic Plymouth, where a local TV news station acknowledge the June 22 event was met with protesters outside Plymouth Public Library... The city library's website states its Drag Queen Story Hour "captures the imagination and play of the gender fluidity of childhood and gives kids glamorous, positive and unabashedly queer role models..." But the sexual perversion not only showed up in public libraries in recent years but as brazenly tied to wholesome children's story hours, where reading Dr. Seuss is replaced with pro-LGBT children's book... The obvious attempt to influence and indoctrinate children found a willing partner in public libraries, where "tolerant" liberals are often on the payroll and often clash with the community at large.[61]

Teaching Perversion Will Open the Door to Pornography

We have to take into account that children and young adults are viewing pornography at an increasing rate. With schools teaching children to appreciate perversion, seeds are being planted in their undeveloped minds. Eventually, a curiosity will lead them to experience for themselves the abysmal lust. Jeff Minick provides five alarming facts to support this claim:

1) The top customers for "porn" are "12 to 17,"

2) "89% of youth admit to receiving sexual solicitations in chat rooms,"

3) "20% of teens have sent or posted nude or seminude photograph or videos of themselves,"

4) "51% of 11 to 13 year olds have at some point seen porn," and

5) "12% of parents of teens know their children are watching pornography."[62]

We are losing our children to perversion. When will we wake up?

Famines and Pestilences and Earthquakes

While these societal issues barrage us, natural disasters are becoming increasingly common globally. It seems that every time the television is on, there seems to be a story of some hurricane off the Gulf Coast or of another region flooding. Do people really understand that Jesus' message is speaking of a time which believers will never experience? I don't think so. What is important is that the strange weather patterns will only increase as the wickedness increases. Evidence is found in Revelation 6:5-6 & 12-17 that represents the Third and Sixth Seal Judgment (the black horse and heavenly phenomena), being the Lord's prescription of unimaginable harsh conditions. There will be great earthquakes where mountains will disintegrate, and famines will become the norm as record heat scorches the earth. We have seen nothing yet, but what is happening is a warning of the judgment to come.

Throughout the Bible, God has used famines, pestilence, and earthquakes as agents to punish nations for their disobedience, and in some cases against His enemies. Even in Isaiah 19:2-8, God used civil war to administer judgment upon Egypt, and in verse five told of the drying of the Nile River, as a sign of His displeasure over their wicked activity. Indeed, these passages supply an up-close look at how a nation with an abundance of natural resources (e.g. water) can fall due to a group of calamities. Certainly, the United States is experiencing these pains at Biblical proportion.

Famines

In 2021, California Governor Gavin Newsom proclaimed an emergency drought-declaration for the state's forty-one counties. Even during the summer months, Californians were encouraged to preserve water. This challenge exists because a lack of precipitation resulted in an abysmally low water table. There have been discussions regarding using the water that melts from the Colorado mountains and passes through Arizona to California. Some dry states, such as California, are disputing restriction over water, to the point of threatening litigation. Colorado believes that they have the right to restrict the water that flows from their mountains to other states. Since Colorado has experienced a population boom, they have had an increase in demand. On the other hand, states experiencing water shortages believe water cannot be restricted under any circumstances. This is only serving to cause further strife within our great nation.

Pestilences

In Exodus 8-10, God had Moses deliver a warning of an imminent judgment, because Pharaoh's heart was hardened, he refused to let the people go. Pharaoh neglected the warning. As a result, Egypt experienced an abundance of frogs (Exodus 8:1-7), lice (8:16-19), flies (8:20-24), and locusts (10:12-20).

Adriana Brasileiro reports on a new, very aggressive mosquito known as *Aedes scapularis*. It has since became a nuisance to greater Miami, Florida. Although indigenous to "South America," its "origins" culminated along the "Key West" over half a century ago.[63]

In California, black-legged ticks called "arachnids" have been discovered at beaches. These arachnids are known, according to Susanne Rust, to attach themselves to Western Grey squirrels and lizards.[64] Arachnids are known to carry Lyme disease, which makes it imperative for beach goers to use caution along the Oceanside.

China has also reported a rare infection called the Monkey B virus, which has claimed its first victim. *The Epoch Times* described the virus as having an 80% fatality rate. By God's grace, there have been no reports of this deadly Monkey B virus in the United States.[65] Oddly enough, China has been wrestling with several plagues in the last five years. First, the

CCP had to slaughter over 30,000 hogs, due to G4, a variant of the swine flu virus. Consequently, this forced China to import the majority of their pork from the United States and Brazil. In Texas, Dallas County Health and Human Services identified an infected person with the rare Monkey Pox virus, after arriving from Nigeria. It is the first time this virus was discovered in Texas. One thing that has not occurred in the United States is the onslaught of locusts, which has occurred in several countries.

I remember hearing about the locust invasions that have ravaged Africa and some Middle Eastern nations, notably skipping Israel. These locusts, nevertheless, have travelled thousands of miles into China, devouring trees, crops, and vegetation. There are pictures of people stranded in their homes, as the insects were completely covering the entire patio. In Africa, it was estimated locusts had destroyed trees and crops in only "30 minutes." You know what's most intriguing about these reports? They all struck within the first half of 2020, around the same time span as the Coronavirus infected the world. In addition to this assertion, it is likely that man-made viruses created with gain-of-function research are extremely lethal and capable of killing a fourth (2 billion) of the world's population (see Revelation 6:8). It is possible God could include man-made viruses as an agent to do His Will on the earth. For instance, the CCP has been busy. There is new evidence that scientists at the Wuhan Institute of Virology have develop the new "Nipah viruses," which has an 80% mortality rate, more deadly than the Coronavirus.

Earthquakes

During the summer of 2021, Alaska experienced an earthquake that frightened thousands of citizens. Earthquakes are nothing new. In fact, May 24, 2021, Congo, in Africa, experienced an earthquake so powerful that it triggered a volcanic eruption. There were reports of lava spewing towards cities and villages. Remember these are just the groanings of birth pains.

In conclusion, Jesus gives us clear warning that these calamities will take place in His future, our present. Always keep in mind that everything we are experiencing today is not the end – only the beginning of the pains that are pointing to the final play. First, the Rapture, then the Tribulation.

CHAPTER 10

#THERE ARE 'WOKE' PIMPS IN THE PULPIT!

"We know they are lying, they know they are lying, they know we know they are lying, we know they know we know they are lying, but they are still lying."

- Alksandr Isayevich Solzhenitsyn

How often have you thought about Jesus warning to beware of false prophets that will deceive many believers? Woke pimps in the pulpit shall rise coupled with contemporary heresies birth from the womb of the New Age movement. For its imposters whom has seized the Gospel message by twisting and deleting, pulling and adding to the interpretation of the Word of God. What is befalling the Church is a religious coup slowly gaining momentum to infiltrate the body of Christ softly, through culture. Churches are becoming cultic centers that espouses wokeness as to "having a form of godliness but denying the power thereof: from such turn away" (2 Timothy 3:5). There is a consuming moral and spiritual dumpster fire impelled by men and women calling themselves pastors whom, likely, never experienced the New Birth. These are charlatans whom actively pilot the Lord's servants, with lies, far away from sound, Biblical truth.

Thyatira Church: Blazing Wokeness within

Notwithstanding I have a few things against thee, because thou sufferest that woman Jezebel, which calleth herself a prophetess, to teach and to seduce my servants to commit fornication, and to eat sacrificed unto idols. And I gave her space to repent of her fornication; and she repented not.

– Revelation 2:20-21

Case Study

In Revelation 2:20 it is our Lord and Savior Jesus Christ speaking to the Church of Thyatira, once a prosperous city, in Asia minor (common day Turkey), was known for its manufacturing and purple dye. It was common for residents to affiliate with local guilds because it was a fraternal order to one's vocation, or a specific form of arts. Most importantly, membership carried among other things a style of political veneration therein emperor worship; people would hold these men to be Zeus reincarnate. Overall guilds were inherently nonpolitical carriages to pay homage to an especial pagan god. Visualize, hypothetically, if one were to dine at Burger King, one is required to dedicate a sacrifice to ones patron god; to shop at Sams Club – a sacrifice to that god. For it was common for social elite's to receive invitations to dine with a patron god in the temples, consuming the meat sacrificed to demons.

Depending on the patron god, prostitution was a by-product of temple worship that encompassed orgies, drugs, and alcohol. And yes, during the First century drugs were a systemic problem within pagans worship system; to even include, some Church members exploited illicit drugs to reach levels of ecstasy. For instance, in Revelation 9:21 – introduces the term "sorcery" (GK. *pharmakon*; means drugs or magician), where in the English, it translates to pharmacy. Many people do not know that God depicts "illicit drugs" (not medication) as the "sin of sorcery."

Jesus' message was clear. First, commending this congregation for "thy works, and charity, and service, and faith, and thy patience, and thy works; and the last to be more than the first" (verse 19). However, He held a "few things against" this Church because many of its members "sufferest that woman Jezebel" (verse 20).

To understand a connotation for the "Jezebel" moniker refers back to 1 Kings 16:29 – 22:40, where King Ahab, and his wife, Jezebel, were described as being more evil than Jeroboam. For twenty-two years he and Jezebel, had inaugurated the largest cultic institution in the land for worship. What made it worse, however, their deeds infuriated God by seducing Israel to idolize baal-melkart. In addition to this evil indoctrination, Ahab had "reared up an alter for baal" and "made a grove," as a fertility god; thus effectuating this form of worship for half a century (1 Kings 16:32-33).

It is from this same cesspool of debauchery as described in Thyatira, hence having its origins from the spirit of 1 Kings cultic, institutional stage. Jezebel had managed to usurp her husband's authority, who was, at that time, king. Yet she was subtle enough to influence the spiritual climate affecting generations. Just by Jezebel's comportment alone, proves God was not the head of her life. Likewise, in the book of Revelation, Jezebel was not the name of an actual person. She was the spouse, of a pastor, of the Thyatiran Church. It was because of her subtle comportment that led Christ to bestowed to her this name of shame. Remember when He introduced her, it was not a pleasant announcement. Back in chapter 6, I told you how Christ had referred to Jezebel as "that woman" who "calleth herself a prophetess," as it does, removes any authenticity to her title. Considering the Greek participle is presented in the present tense, meaning "while calling" herself does affirm Jezebel being a "self-proclaimed" preacher-teacher. Furthermore, there is no favorable historical evidence that proves she was authorized to speak on the behalf of the Lord, which is a meaningful problem.

Does Jesus statement collaborate with Apostle Paul's' directive in 1 Corinthians 14:34 and 1 Timothy 2:12, when he said, "But I suffer not a woman to teach, nor to usurp authority over the man, but to be silence?" It is important to carefully explore the historical, cultural and grammatical forms of interpretation to understand the true meaning of Paul's instructions.

Why did Apostle Paul provide these instructions?

The Church was very young, exploding with new converts from the Jewish but mostly Gentile (Roman) communities. These babes in Christ would often reserve former worship traditions, at the cost of injecting different applications into Church meetings. For instance, soul-winning had paid off for the Apostle Paul, and the other saints, as they led many pagans, such as "temple priest" and "priestess," to Christ. After receiving the new birth many of those "post-devil-worshipping-ministers" struggled to relinquish their dysfunctional traditions.

For this reason, Apostle Paul had felt, as it was, imperative to address all the gross, carnal behaviors. This opened the door of opportunity to teach, coach and mentor these individuals and congregation, on how to embrace a godly decorum and behavior pleasing to Christ (1 Timothy 2:9-11). For instance, people whom once functioned as a temple priest were accustomed to wearing head coverings (like women) while performing their duties (1 Corinthians 11:4, 14). Therefore, Paul reckoned this issue as a conflict of interest. Under Christian and Jewish traditions, women were accustomed to wearing head coverings (type of Habit), not men.

Another issue, women whom once functioned as temple priestess would wear their heads shaved, as a representation of that cultic practice. But Paul's letters would emphatically instruct women to observe wearing the proper length of hair longer than men (1 Corinthians 11:5- 6; 13). Many wore expensive garments with gold, and pearls that reflects their social economic status (1 Timothy 2:9-10). Imaging those saints from a less social economic status, left feeling inferior. Paul did not approve of flashy attire.

Keep in mind, the Roman society was a male dominate society. So females in the Roman and Jewish cultures shared similar societal requirements where women were subordinate to their husbands. There was an ambiance of feminism that gradually developed during this period. Females were afforded more freedoms while worshipping their patron gods. Even their dress code inside the temple was a reflection upon their patron god. In certain observances it was common practice for women to participate half nude. For instance, Ephesus had once housed the temple of Artemis, the patron god of fertility, where temple prostitution and orgies were the source of activities. It is likely that women may have participated in sexual immorality with male and female temple prostitutes.

Hyperspiritual Worship

The church was another place appealing to women because for a short time, they were liberated from the depressive societal limitations. They could be in the company of other men and not fear any pressure to separate. There were instances where women would depart their spouse's patron god and strictly devote their lives to Christ. Surely, though, this took courage and forbearance to serve Christ despite some societal consequences. Regardless of the weighty obstacles, these women were successful in winning their husbands to the faith from the evidence of their faith.

In the temple men and women enjoyed the liberty that was offered to ritual leaders. However, in the Church, many struggled with the challenge of understanding that their pagan style of worship caused confusion. There were some women that habitually disrupted services by speaking out of order during services (1 Corinthians 14:26-32, 34, 35). So Paul would say, "For God is not the author of confusion but of peace, as **in all** churches of the saints" (1 Corinthians 14:33a, emphasis added). He also made clear to "let all things be done decently and in order" (1 Corinthians 14:40). Perhaps Paul came to an impasse while attempting to correct these foibles, only to arrive at the state of more drama. But what we do know, he did not provide these instructions for just, the sake of it; no –there were challenges detrimental to the structure and integrity of the church. He followed the unction of the Holy Spirit to provide these relevant instructions to the Church in perpetuity.

I have arrived at this point, to say, we can concede there is no question Paul's instructions are still disputed today. In the Me-too era, for many, a woman's role, specifically in church leadership, has been the heart of contention. But most importantly, the real inquiry pertains to women being called "pastors" over men. Needless to say, women have played an important role throughout church history, to include, church leadership. It is no question, throughout the New Testament women have been great "helps" in assisting the men of God. We acknowledge how instrumental they are in accepting the responsibility to train other women, and regarded as exceptional soul winners. Therefore, women deserve respect and their place in history.

1 Timothy 2:11-12 are Paul's words indeed

When Paul wrote verse 11, it was done under the apostle authority, he issued, "Let the woman learn in silence with all subjection," gives inference to Paul's expectation for women to adopt a modest form of conservative decorum that's antithetical to western culture. And in Verse 12, the apostle continued, under the same authority, establishing, "but I suffer not a woman to teach, not usurp authority over the man, but to be in silence." Paul's statement is based on his years of administering every, single church; thus he had witnessed the same problems over, over and over again, reaching a boiling-point that exceeds that which is over-whelming. Basically if Paul was here today, I could see him pointing a finger, while exclaiming, enough is enough!

Did you ever encounter a problem for so long, it frustrated you, em-barrassed you; whomever or whatever "pluck that last nerve" (like my mother use to say); hence to a point you had to confront it; and say – no more! Stop it? On the contrary, I have heard different translations to this passage to reflect a more liberal view, where preachers have accredited this instruction to apply "only" to the first century Church. However, is this true?

It's simple; when Paul asserted, "I do permit," (Gk. *epitrepō*) is in the present tense with an adverb (not) being the negation, introducing Paul's intended meaning to render, "I do **not** permit." The "aspect" is a contin-uous action that is followed by an infinitive (in the present tense). This continuous action thereby translates to, "But I suffer **not** a woman to **continually** teach, nor to **continually** usurp authority over the man, but to **continually** be in silence (emphasis added)." Again the Greek verb is in the present tense, and there is an infinitive, also in the present tense. Therefore this passage in-chief, translates to a continuous action. It is still in effect, right now.

Just think, if Paul would have intended to say, "I do permit women" (without a negation) people would kick and scream thus stressing for the meaning to be a continuous action in the present tense. Well it does not.

Case in point – in 1 Timothy 2:3-4 says, "For this is good and accept-able in the sight of God our Savior; Who will have all men to be saved, and to come unto the knowledge of the truth." Does this passage apply to the twenty-first century? Did Apostle Paul's statement: "God our Savior" desire that "all men to be saved" refer to the first century Church only? Or does this desire of God pertains to both, men and women today? God's desire is in the present active – translating to a continuous action. In other words, God's desire continues for people to be saved and learn more about Him, right now. We cannot cherry pick Scriptures to tickle people's ears. We have to take the Apostle Paul's words literal because it is the Word of God.

Post-evangelism movement:
A New Age cult having the spirit of Jezebel

In an article written by Sarah Pulliam Bailey, of the *Washington Post,* was featured on the front page of the *St. Louis Post-Dispatch*, describing in October 2021, a gathering of pastors to discuss the future of their faith and develop a professional group of individuals self-describing themselves as "post-evangelicals" (PE). First, I want to be clear; in no way does Bailey's article insinuate any participants, described in this article, are partaking in any nefarious activities. Thus viewing this article through a secular lens, what took place in Indiana was acceptable. However, when these activities, I'm about to describe are processed through sound, biblical orthodoxy – on the contrary.

The majority of the attendees were millennials, whom shared a similar belief in Christ; but what they are accepting is in conflict with New Testament teachings of Christ and the Apostles.

For one, all in attendance agreed that post-evangelicalism supports having an "affirming church" that would not refuse to perform "gay weddings" nor prohibit "LGBTQ people in leadership."[1] Bailey writes these pastors have aligned themselves with this PE philosophy suggesting "curiosity" being more significant than "certainty" and "inclusion" outweighing "exclusion" as a basis for their exploration of truth.[2] The root of this philosophy is centered upon two contentions that ushered them to "deconstructing", or "reevaluating, their faith" based on "LGBTQ inclusion and racial justice."[3] These factors have led PEs to abdicate from evangelical circles, seeking to locate a congregation that follows their similar views, perhaps in another Protestant denomination. One particular, Amy Mikal, is the pastor of *A Restoration Church*, boldly instructed her Church members to alter the name of God, according to Bailey, "she's encouraged her congregants to reconsider God with male pronouns," to include rethinking the Bible "to see what they think collectively."[4] Basically, I wonder which personal pronoun will Mikal refer to God as, "HE" or "HIM," as a substitution for saying "God" and "Lord"? Sounds familiar? In the garden the serpent did the same thing to Eve, minimizing God's name from Yahweh "Lord God" as seen in Genesis 2:4-3:23, to just "God" saying, "**For God** doth know that in the day ye eat thereof..." (Genesis 3:5, emphasis added). The Lord emphatically said, "Ye shall not **add** unto the word which I command you, neither shall ye diminish ought from it, that ye may keep the commandments of the Lord your God which I command you" (Deuteronomy 4:2, emphasis added).

Here's a warning that stands out in the book of Revelation, yet overlays every Scripture therein the Bible. "For I testify unto every man that heareth the words of the prophecy of this book, if any man shall **add** unto these things, God shall add unto him the plagues that are written in this book: And if any man shall **take away** from the words of the book of this prophecy, God shall **take away** his part out of the book of life, and out of the holy city, and from the things which are written in this book" (Revelation 22:18, 19, emphasis added). Here is why: "For I am the Lord, I change not" (Malachi 3:6). Mikal is doing just that with the intentions to soften up God, thus making Him more appealing to the woke cult.

Post-evangelism causes Cavity Faith

In all certainty, I cannot say all pastors in attendance are false prophets. However the problem are those who claim to be a pastor and peddle apostasy by steering saints from orthodoxy theology into accepting pluralism, inclusivism and relativism intertwined with a social gospel and LGBTQ+ agenda. Participants at this gathering do not share a Biblical worldview in practice or within managing issues. What is being presented by this group are tools of Satan to deceive people; thus believing their truth falls within a universal correctness. Moreover their truth suggests that LGBTQ+ members will not suffer God's judgment, as Scriptures proffers. And many, if not all attendees, emphatically believe social justice is more weighty than preaching about God's holiness, obedience and sin. Doctrinal wise, their ideology has nothing to do with all of the evidence written therein the whole council of God. But instead it is insulated with Gnostic tones of feelings and objective opinions from others to strengthen the shadowing Beast system. These so-called pastors lust after anyone whose willing to scratch their itchy ears, as Paul points-out, "For the time will come when they will not endure sound doctrine; but after their own lusts shall they heap to themselves teachers, having itching ears," and Paul continues, "And they shall turn away their ears from the truth and shall be turned unto fables" (2 Timothy 4:3-4). One expects for a pastor to be "rooted and built up in him [Christ], and established in the faith, as ye have been taught, abounding therein with thanksgiving" (Colossians 2:7, emphasis added). In order for someone to be rooted and established in faith, one must be taught. Once taught, who would not display gratefulness for Christ saving them. It is in Christ the treasures of wisdom and knowledge dwell. Do they not know it is by grace each one of them were saved through faith? It appears their faith is corrupted with decay, having holes like a cavity.

Keeping this in mind, Bailey's interview exposes Mikal for having seduced her church, with the teachings of, doctrine of demons. Mikal explains, "The hardest part is that we were taught to take the Bible literally... We want to be a place that asks more questions than provides answers."[5] To interpret Scripture in the literal sense, the Word of God will require them to be held accountable for sin. But to say, interpret the Scriptures allegorically, however, would permit false prophets to stand as the authority of Scripture, not God. Why? People, like Mikal, can spiritualize a Biblical text to say whatsoever she pleases. Too many churches are moving into similar cultic groups that prefer to ask more questions than to provide solutions. What happens the more (Christ) questions goes unanswered the more confusion creeps in; for it is within those solutions (answers) that are discovered in the Word of God, wherefore is where one will learn that spiritual renewal only comes through Christ Jesus. Do you think Jesus desires for people to have more questions than solutions? He is the answer and everyone can find valuable solutions within the sixty-six books of the Bible. Unfortunately, if you accept Mikal's idea for ministry, then those of whom are lost within her thickets of folly, nevertheless will remain in a field of confusion. No longer will Christ be the center of their lives, but man's truth will stand in the place for God's truth. In the end, people will capitulate to becoming man-centered (anthropocratic) overall. Beloved these are dangerous grounds to be planting seeds.

Post-evangelism 'Spiritual guide'

Bailey introduces a young, charismatic woman named, Brit Barron, thus describes her as a "Black-Mexican lesbian," designated as the "spiritual guide."[6] Although Ms. Barron was unfamiliar with the grand scheme of a post-evangelical movement; she established the goal to generate a conversation, as a vehicle to help others reexamine their faith. She said, "You shouldn't have to believe anything in particular to be a part of this group… Well, if you're racist and homophobic, you might be uncomfortable."[7]

Many in attendance left the evangelical traditions to pursue affirming churches to appease their "gay friends," or like, David Roberts, pastor of Watershed Charlotte Church, lamented about a time he was "kicked out" of his old church after revealing his homosexual lifestyle.[8] The problem is their love for the world outweighs their love for God. No matter what anyone can say or write, will never change the psychology of these attendees of an up-in-coming-cult. Apostle John said, "Ye are of God, little children, and have overcome them: because greater is he that is in you, than he that is in the world." John prepares to describe the differences between what post-evangelicals uphold verses orthodoxy Christianity, by asserting, "They are of the world: therefore speak they of the world, and the world heareth them. We are of God: he that knoweth God heareth us; he that is not of God heareth not us. Hereby know we the spirit of truth, and the spirit of error" (1 John 4:4-6). Bailey mentions that Ms. Barron had asked the group "whether it was necessary to believe in a literal resurrection of Jesus Christ."[9] Unfortunately, this statement is evidence of a spirit of error; demonic oppression at work. According to Apostle Paul, in 1 Corinthians 15:12-19, are spiritual truths to destroy the wicked arrows of Satan; He proclaimed:

Now if Christ be preached that he rose from the dead, how say some among you that there is no resurrection of the dead? But if there be no resurrection of the dead, then is Christ not risen: And if Christ be not risen, then is our preaching vain, and your faith is also vain. Yea, and we are found false witnesses of God;

because we have testified of God that he raised up Christ: whom he raised not up, if so be that the dead rise not. For if the dead rise not, then is not Christ raised: And if Christ be not raised, your faith is vain; ye are yet in your sins. Then they also which are fallen asleep in Christ are perished. If in this life only we have hope in Christ, we are of all men most miserable.

What flowed from the lips of Ms. Barron are signs of misery, according to Paul, Romans 10:9-10 asserts, "That if thou shalt confess with thy mouth the Lord Jesus, and shalt **believe** in **thine heart** that God hath **raised** him from the dead, thou shalt **be saved**. For with the heart man believeth unto righteousness; and with the **mouth confession** is made unto salvation" (emphasis added). Does the fruit from Ms. Barron's mouth prove her having the "good fruit" of salvation? She does not believe in her heart Christ risen. Therefore how can one be saved? Such bold questions will confuse anyone unsure of Christ's death, burial and resurrection and ascension. Now, according to this article, she has claimed to be a "spiritual guide" proclaiming these false words, as it does, fall in line of being a false teacher. Either way, instead of pastors' shrinking to her words, someone should have interrupted and explained the Gospel message, if it has been revealed to them. Consequently, what was so disappointing about this moment, no one was bold enough to stand up for biblical truth and depart in protest – no, not one.

Apostasy: Post-evangelism resembles Jezebel's Thyatiran cult?

Jezebel was wicked, according to Christ, audaciously seduced people whom were recognized for their love and service to Christ, as it was made manifest through an outward expression of faith to Him. In their ministry efforts glorified Christ in every positive way. They were the epitome of godly church folks. But Jezebel had persuaded too many members to share their wives, and justified it by saying something comparable to, "as long as you are of God it will be fine." When it came to eating the meat sacrificed unto idols. Further suggested it was acceptable to enter the temple and dine, to eat meat from the sacrifice. She even taught there was nothing to fear because these idols were fictionalize. A little meat won't hurt anybody! You are in Christ Jesus. She taught them to ignore certain passages in the Word of God, hence delivered to this Church thirty years prior, by the Apostle Paul and other preachers. Jezebel was out of control; she had these church folk thinking, what they were doing was in concert with God's holiness. Jezebel did not care if the Apostles came before them preaching against prostitution. She did not care about the preachers whom preached about touching anything that is associated with idols – she became the authority in her eyes by distributing a doctrine of Satan. What people need to know about this time was the growing trend of acceptance humanism and Gnosticism. She became a cult leader by bending saints' mental intelligence to the breaking point.

The Rise of Cults

Many Christians do not realize what is going on around them. People hear about the CRT issues that are bombarding the schools. People hear about some of the political fights that are congesting their television screens. But what about their Church? People do not consider their pastors may align philosophically with cultic doctrines. What I have described in this chapter, all relates to cults. Unless one has taken the time to research on their own, in order to identify signs within their church fellowship, employment, or even school curriculum, you will never know. Well this is about the change. We will explore several categories and peculiarities of cults, which are hard to distinguish.

When I was in college, nearly 30 years ago, I was seeking a church body and came across this group of students that attended a small fellowship at a couple's home. The group consisted of, perhaps, over ten people, with the majority being female. The group was led by a young, interracial couple, in age range, to my best guess, in their late twenties to early thirties. In fact, I received my first Bible through them. Needless to say, as time went on some of the females became very hyperspiritual; one particular account, I was in the University Center conversing with one of the other female members, when this young woman came out nowhere in a frenzy – loud, as a result, made me very uncomfortable. I did not know what was going on, for I never encountered anything like that moment.

As I look back to that day, I wondered if the person I was talking to, may have been the personal companion of that spirited young woman. Regardless, I decided to never return to that group. What came to my mind: did I just leave a cult? I remember walking to class one afternoon, on an information board there was a notice of a religious group being banned by the University for cult-like activity. I never found out if that was the same group; nevertheless, I would from that time forward associate, only with traditional churches.

What is a cult?

There are numerous movements in America that meet the category of a cult. Such movements' are aligned with a specific goal centered upon philosophy shaped by a center of belief. Second, the person leading the group, tend to be charismatic, but some look like pedophiles thus skilled in the ability to persuade people with their dynamic play on words. They strive to be revered by those subordinate to them. Third, they appear to possess answers unfamiliar to anyone else; yet for one to enter into this enlightenment must be willing to adopt their precepts. It is not unusual for a leader to establish him or herself as having some special gift or knowledge because of some heightened spiritual enlightenment. In this chapter, I will examine four classifications of cults:

Religious

Cults tend to share similar characteristics in their decorum, like in the New Testament, and in the second and third century, there were groups that practice ascetic lifestyles (i.e., Seven Churches), to even refusing to provide ones spouse their conjugal rights. The Apostle Paul spoke against cults imposing celibacy and diet restrictions as being part of their devotions (1 Corinthians 7:5). Even today, I have witnessed cult leaders claiming to be a twenty-first century prophets. What testifies against such cult leader is their tendency to lie. They will restate facts overheard or what someone had told them in a previous conversation. Then claim months later the whole story was given to them from the Holy Spirit or God. For instance, Mr. X on numerous occasions shares his plan with Mr. P (for prophecy) to purchase property. A year later, during a conversation with Mr. X, out of nowhere, Mr. P proclaims: "God said, you going to buy multiple properties (then assume the locations)." These people are quick to tell someone "God said..." or "the Holy Spirit told me to tell you..." when their predictions are instigated by ones bias, conversations, assumptions, or imagination.

Even spiritual gifts are weaponized to manipulate people to pay homage to the bearer and to control people. For it is not uncommon for someone is told if they do not speak in tongues, they are not filled with the Holy Spirit. Leaving the victim feeling lost, unworthy, believing God does not accept them. All the person has to do is delve into the Scriptures to know, once saved God, the Holy Spirit indwells in all believers. Definitely most religious cults are hyper-spiritual, abusive and controlling; thus if anyone attempts to disagree with their doctrine are shunned into isolation. Any member that is accused of being disloyal will suffer mental and emotional abuse. The leader will not acknowledge them but will be slanderous towards that person. *ARCGIS* suggests religious cults "practice and influence techniques include speaking in tongues, chanting, praying, isolation, lengthy study sessions, faith healing, self-flagellation, or many hours spent evangelizing, witnessing or making public confessions."[10] Looking at this list, one might say, these practices covers many evangelical circles; which are not cults. I have worshiped in many evangelical traditions where, praying, evangelizing, public confession and Bible studies tend to be long. It really depends on the Church tradition. I believe what *ARCGIS* is referring to are activities that rises to being out of the ordinary, impulsive, unbiblical acts that tend to be packed with ultra-spiritual demands on its members. Like participating in grave soaking or people fall and rolling all over the ground screaming and yelling uncontrollably. It is not uncommon for these cultic leaders to take Scripture out of context, claiming God give them a "new revelation" from Scriptures while witnessing to their teachings, or just give new meaning to the Gospel depiction of Christ (i.e., Unity School of Christianity).

There are some whom claim to be the messiah, or have certain powers to do things no other person can. And there are some whom will use manipulation to garnish sexual favors from vulnerable acolytes (e.g. David Berg's, Children of God cult).

I had an opportunity to have the exposure of many different faith groups and cults. One would not think that those within the Catholic Church, specifically, in South America and Mexico practice witchcraft as part of their worship. Not too long ago, I had an opportunity to minister to this Mexican woman, of whom was adamant to never allow anyone to keep locks of her hair after being serviced at a salon. I asked, "What benefit do you have with useless old hair. You can't stuff it back into your scalp?"

"I burn it," she replied.

She believed, someone's hair in the wrong hands will open oneself up to an evil result. She even expressed vehemently about discriminating against Dentist who fail to honor her wish to depart with her extracted wisdom teeth, and said "I will find someone else that is willing." Like hair, I asked her what is the benefit for keeping extracted teeth? She explained of being in possession of her own baby teeth; which gives inference her mother was a practitioner of witchcraft. "People make necklaces with children's teeth to bring good luck. You can do many things with teeth," She asserted.

Even though this young woman claimed to be Christian, yet considers herself to be a witch because of the white magic. I was given a light lesson that many native Mexicans, as she claimed, practice "white magic" verses "black magic," also known as Santeria. Just like there are those who pray to the Saints, nevertheless there are those who consider themselves as a Catholic but practice witchcraft. Gently, I proceeded to explain to her the Gospel message and what was being practiced by her was "not" honoring God but Satan. Surprisingly, this woman's age, at the time of our conversation, was only 22 years old.

New Age

Pew Research Center estimates "six-in-ten Americans adults" accept at least one new age belief. "Four-in-ten" believe in "psychics" and "spiritual energy" dwells in tarot, shamanic, crystals, and runes.[11] Equally important, "Thirty-three percent" believe people will experience "reincarnation" while "twenty-nine percent" believe there is significant power in "astrology."[12] In another Pew Research data called the "Religious Landscape Study," captured the biometrics of one's age, race, gender, maritrimonial status, et cetera, of the most common actors in the New Age Movement:

- (85%) White

- (61%) Woman

- (43%) Age 30-49, followed by (33%) 18-29 years of age

- (30%) Never Married, while (29%) Married

- (72%) Non-parents

- (87%) Believe "the Holy Scriptures are not the Word of God"

- (43%) Democrat, (41%) Liberal[13]

In his book, *Invisible Master*, Leo Lyon Zogami has identified that many of the cult leaders in the New Age movement are women. Since the late 1800s, Helen Blavatsky, has been considered the mother of the New Age Movement. She was successful in winning people's attention with outlandish, supernatural stories pertaining to a demonic being named "Koot Hoomi," whom was portrayed as having an omnipresent nature. One of Blavatsky's contributions, most notably, came in the form of writings, known as "*The Secret Doctrine*," being a racist dogma suitable for Nazism –synthesized as an Aryan hypothesis thus claiming to be ethnically superior. Moreover, the German's fell in love with her theory that eventually shaped into what is known as the infamous race theory. So depraved, it is widely known that Blavatsky's revelations were believed to have been supplied to her by mysterious figures enveloped in a dangerous religion, she called, Theosophy.[14]

Today, however, we are witnessing the rise of Theosophy by the globalist push for intellectualism, science, to include the supernatural. In the coming future the expansion of New Age philosophy is believed to be a vehicle for the Beast system. I'm not into conspiracy theories, however, some prophecy watchers believe this could be the religion that is integrated into the new Temple in Jerusalem.

Over a decade, yoga has grown in its popularity within the Christian church. Despite this form of worship falling within the Hindu religion. However, I will place it in the new age because of the Church acceptance being in the same category of Christian Tarot cards and crystals. People that practice yoga do not realize how dangerous the art is to their soul.

Hinduism is polytheistic – having a strict observance to more than one god. In this case, Hindu's worship over 330 million gods. For Christians, however, ought to know Hinduism emphatically denies Christ Lordship. Here is why; Jesus is considered an avatar, or a symbol of a person. To Bible believing Christians, Christ is our Lord and Savior, right now – sitting at the right hand of the Father. No true Hindu will agree with this fact. Yoga is, nevertheless, a form of **pagan worship**. The name "yoga" means **union**, where the practitioners goal is to reach a heightened spiritual embodiment, called the Kundalini; which coils at the base of ones spine. Each yoga position has an actual figure representing one of its 330 million gods (demonic spirit).

What people are practicing is not an exercise but an actual worship that unites the victim with a Hindu god. Frankly, during this process of being yoked with many devils, a form of meditation is done simultaneously. It is during the meditation a person will assume one of the demonic positions. And proceed to make this vibrating, mumbled sound (uh-hh-maa) allowing these vibrations, to connect the person to the spiritual realm. Consider this – what is the purpose for placing a yoke on horses? Simply to keep them in unison. Whenever someone is practicing yoga, what is occurring, the practitioner is harmonious with demons. For further education on this topic, I suggest viewing a video called *yogauncoiled* that can be found at www.brokenbutnotcrush.com.

Terrorist – political cults

I have spoken in depth about groups like Antifa and BLM activities after the George Floyd murder. You will not hear any of the media outlets label these entities as a cult, despite exhibiting cultic traits. Hence, if it looks like a duck, walks like a duck, quacks like a duck, and smells like a duck – it's not a pigeon. It is a duck. Terrorist cults tend to act as enforcers for secret societies that is energize with ambitions to change society through revolution, as a process to over throw an archenemy, according to *arcgis*.[15] Such groups operate as paramilitary outfits executing operations that resemble layers of military support assets. During the summer of 2020, it was reported how Antifa had pre-positioned weapons (pallets of bricks and wood) in parks and street corners. Also prepositioned were mobile aid stations that had large supply of milk, specifically for protesters to flush their eyes after being sprayed with tear gas. These tactics resemble ancient battle strategies where the front line would have the font-line warriors with swords and spears. While the marksmen firing arrows from two rolls behind the front-line. Likewise Antifa had people holding extended umbrella's to deflect fired tear gas. Behind them, people were throwing bricks and flammable items in the direction of law enforcement.

Communication was a major node as many wearing black were shown on the news having an ear piece and hand-held radios. Those arrested had secret codes that identified certain areas and teams. It is likely there was a command center where the key leaders disseminated orders to all down-trace "units" therein Antifa. We will see more of Antifa and other political cults rise during the end-times.

Occult

Whenever one thinks of the occult, the first thing people say is satanic, or witchcraft, while others may say Freemasonry or the Illuminati. All is correct in describing secret networks that falls within the spectrum of the occult magnet. For the word occult means "secret," which indeed explains the foundation is clandestine, mystical and embodies spiritualism controlled by the demonic. The leaders of these groups tend to boast of having extra-ordinary knowledge being delivered to them through some extra-dimensional entities (e.g. Jinn – a demon, or Set). These groups tend to practice animal and human sacrifices, sex perversion as part of their rituals.

Be that as it may, Hitler's regime had practiced black magic and other occult practices to no surprise. Many of their practices and inventions were said to have been the result of advice and guidance sought from supernatural techniques. Even the United States, after Operation Paperclip – many Nazi scientists and technology were brought to America then integrated into clandestine programs. It is no secret that many of those techniques had dealt in the occult. Whereas today, I would have never imagined the United States Government using black magic as a weapon; let alone being in a partnership with CERN or CIA, that manages an authentic division that research occult activities (mind control). You will be surprised to discover which U.S. allies routinely flirts with the occult, which is public record.

Christian radio host and author, Jan Markell, shared a case of occult activity tended by many world leaders, at the Gotthard Base Tunnel, Markell explains:

In June 2016, an event came along that few noticed. You had to be an online reader to know of its existence. But if you were and you researched the Gotthard Base Tunnel ceremony in Switzerland and watched it on YouTube, you had to be alarmed! The tunnel connected Italy to France and wound underground through Switzerland. It was a gigantic globalist celebration and ceremony. It was also satanic. *The two often go together.* Many world leaders gathered and watched an eight-hour ceremony that was so blatantly evil it was stunning. It even had a Baphomet – a goat-man, a notorious satanic symbol – running around and being celebrated.[16]

On November 5, 2021, during hip-hop artists, Travis Scott's concert, at the Houston Astro World, ended tragically; unfortunately at the time of this writing, 9 died and over 300 people were injured in this disaster. Scott, a known occultist, frequently injects satanic symbolism in his lyrics, videos and, of course, during this concert. For example, if you would like to witness for yourself, view his *Goose Bumps* video, which is adorned in an occultic fashion.

At the time of publishing, the Center for Desease Control and Prevention (CDC) had joined a diabolical plot to promote occult activity to minors. *The Epoch Times* purports the CDC's website connects children to a live-chat room called QChatSpace. Jackson Elliott wrote that the main function of QChat is to deliver "on-line advice on sexuality with content that promotes transgenderism, anal and oral sex, and occult superstition."[17]

In conclusion, we are witnessing more and more young adults engaging in the cult, and occult, having no interest to serve God of the Bible. Satan is busy corrupting the minds and diligently searching to take as many people with him, to hell. For Satan understands his time is running out. Satan's objective is to destroy God's prize possession, His creation.

Satan's plan was to rob Jezebel of her victory, therefore, Jesus was prepared and ready to give Jezebel another chance to repent and turn away from her wickedness. Even though, she had led many people astray within the Church. Regardless, Christ's grace, mercy and love was still extended to Jezebel and those whom followed her. All she had to do was repent. And say, "Lord forgive me for teaching and seducing Your servants to commit fornication and eat things sacrificed unto idols," afterwards, she would need to make a decision to do right until the end. But she refused to humble herself and return to the arms of the Lord; which is foolish on her part. In the same manner, the post-evangelism is in this category, which pastors are joining a cult embryo that eventually will birth biblical compromise affecting generations. Therefore, it is essential for churches to have Biblical standards to shield against cult activity. Pastor Jim Townsley mentions, "It requires no courage to compromise; simply follow the crowd. Standing for the truth may be lonely, but it always honors God."[18]

Christ will change your life

You may not have sinned to the degree as the woman called Jezebel, but did you even commit a sin that Christ needed to forgive you? Maybe cheated on your spouse, lied or took something that wasn't yours. I did. Christ is love was extended to me after I had taken a life. Beloved, it is the same opportunity Jesus gave to Jezebel, as well as extended to you and all believers. Repent! Beloved, no matter the sin, it is wickedness in the eyes of God. Jesus said, "But that which ye have already hold fast till I come. And he that overcometh, and keepeth my works unto the end, to him will I give power over the nations" (Revelation 2:25-26). Jesus further asserts, "Behold, I come quickly; blessed is he that keepeth the sayings of the prophecy of this book" (Revelation 22:7).

A customer wanted to buy a chicken and the butcher had only one in stock. He weighed it and said, "A beauty. That will be four dollars, lady."

"Oh, that's not quite large enough," said the customer. The butcher put the chicken back in the refrigerator, rolled it around on the ice several times, then back on the scaled again.

"This one is six dollars," he said, adding his thumb for good weight.

"Oh, that's fine!" said the customer. "I'll take both of them."[19]

There is no mistake about it, Christ will not twist anyone's arm nor force Himself upon anyone to worship and love Him. You have a choice to take it or leave it. With clarity, Jesus asserted, "he that is unjust, let him be unjust still: and he which is filthy, let him be filthy still: and he that is righteous, let him be righteous still: and he that is holy, let him be holy still" (Revelation 22:11). The Apostle Paul reminds us, "But if the Spirit of him that raised up Jesus from the dead dwell in you, he that raised up

Christ from the dead shall also quicken your mortal bodies by his Spirit that dwelleth in you" (Romans 8:11).

Jesus died on the Cross, He took on your sins, and God raised Him from the dead on the third day. To raise you up from your old-dead-self to who you are now, in Christ Jesus. "For he hath made him **to be** sin for us, who knew no sin; that we might be made the righteousness of God in him" (2 Corinthian 5:21, emphasis added). It was in that very moment you received Christ, and immediately your sins were blotted out. "There is therefore now no condemnation to them which are in Christ Jesus, who walk not after the flesh, but after the Spirit" (Romans 8:1). You no longer have to dwell on your past offenses, because Christ had paid the ultimate price by the shedding of His blood, and being subsequently nailed to the Cross. Amen!

CHAPTER 11

FINISH STRONG

Our greatness is birth from the womb of our greatest pain and setbacks, then metabolizes into remarkable strength.

-D. A. Kelly Sr.

One morning I woke up with this burning thought to "Finish Strong." All week this winning theme tarried in my mind, about how imperative it is to go-all-in until the end. I often envision the many depressed people I have encountered this past year. At one time or another, many perceive the urgency "to build" has lost its relevancy. And the determination to second guess their motivation has become more attractive than succeeding. Thus I began to reflect upon several kings in the Old Testament, specifically, within the book of Kings and Chronicles. A few of these men of whom had started off strong but ended wrong. One particular king was Solomon, the son of David, of whom God had endowed with great wisdom and treasures of blessing beyond human imaginativeness.

Indeed his appetite for ungodly women over God ultimately became his ruin. A commonality are three vices that causes people of God to fall and tap-out, being that it's: sex, money, and fame. In the case of Solomon, nevertheless, had touch, at least, one of these takedowns that qualified him to end wrong. For the time, that which, we live requires the people of God to pursue the hard right over the easy wrong. Simply true believers are called to live a life pleasing to God. We are not to live as one whom is of the world.

In the Matthew 24:13 account, Jesus declares to the disciples. "But he that shall endure unto the end, the same shall be saved." We can turn to the seven churches in Revelations and receive the encouragement to overcome. The message to the Church, it is through His grace and shedding of Christ blood, "that he might reconcile both unto God in one body by the cross, having slain the enmity thereby" (Ephesians 2:16). No doubt the world we live in is spiraling out of control. Today it is hard to remain positive in a society that is casting explosive unbiblical worldviews. It is like finding yourself, in a revolving process of getting into a cold bath. And even though the world is going bad doesn't mean that we have to follow the convoy. Therefore, it is my goal to encourage you to stand on the faith that flows from the grace of Christ Jesus, and Finish Strong.

There is a prerequisite that requires us to be a willing vessel to serve others, and influencing others, by demonstrating how valuable people are to us. In this process to Finish Strong declares our greatest accomplishments come from some of our most unpretentious goals and decisions. Wherefore it leads us to insulate ourselves around people whom are faithful to Biblical truths, ultimately giving themselves to being conduits of hope. Once, Winston Churchill said, "success is walking from failure to failure with no loss of enthusiasm." To live in a place where enthusiasm dwells will require others to witness the Lord's power through our overcoming difficult times.

Don't believe the devil, when he say:
"Your problems are bigger than God"

First thing, tell yourself that "my trials are just an undercover blessing!" In the words of Jesus' brother James, in 1:2-4, 12, points out: "My brethren, count it all joy when ye fall into divers temptations; knowing this, that the trying of your faith worketh patience. But let patience have her perfect work, that ye may be perfect and entire, wanting nothing." And verse 12, continues, "Blessed is the man that endureth temptation: for when he is tried, he shall receive the crown of life, which the Lord hath promised to them that love him." James waste no time in verse 2 by encouraging believers to "count it all joy," when we "fall into" many temptations, trials or troubled. A trial (Gk. peirasmos) refers to "an attempt to learn the nature or character of something" by God to satisfy His divine purpose.[1] A trial and temptation are synonymous to the other. For they are not sin within itself; however only becomes sin predicated on the response of the one being tempted. What James is suggesting, whenever we pass into a specific condition, whether captured by unhealthy thoughts, to even being attacked by haters, or met with many questions about handling a relationship is for the good.

When James suggest that we are to "count it", consider this as some means to understand the "it." Your "it" can be hinged upon a decision to leave that stale job to pursue your dream. Your **it** might be the fear of "what's next" after losing a spouse or child to the coronavirus. It may be the people at your job that has plucked that last nerve, and you know not what to do. Perhaps your dream to starting a business, in order to escape melancholy is frustrated by the disingenuous spouse. People think of starting over at the age of 40 is a challenge. It can be, if you allow it to be. I must add, in the foreseeable Great Reset lucrative vocations will no longer exist under the globalist Build.Back.Better bill. We will start to see the unemployment rate incrementally increase then there will be more, more and more murmuring and complaining that follows. Regardless, don't quit. A preacher named Oswald J. Smith, once said:

My friend, you may grow in grace; but there must be a starting point. You get nothing until you start. There is a beginning to everything. There must be a beginning to victory. There must be a moment when you step out of defeat into victory when you turn from the old to the new, when you leave the wilderness for the Promise Land, when you cross the Jordan River. I say, there must be a definite crisis experience. There must be a start. Have you started? You can't get anywhere till you start. If you started, then, if I were you, I would start at once.[2]

The bottom-line, a perceived trial is an attempt to develop your character to build you up, so that, you can become more than a conqueror and not be moved by the weight of circumstance. Imagine this, James is communicating to believers that a problem is not a problem unless you see it as such. More importantly the way we perceive ourselves in the midst of trial will determine our survival. When we go through trials, or calamities, we are to receive it with joy, like it is a delightful thing. Sounds a bit crazy; but it is far from fiction.

To understand this perception requires believers to be honest with oneself. Then diligently dig deep while committing these concerns to prayer. God, the Holy Spirit will upload wisdom for us to navigate through these arduous periods of testing of our faith. To initiate this self-assessment ask yourself, "how do I view myself in the midst of this ordeal?" Keep in mind how we cope with a trial will determine our satisfaction of results? It is not about how we feel or what we perceive as being right, but whether, how we meet God's standards to Finish Strong. Too often people want to make God in their "own" image instead of being made in Christ's image. For instance, in Isaiah 55:8-9, God affirms this claim by asserting, "For my thoughts are not your thoughts, neither are your ways my ways, saith the Lord. For as the heavens are higher than the earth, so are my ways higher than your ways, and my thoughts than your thoughts." Many times trials can entice a person to partake in some immoral activity because of mishandling a problem that is spiritual and emotionally draining.

The fishing-frog (known as the sea devil) has hanging over its mouth, an attachment that uniquely resembles a fishing lure, with a worm assembled to it. Once its prey is attracted to this decoy, the sea devil devour the deceived fish. Likewise, trials and temptations are similar to the sea devil. Temptation (tempted-to-taste-sin) can be attractive, and with the wrong decision can be the difference of overcoming or suffering an unfavorable life altering consequence.

Why should I consider trials a delightful thing (blessing)?

In James 1:3, "Knowing this, that the trying of your faith worketh patience." At times, when we are under pressure, our faith-life is forced into the open, eventually exposing our true colors. If you want to know whom people really are, just watch them go through the lens of their calamity. The **trying** of your faith" (Gk. *dokimion;* means testing). In the BDAG, the Greek spelling rendered is *dochimion* to refer to as "means of determining the genuineness…as a result of a test."[3] Temptation is also a means to which prove whom you are, and whose you are either in Christ or not. God uses this academic term to teach us through our greatest challenges.

It is often suggested that one's greatest teacher is ones trials and hardships that are born from temptation and even, transgressions. The testing, at times, produces frustration because of being stuck in a holding-pattern around disappointment. Thus opening us to experience the familiarity to suffer hurt again. Do you have something hard in your life that has become a heavy burden? The testing is the struggle of your faith, which is the application of nurturing patience to its maturity. Once King David had mentioned, "For there is not a word in my tongue, but lo, O Lord, thou knowest it altogether" (Psalms 139:4).

Indeed, God knows altogether our heart and definitely understand our limitations. Apostle Paul even noted, "there hath no temptation taken you but such as is common to man: but God is faithful, who will not suffer you to be tempted above that ye are able; but will with the temptation also make a way to escape, that yet may be able to bear it" (1 Corinthians 10:13). In this season, all we need to remember is that God will never let us down; moreover, He will never allow for us to be pushed over our limitations. He will always be there to help us through it all. People often opine Jesus is not on the job because of the climate of their trials. For it is not uncommon for believers to think their faith is unmatched with Christ expectations because of how the emotional toil has affected them. For God is succinct, hence "let your conversation be without covetousness; and be content with such things as ye have: for he hath said, I will **never** leave thee, **nor** forsake thee" (Hebrews 13:5, emphasis added). Jesus is the cure to anxiety. For He said, "therefore I say unto you, Take no thought for your life, what ye shall eat, or what ye shall drink; nor yet for your body, what ye shall put on. Is not the life more than meat, and the body than raiment? Behold the fowls of the air: for they sow not, neither do they reap, nor gather into barns; yet your heavenly Father feedeth them. Are ye not much better than they" (Matthew 6:25-26)? We are important to our Heavenly Father, who loves us unconditionally. Even when everybody has turned their backs, but God will never turn away from us. Even when Slick Willie, goes outside his marriage, thus turning away from his wife for another woman. God is willing to mend that gaping wound in her heart. We just got to trust in Him.

Every trial has its purpose to build endurance

During Jesus Sermon on the Mount, Matthew 5:10-12, demonstrated His sincerity concerning the challenge believers will endure through the hands of abusers, and haters of the Cross. He declares, "Blessed are they which are persecuted for righteousness sake: for theirs is the kingdom of heaven. Blessed are ye, when men shall revile you, and persecute you, and shall say all manner of evil against you falsely, for my sake. Rejoice, and be exceedingly glad: for great is your reward in heaven: for so persecuted they the prophets which were before you." For me, the most comforting part of this message is the prophets had gone through similar challenges we have encountered. Even writing this book as controversial as it is, I will be within the cross-hairs of haters and a "grateful" recipient to derision. I just say, amen, and hallelujah anyhow. It is never about the person who does you wrong, rather it's how much you're willing to handle and respond.

There is a flower indigenous to Southern Mexico and Southeast Asia that blooms only in darkness called the "queen of the night." Wikipedia describes it as having sensitive "flowers [that] wilt before dawn;' and most importantly, a flower that is commonly harvested to treat "respiratory," "inflammation" and "bleeding conditions."[4] Just like the queen of the night, we are living in a dark world where God is calling all believers to blossom where they are planted as to Finish Strong. We have spiritual gifts that are provided to us to bless the world by delivering the Gospel message that man might be saved.

We are called to Finish Strong even in the spotlight of dissenters. I have good news for you. Whenever we are persecuted, reviled, or confronted with sin, it is a sign as to whom we are in Christ Jesus. Spoiler alert – it only applies when we are living for Jesus. So do right. Jesus drew in the hearers during the Beatitudes discourse by confirming the prophets were persecuted, His apostles were reviled for His name sake. Jesus was beaten, lied upon, hated, and put to death.

Did you know there is a blessing within the process to endure?

Do you remember the declaration in James 1:12, that says, "Blessed is the man that endureth temptation for when he is tried, he shall receive the crown of life, which the Lord hath promised to them that love him."

Do you love our Lord and Savior Jesus Christ? Well – He surely loves us in return. For He loved us before we knew what loving Him was all about. Beloved be happy about your circumstance; be very glad! For a great reward awaits us in Heaven. Praise the Lord, and thank God for the haters. They are just doing their part to strengthen you. Thank God for the difficulties that find its way in your life. You know why? Christ is not finished with you yet.

To Finish Strong points us to Mark 4:35-41 as a reminder that Jesus will calm the storms. There are times when we need Jesus to calm the storms in our lives. One late night, the disciples were on the boat, in the middle of the Sea of Galilee, had experienced a chaotic storm where the "waves beat into the ship." This was no ordinary storm; it probably resembled a roller coaster ride, with the disciples in crisis mode. If they could have dialed 911 the switch board would have blown up due to the overwhelming demand to be saved. But guess what Jesus was doing at that given moment? He was "chillin" while sleeping on a pillow. Pregnant with fear, each disciple witnessed the ship accumulating so much water to the point, it appeared it was not going to hold together much longer. Did you ever have situations beating at the four corners of your life? At one point it seemed the expectations you grew accustomed was not likely to hold together?

Hopeless. Fear could not find Jesus anywhere because the disciples attention was fixated on the storm, while being consumed by an imaginary fate that neither existed. But when someone gained the courage to call out, "Master, carest thou not that we perish (verse 38)?" Indeed, one thing the Bible doesn't mention is if Jesus had stretched out; but what it does mention, is our Lord and Savior showed up to calm the storm. The next time you find yourself on a boat called hardships of life being tossed about. And the sea of emotions are consuming your every thought. Even when it may appear there is no help in sight while more and more sea of trials are gushing on the floor of your finances, marriage, and health. At that moment is the right time to stop, and tell yourself, Jesus is on the boat! Just because things don't turn out like you predicted, doesn't mean Jesus is not working it out. On the contrary, Christ will work it out. The Bible says, "hope deferred maketh the heart sick: but when the desire cometh, it is a tree of life" (Proverbs 13:12). In the Black church tradition, we have a saying that "hope deferred is not hope denied."

Psalter Continuum: Depart. Do. Seek. Pursue.

When we are on the journey to Finish Strong, I believe the people of God ought to follow what I call the Psalter continuum found in Psalm 34:14, that reads, "Depart from evil, and do good, seek peace, and pursue it" (see figure 11.1). By taking the time to apply this passage to memory will enable anyone to remain on track to Finish Strong. How do you want to be remembered after graduating to Heaven?

Depart from evil

Nowadays, it is easy to find oneself being vacuumed into foolishness that is in pursuit of us. Satan loves foolishness because it always encircles sin. Like I said before, sin is the pork of humanity. It tastes good, but extremely bad for us. In the news there are young adults participating in "flash-robbery's", a version of flash mobs. They consist of invaders breaking and smashing into high-end stores; subsequently performing snatch and grab of expensive merchandise. Perhaps that was an extreme example; however, to depart from evil will require people to change the way they think. Thus change is only conceived through that which is produced in one's heart, and then expressed outwardly. The fruit from what one thinks can be seen in one's speech and in one's physical actions. But the bottom-line, one must alter the way one think in order to make a departure from evil. I believe this issue is illustrated in a September 2021 study published by *The Roys Report*, which chronicles George Barna and Cultural Research Center (CRC) discovery that 9% of "born-again

Christians" possess a biblical worldview. While among American adults, just 4% hold the same.[5]

I find the problem rests where most self-identified Christians do not have an appreciation for God's holiness, nor the relevancy of faith. Jesus said, "not everyone that saith unto me, Lord, Lord, shall enter into the kingdom of heaven; but he that **doeth the will** of my Father which is in heaven" (Matthew 7:21, emphasis added). Just think, only 9% out of 69% of the U.S. population consider themselves born-again, with a biblical worldview. While only 60% of so-called believers live day to day with a carnal worldview.[6] As sad and frightening as this may be, it is possible these are the people Jesus is referring to.

We are called to live a spiritual life being aware of the law of sin and death. To have a biblical worldview means "now we have received, not the spirit of the world, but the spirit which is of God; that he might know the things that are freely given to us of God" (1 Corinthians 2:12). However, look at the difference between those having a biblical worldview verses a non-biblical worldview from Apostle Paul's perspective. He said, "for they that are after the flesh do mind the things of the flesh; but they that are after the Spirit, the things of the Spirit. For to be carnally minded is death; but to be spiritual minded is life and peace;" Paul continues, "Because the carnal mind is enmity against God; for it is not subject to the law of God, neither indeed can be. So then they that are in the flesh cannot please God" (Romans 8:5-8).

In 1 Corinthians 2:14, Paul argues, "But the natural man receiveth not the things of God: for they are foolishness unto him: neither can he know them, because they are spiritually discerned." What Paul is referring to are those people who always attempt to discredit any biblical truths are mere hate. They push back on Paul's message only being relevant during the time it was spoken. And it is not applicable in the climate of the neo-socialist world. In fact they love to apologize for the tone of Scriptures as being too masculine, I want to encourage you. If you are part of the 60% after reading this book, read it again slowly. The next part of the continuum is for us to do good.

Do good

To do good requires true believers to be obedient unto the Lord. Thereby making the best effort to exercise the Word of God in every space of our lives. What this means, we are called to take up our cross and follow Him daily. Not just on Wednesday nights, or only on Sundays; but to carry that cross every minute and every hour. No one said it will be easy; which is why we need Jesus. Life wise, if it was not for the Blood of Jesus Christ, I would be on a collision course with Hell. It is only because of His grace, I can have a smile on my face.

Titus 3:8 says, "This is a faithful saying, and these things I will that thou affirm constantly, that they which have believed in God might be careful to maintain good works. These things are good and profitable unto men. But avoid foolish questions, and genealogies, and contentions, and striving about the law for they are unprofitable and vain." To translate this plainly, Paul is insisting that we devote ourselves to believers by sharing the Gospel message and our gifts with them to build the church up. But most interesting, he was poignant about believers to shun "foolish" (Gk. *moros;* means foolish or stupid) people.[7] The word *moros* translates in English to the word "moron."

In verse 10 the Apostle Paul issues a second warning about these heretics, specifically to avoid them because they are enemies of God. Despite having these forms of distractions, we are, though, called to evangelize the world with the Gospel. And teach people that we know, so that, what we know will outlive us. While keeping in the back of our minds, to refrain from being a partaker in other people's sin; hence anyone's foolishness. Look. A persons malfunction or dysfunction is not my ministry function. In other words, we do not have to absorb their foolishness in any aspect of our vocation. Moreover, we do not have to allow ourselves to be vexed by their ignorance; especially after telling them multiple times to abstain from their shenanigans. You don't know who you are or capable of going through until given the chance to prove it.

Seek peace

When you hear to "seek peace", what is the first thing that comes to mind? Stop for a moment and think about this question before you go any further. In the Old Testament peace comes from the Hebrew word *salom*, utilized over 250 times within the Old Testament. It is used extensively to refer to righteousness (Isaiah 48:18) and "sharing the gift of the gift of salvation" (Jeremiah 29:11).[8] It is important to remember that the Old Testament always points towards Jesus and His Messianic Kingdom. While in the New Testament, the Greek form of peace translates to *eirene,* and it refers to an act of being harmonious within some "personal relationship."[9]

To seek peace, of course, is to understand the deliverer of peace is Jesus Christ. We can begin in Isaiah 9:6-7, as the prophet fore-tell the birth of Jesus Christ, and calling Him the Prince of Peace:

> For unto us a child is born, unto us a son is given; and the government shall be upon his shoulder: and his name shall be called Wonderful, Counsellor, The Might God, The Everlasting Father, The Prince of Peace. Of the increase of his government and peace there shall be no end, upon the throne of David, and upon his kingdom, to order it, and to establish it with judgment and with justice from henceforth even forever. The zeal of the Lord of hosts will perform this.

The Apostle Paul further expresses how Christ is the source of our peace, and emphasizes, "For he is our peace, who hath **made** both **one**, and hath broken down in the middle wall of partition between us" (Ephesians 2:14). Christ's work on Calvary's Cross tore down the partition and broke the chains of bondage, so that, He might bring us into harmony with the Heavenly Father. Paul affirms this assertion, when he explained, "Having abolished in his flesh the enmity, even the law of commandments contained in ordinances; for to make in himself of twain one new man, so making peace. And that he might reconcile both unto God in one body by the cross, having slain the enmity thereby" (Ephesians 2:15-16).

Christ's death, burial and resurrection was the bolt-cutters that freed us from the enmity (sting of death). And through His redemptive plan, we are not burdened as the world in the end-times. For anyone that has rejected Christ and His salvation (peace) will ultimately pay the price for the rejection, as a payment for their sin debt. In Revelation 1:18, Jesus explains, "I am he that liveth, and was dead; and behold, I am alive for evermore, Amen; and have the keys of hell and of death." O what a pity; for anyone that rejects the One True Living God whom has freed the captives from the wages of sin.

To have peace means, we are "therefore being justified by faith, we have peace with God through our Lord Jesus Christ" (Romans 5:1). He will fill us "with all joy and peace in believing, that ye may abound in hope, through the power of the Holy Ghost" (Romans 15:13). "Finally, brethren, farewell. Be perfect, be of good comfort, be of one mind, live in peace; and the God of love and peace shall be with you" (2 Corinthians 13:11).

Pursue it

What are you and I going to actively pursue? Real simple. Finish Strong. Christ has given us the tools to persevere to sustain us until the day of glory. Whenever I preach, teach or witness to people, I emphasize the importance in finding a good Bible teaching church. Not some water-down Gospel that is soggy, but delivered by a Holy Ghost filled preacher that is not afraid to proclaim the whole counsel of God. But showing love by providing tools that will assist you in being that salt in undesirable places. Here are seven "salt shakers" to improve and strengthen your faith:

1. Make the decision to live for Jesus (John 1:12)

2. Pray without ceasing (1 Thessalonians 5:17)

3. Tell everyone about Christ's redemptive plan (Matthew 10:32)

4. Serve Christ (Matthew 25:29)

5. Keep pushing and not give up (Philippians 3:13)

6. Read your Bible (Gospel chapter a day – 1 Peter 2:2)

7. Support a ministry or church financially (2 Corinthians 9:6-8)

I like to share a word from a dear friend and brother in Christ, Minister Graham. He was excited about this chapter and had this to say:

> To Finish Strong, we must be willing to do our part with the knowledge that is from God, and to allow Him to do the heavy lifting. We must trust in our Lord to Finish Strong. With this in mind, I realize that to Finish Strong, I must acknowledge that

God establishes the winning strategies. God sets the pace and His Holy Spirit guides me and keeps me on pace to Finish Strong. It is our choice to make the decision to be strong by pursuing our Lord's divine counsel. Who is stronger than our God? No one. Overall, to Finish Strong is really not about us, but about God whom is in us.[10]

Last and final, in Psalm 28:7 says, "The Lord is my strength and my shield; my heart trusted in him, and I am helped: therefore my heart greatly rejoiceth; and with my song will I praise him." As a watchman itis imperative for me to sound off and warn people what is to come. But also to exhort God's people to Finish Strong. Therefore, by digesting this exhortation, we can touch and agree to embrace Christ alone. Faith alone. Grace alone. Scripture alone, and walk victoriously. I will leave you with Isaiah 40:31, that says:

But they that wait on the Lord shall renew their strength; they shall mount up with wings as eagles; they shall run and not be weary; and they shall walk, and not faint.

Finish Strong

CONCLUSION

I have set watchmen upon thy walls, O Jerusalem, which shall never hold their peace day nor night: ye that make mention of the Lord, keep not silence, And give him not rest, till he establish, and till he make Jerusalem a praise in the earth.

-Isaiah 62:6-7

As a watchman, it is important for the people of God to stand with us. We must sound the alarm, and not get distracted over people neglecting the enormous inventory of favorable evidence, that is fundamentally necessary to gauge the current, social pathology. I often wonder why are believers capitulating to the culture? I'm sure we can create valid reasons to make sense out of all this mess. I stand with many who believe the problem starts with, so many, Christians whom fear of being ostracized as a conspiracy theorist; or, at best, reviled. For one, I have to continue to remind myself with everything that has happened is not a Democrat or Republican issue, nor is it a race issue, it is a heart problem. W. B. Riley once said, "The head may be well stocked with Scripture; yet unless the heart, the seat of emotions and director of wills, be also the habitation of God, the feet may stray." Equally important, the demonic has found its way to exploit the multiplicity of believers. As a result, people everywhere are moving expeditiously to point their fat finger at somebody for somebody. Charles Spurgeon, a 17th century preacher, once said, "There must come with decision for truth a corresponding protest against error." We do not hear a lot of people speaking up and out about the vast errors from COVID mandates to the Great Reset agenda. At this point, what decision have you made?

I challenge you to strive and be a bastion of encouragement, for we, as believers, must get on our knees to pray for our leaders, our pastors, grandchildren, school teachers, military members and their families. Dwight Eisenhower emphatically believed communion with God is essential to ones greater success; he asserted, "Prayer gives you courage to make the decisions you must make in a crisis and then the confidence to leave the result to God." There is no better time to practice praying, especially in times like now. I believe this is the right place to provide some situational awareness relevant to what is occurring within the rising stages of the Beast system. The foreseeable future does not look good, please do not neglect what some of the most evil people on the face of this planet has their hands in. Each day has to be examined for its authenticity. "The best thing about the future is that it comes only one day at a time," said Abraham Lincoln.

Remain awake and keep watch for issuations

I cannot stress this enough, almost daily there is some drama or crisis budding. Take California, for an example. It is the first state that has passed a law, SB 742, which restricts freedom of speech to such as on sidewalks or public places. One must understand that this action is pure lawlessness. And the underlining argument of this law is unconstitutional, because the U.S. Supreme Court has ruled, already, in similar cases that such laws violate the Constitution. Therefore this law lacks any judicial teeth thus leaving the Federal Courts to subsequently rule against it soon.

The axiom of the bill will criminalize people for carrying signage, passing out flyers, particularly religious base materials. It seems, nevertheless, that California has conformed to being the country's lawless proving grounds; furthermore harmonizing everything imaginable that celebrates debauchery. I picture California as a jet stream of socialism that is sweeping its way towards the eastern half of America.

Next, you and your family could be heading for the Department of Justice (DOJ) domestic terrorist list. I wrote about this previously, but what I did not mention, the DOJs has an active database with the names of concerned parents, wanting to exercise their right to publicly oppose the leftist attempt to poison the minds of their children. What the government is really saying, in the voice of Satan, "I want your children; they belong to me. And I will destroy their future and their relationship with God." Satan is operating through the official and advocates for CRT, sex education, to name a few.

It is possible for the COVID doom and gloom to continue until the presidential elections in 2024. At the time of this writing, the Omicron variant was reported in South Africa, with many case reported in across America. What is puzzling the victims have been fully vaccinated, even with the booster shot. It amazes me how the Delta variant had subsided towards the end of 2021, then all of sudden, omicron was gently phased-in to restart the fountain of fear. It is my bold opinion, we will witness variant after variant that many will claim to be more dangerous or contagious then that previous variant. As long as people are paralyzed in a state of fear, technocrats will continue to collude with the government to seize control. Remember the **Constitution** stands as a giant, fortified wall against the Democrats path to socialism. There is great effort by those wanting to transform this country by maneuvering around our Constitution – a remarkable protector of freedom. Understand the private sectors are immune to many of the stipulations engraved in the Constitution. Further the Constitution protects citizens from government intrusion but not private sectors infringement on citizens' rights; which is why certain States are, now, passing legislation to contend with these micro-aggressions. This is how we can identify the activity of social media censorship, and widespread coronavirus vaccines mandates, hence are socialist in nature. Biden Administration has already been sued and prevented from imposing many of their socialist mandates, which are disguised under COVID. For this reason, the onus is on the Federal Courts to enforce the Constitution; which is why the Democrats are screaming, as though, their hair is on fire every time the Federal courts rule against their mandates. However, they tend to find a way to by-pass the Constitution by using a surrogate-private corporations. We are witnessing the Government methodically execute their micro-mandates down to private companies. I admit; we are witnessing a well thought out and executed plan by evil people that are getting away with it.

Did you know that Congress, Federal Judges and the U.S. Postal Service are **exempt** from taking the COVID vaccine? Why? When the same government that is pushing and pressuring their citizens to get vaccinated or else? Well, surprise! You are now receiving a glimpse into the nature of socialism-communism as to "do what I say, but, not as I do." All socialist nations are accustomed to wholesale hypocrisy. It is obvious, though, those top-officials exemptions gives inference there is something "extremely" wrong with COVID vaccines. If not, then, allow me to be the one to encourage the White House staff and other officials to lead by example and get-a-needle-in-your-arm.

The Word of God teaches us to be cautious but, at the same time, be wise. Wisdom is given to us to research, research, and research data that is available to make your own decision about the times. I'm not afraid to mention don't take "Dr. Strange glove" (Dr. Fauci) orders to "just do what you are told" or "follow the science;" here is why. Did you ever hear there are three distinguished research Universities that concluded, over-the-counter aspirin can protect lives and reduce COVID symptoms? Sarah Taylor, wrote in *The Blaze,* that research data consisting of over "four hundred Americans" hospitalized for COVID-19 were used for this study. The results are remarkable. There is strong proof of successful COVID treatments other than, the Moderna, J&J and Pfizer vaccines. George Washington University, in addition University of Minnesota, and Basel University – located in the country of Switzerland, all concluded that simple aspirin used during treatment of COVID patient's has efficacy that "reduced the risk of severe illness by nearly half."[1]

It was further concluded that many, "hospitals across the United States [had] cut the need for ventilation by 44 percent, slashed ICU admission by 43 percent and reduced overall in-hospital mortality rates by 47 percent."[2] I classify this as a miracle from God. A drug so simple and affordable; how many people have you heard died from taking aspirin? I'm sure there are people that have died over the drug's lifespan. However, I bet it is less than those whom has died due to the COVID-19 vaccine? Why haven't ABC, NBC, CBS, CNN, or other news outlets spread this message to calm the nerve of America? Should there be media special reports on this breakthrough? I believe we will hear in the near future about other effective treatment against COVID. Also we will hear of the horrors and the mortality rate after we have received these vaccines injections. Why haven't the news media aired the discovery from Japanese scientist of contamination therein several COVID vaccine vials? Another media blackout. Keep your eyes on the Nipah virus as it has an eighty percent mortality rate. And I wonder if this will eventually become the virus that will spur another global lockdown?

Keep your eye on the lock downs in Australia. You would think this Western nation was a communist country by the way Australian government has been treating its citizens. Also, New Zealand has begun to impose similar restrictions as their Eurasian neighbor. And soon, it is possible, European countries will invoke similar socialist practices as lock downs, perhaps even flirt with an idea of confiscating personal property, as extra-judicial punishment for lock down violators. For there are leaders in the EU hinting towards this method. They are waiting for another variant to provide a window of opportunity to infringe on its citizens freedom. In basic science, when a virus consistently mutates, does it not become less lethal? Something for you to think about.

I have often thought along the lines, the way our government and businesses has mistreated, harassed and even fired people for refusing to receive the COVID vaccine, rhymes with end-times prophecy. Imagine comparing today's persecution via the Tribulation's "mark of the beast," where people, left behind, from the rapture, thus respond by refusing to take the mark (after reading their Bible and this end-times book). Even though the COVID shot is not the mark of the beast but a prelude, where God has allowed for Watchmen to translate today's persecution: the harassment, rejection of religious exemptions, mandates where one cannot buy, sell, or travel without proof of having the "jab" as a loud warning. Consequently, those of whom refuses to take the mark of the Beast, according to Apostle John's account, "…I saw the souls of them that were **beheaded** for the **witness of Jesus**, and for **the word of God**, and which had not worshipped the beast, neither his image, **neither** had received his **mark** upon their **foreheads**, or in their **hands**; and they lived and reigned with Christ a thousand years" (Revelation 20:4, Emphasis added). There will come a time people will suffer the consequence of beheading for refusal to accept the Beast government mandate.

In America, the emphasis to vaccinate children may come to the point of becoming a requirement for the fall school year. I would not be surprised if child protective services were to investigate families for refusing to vaccinate their children for school. Failing to do so, means the child is no longer in school. And the schools, subsequently, turn in to authorities a non-compliance list of parents. It could get as bad where, parents refuse to comply with a school vaccination policy, it could result in the removal of children from the home. My question; why vaccinate children when it causes inflammation of the heart? Eventually those whom are suffering as children will become adults with greater risks for heart attacks, strokes and blood diseases. Then any suggestion of possible linkage to COVID vaccines may be followed up with a statement of deniable plausibility. We have to, just, wait and see.

There are politicians waiting for the right opportunity to institute similar restrictions on Americans. Remember that one of the reset goals is for the economy to crash. For the globalist need a crisis to establish their New World Order (Build. Back. Better plan). Why is there a need to build America back better? Especially when the American economy, in late 2020, showed evidence of being the number one exporter of oil for the first time in history. Instead, Biden express a desire to "do" better; when all Biden had to do, remove the current crippling restrictions. Then take initiative to institute a national emergency to kick start our great American industrial machine. Fortunately a Democrat senator, from West Virginia, refused to support Biden's $2 Trillion socialist bill, leaving the Democrat Party furious. Biden's intention was to pass a destructive bill instead of supporting the "Make America Great Again" by administering an executive order to help with the logistical constraint similar to World War II.

Seymour Morris Jr, book, *American History Revised*, wrote during World War II, Joseph Stalin said, "without American production the Allies could not have won the war."[3] During the war American ships had to worry about being destroyed by Japanese submarines. Regardless the logistical operations were a non-stop pipeline of "troops, food, planes, tanks, landing craft, airfield equipment, guns, ammunition, and fuel," said Morris.[4] This enormous success was credited to Henry J. Kaiser for exhibiting optimum material management. Notable, in two short years "1,383 ships" were built for the war effort.[5] Similarly Trump mobilization of Operation

Warp Speed resembled Kaiser's playbook to throughput three vaccines into production. Private companies were given the mission to shift their operations into a PPE and respirator refinery. All was done in short-order and with impressive results in 2020. Now, our nation is experiencing a major resource depletion and inflation reaching all-time highs.

Perhaps people need to demand from their representative, in Washington, to press the Biden Administration for solid answers, with facts. Then devise a bill to spur the ruling party to respond in kind. What does it profit a nation when its citizens neglect their responsibility to hold the president's feet to the fire. Somehow the American people did not only contract COVID, but a case of the tight-lip syndrome.

The Great Reset is a dysfunctional communist fantasy

The United Nations Agenda 2030, or 2030 Agenda for Sustainable Development was drafted in September 25, 2015 with the intent to establish a global stakeholder partnership to heal the world. Subsequently this meeting created seventeen goals believed to be a necessity for the world citizens to achieve the Marxist utopia. We are witnessing bible prophecy coming to pass with greater cries for every nation to accept this transformation into a communist nightmare, as we are told, doing so will secure safety and security for every nation. A fallacious fantasy for an inclusive economy that ultimately translates to a redistribution of wealth from nations like America. Higher taxes if you drive from the suburbs to work, higher cost of food, coupled with Klaus Schwab's Marxist forecast – loss of legacy systems. In order for less developed nations to enjoy the fruits of your hard, earned labor. It's not right; neither is it fair, particularly when America has been the most generous nation on the planet. We have provided billions of dollars to poor countries for decades. Yet there are people who hate this country for which it stands. One should consider the UN, Dr. Schwab, and thirty-nine more globalists as seekers to inject repressive socialism on the globe.

As to prove a point, below are 17 unpretentious goals envisioned by the United Nations: (I challenge you to compare each goal against what Marxism – socialism utopia requires)

1. End poverty in all its forms everywhere

2. End hunger, achieve food security and improved nutrition and pro
mote sustainable agriculture

3. Ensure healthy lives and promote well-being for all at all ages

4. Ensure inclusive and equitable quality education and promote life
long learning opportunities for all

5. Achieve gender equality and empower all women and girls

6. Ensure availability and sustainable management of water and san
itation for all

7. Ensure access to affordable, reliable, sustainable and modern ener
gy for all

8. Promote sustained, inclusive and sustainable economic growth, full
and productive employment and decent work for all

9. Build resilient infrastructure, promote inclusive and sustainable in-
dustrialization and foster innovation

10. Reduce inequality within and among countries

11. Make cities and human settlements inclusive safety, resilient and
sustainable

12. Ensure sustainable consumption and production patterns

13. Take urgent action to combat climate and its impacts

14. Conserve and sustainable use the oceans, seas, and marine re
sources for sustainable development

15. Protect, restore and promote sustainable use of terrestrial ecosys-
tems, sustainably manage forests, combat desertification, and half
and reverse land degradation and halt biodiversity loss

16. Promote peaceful and inclusive societies for sustainable development, provide access to justice for all and build effective, accountable and inclusive institution at all levels

17. Strengthen the means of implementation and revitalize the Global Partnership for Sustainable Development[5]

The UN document sounds good and reads well but lays out a robust Marxist plan injecting additional 169 stipulations that speak about interconnectivity of the international law, courts that demands every person, on earth to have a basics standard of living, while redistributing wealth from Western nations. I tell you this is not a conspiracy theory but, actually discussed within the sustainment development goals.

Also I have provided in chapter 6 evidence of this plan that you will own nothing. In other words, nothing means not anything! Since the elites are advocating for people to eat less meat and accept protein substitution because of food insecurity in foreign countries. The question still stands; what does this have to do with Americans? For starters, research how the United Nations sustainable goals are attempting to inject the globalist needle to redistribute wealth and force implementation of biotechnologies.

Back in 2013, in *Intelligent Medicine*, Ronald Hoffman, MD, gave an example how people will eventually become unfamiliar with the taste of authentic foods, such as red meat and other traditional proteins. To drive home his point, Hoffman referred to a 1973 sci-fi movie called "Soylent Green," where people could not remember the taste of farm grown eggs. (It is hard to fathom such days are not far off, where by 2050, we might forget how "real" meat tastes). Nevertheless, Hoffman recalls, one scene, in the movie where "nobody can remember what real food used to taste like, so Edward G. Robinson's character reminisces: "I was there, I can prove it! When I was a kid, you could buy meat anywhere! Eggs they had, real butter! Not this…crap!"[6] Hoffman's articulation coincides with the development Dr. Schwab has suggested in his book and within the UN Sustainment Development invitation into a terrorized culture. As far back as 2013, PayPal founder, billionaire, Peter Thiel has invested in plant base, artificial egg product called "Beyond Eggs" that has been projected to replace real eggs in supermarkets. Nearly a decade later faux eggs have not replaced real eggs. However, guess who is the advisor? Bill Gates.

Apparently Mark Prigg, of the *Daily Mail UK*, reports the "firm hopes to allow developing countries to grow and produce their own 'plant eggs,'" said, Beyond Eggs founder, Josh Tetrick.[7]

UN's plan calls for the recycle of waste to be used as food. Indeed these plans are in harmony with the World Economic Forum and UN 2030 Agenda's, seventeen points to break legacy systems.[8] It is likely, leading up to 2030 and beyond, cancer diagnosis are likely to increase. People could potentially die younger, instead of a longer life expectancy. When peoples' diet consist of non-biological foods or plants grown with nano particles thus regularly consumed, that population may suffer diseases and cancers that are uncommon. Moreover these problems subsequently may become more elevated due to chemical properties designed in GMO foods. In the end, once cancer diagnosis and deaths increase, we may hear that climate change is to blame.

Even wild animals may become illegal to hunt as being part of the Agenda 2030 restrictions to persuade people living in rural areas to comply and move into smart-cities. I would not be surprised if a sophisticated disease infected and wiped out a population of deer, and other animal protein that enable the government to restrict wild game consumption. In a controlled world where a one-world government thirsts to control every aspect of humanity. Do you honestly think eating wild life will be given an exemption under the Great Reset? Hunting wild game is part of the western culture, thus considered a resource therein a legacy system. One method to restrict those living-off-the-land from depending upon wild game; simply afford wild animals equivalent rights as humans. Imagine a time when it is illegal to kill, or even, eat wild game, such as deer. Don't hold your breath, it is happening now.

On October 20, 2021, a United Stated Federal Court has sided with the Animal Legal Defense Fund, in recognizing certain animals as a human. Micaiah Bilger, wrote in *Lifenews*, "Animal Legal Defense Fund executive director Stephen Wells in a statement [said], 'The court's order authorizing the hippos to exercise their legal right to obtain information in the United States is a critical milestone in the broader animal status fight to recognize that animals have enforceable rights."[9] In the words of Wells, interestingly mentions "hippos, rivers, orangutan and other non-humans have been recognized as legal persons in various courts in recent years."[10] The Leftists must start somewhere – right? By 2030, many of the wild animals, game and fish people depend upon for survival will likely have recognition as an "interested person." Once this is implemented, however people will be without a choice but to consume non-biological foods.

Geoengineering

On October 2, 1992, the Wall Street Journal reported:

The Russian corporation Elate Intelligent Technologies and its "Weather Made to Order" director Igor Pirogoff promises that for US$200 a day, Elate hurricanes can be steered within a 200-square-mile range, and that even Hurricane Andrew could have been decreased to a "wimpy little squall."[11]

Twenty-nine years later, on December 11, 2021, an EF-4 tornado traveled over 200 miles, through five states, causing millions of dollars in damages and killing over 30 people in winter. These warm temperatures this time of year are absolutely bizarre. Although it is not the first time such weather anomalies have occurred in the month of December (again, I invite you to remember the Dark winter of 2020), however we are seeing these types of storms incrementally becoming more frequent. People like to say, "God is angry..." or "climate change is the cause." The question has to be raised and carefully occupied – why all of sudden there are severe weather appearing in increments? Keeping in mind during the 2020 elections climate alarmist began to scream over one another to take away people's rights in the name of climate change. We have to put all the UN, Bill Gates, and The Great Reset pieces together and ask the question; Could this so-called crisis be what preachers once warned us would be needed for the globalists to impose a one world government? Perhaps. Ten years ago, if someone came to me with this assertion, I would have dismissed them as suffering a mental health crisis. However, after the events over the past five years, to include COVID-19 confusion and the abundance of lies currently being exposed, I would not doubt there are evil works involved.

Therefore, I want to provide facts that might suggest what we are experiencing might be the result of geoengineering. Before I ever consider an issue, a question pertaining to the motive has to be established; and if there is a design present? Thus far it is through the unveiling of facts that we are witnessing fresh evidence parachute out the sky ranging from the identity of known perpetrators to the patents of technology and its methods of operation. Like in chapter 5, it was written with the intentions to raise awareness about what has happened in the past (historical in nature), which undoubtedly rhymes with current events. In no way am I attempting to convince you to think along the lines as me. Moreover, I cordially ask you to take the time to ask thoughtful questions about what is happening today based off of the facts written in this book. To help with this process, I will provide additional grounds to follow this claim: does geoengineering exist today? And is it possible geoengineering is to blame for the crazy weather and other phenomenon? You make that decision.

Bob Fitrakis and Fritz Chess, wrote in *Columbus Alive*, "Typically, contrails can only form at temperatures below -76°F and at humidity levels of 70 percent or more at high altitudes, according to NOAA meteorologist Thomas Schlattes. Even in the most ideal conditions, a jet contrail lasts no more than 30 minutes."[12] It is more common, now, to see what appears to be contrails remain in the sky and transform into clouds hours later. A.K. Johnstone, invested countless hours researching weather by asserting:

> During a chemtrail "weather-creating" flyover, extremely large Xs (markers) are formed in the sky at high altitude, 30,000 feet (9,000 m). They are accompanied by repetitious linear trails laid out from east to west, south to north, or vice versa. Within a few minutes of chemtrails placement, cirrus clouds being to form from the trails, gradually changing into layers of clouds (cirrostratus) and, finally, darkening into storm clouds (cirrocumulus), precursors of precipitation.[13]

Within the last three years, I have noticed more of these "chemtrails" forming into clouds, even recall witnessing the sky developing a milky presentation. According to Freeland, once the atmosphere is ionized (charged electrons) it is likely one might witness "lightning with no thunder." But interestingly as the atmosphere is saturated with "common" chemicals like "barium" and "aluminum" it is then "pumped into the atmosphere creating suitable conditions to produce severe storms like a "tornado."[14] Now taking this into account, do people, after experiencing such weather, think these conditions were an act of God? Even when it was created by man? Absolutely. People do not know what they do not know.

Another form of weather modification is the High-frequency Active Research Project (HAARP), an ionospheric heater with a central purpose of "fine-tuning jet stream diversions." According to Ms. Freeland's research it is possible for the weather (December 11, 2021 tornado) may have been manufactured by any government or wealthy individual desiring dominance with HAARP. Here is one method:

> Ionospheric heaters can generate 3 million gigawatts (giga=-billion) to heat up one square kilometer of the ionosphere to 28,000°C (50,432°F). Control the jet stream and you can reroute storms, hurricanes, and droughts and make a fortune from weather derivatives. Shoot microwaves into the Earth (tomography) and you can discover oil reserves, underground bunkers, earth-moving machinery, "aid," CIA, military, etc. to boost the economy back home and if a country does not comply with transnational and IMF "guidelines," a flood or drought might convince its leaders to reconsider.[15]

Where did this technology come from?

Ms. Freeland reports, "U.S. Patent #4,686,605," belongs to a scientist named "Bernard Eastlund" (look carefully at the title of the technology) called the "Method and Apparatus for **Altering a Region In the Earth's Atmosphere**, Ionosphere, and/or Magnetosphere (emphasis added)."[16] In the patents description, column 1, subparagraph 1 – "Technical Field," explains how this device will alter weather; while in other subparagraphs therein this patent describes other functions as being a type of energy weapon. Eastlund explains:

> This invention relates to a method and apparatus for altering at least one selected region normally existing above the earth's surface and more particularly relates to a method and apparatus for altering said at least one region by initially transmitting electromagnetic radiation for the earth's surface essentially parallel to and along naturally-occurring, divergent magnetic field lines

which extend from the earth's surface through the region or regions to be altered.[17]

I want to keep this as "Barnie" as possible; the full intent of this device is multi-purpose. The American Government can use this device, at will, to alter foreign or domestic weather; as well as, it can function as a weapon system, specifically as a shield to disrupt incoming nuclear weapons, by using high and low frequency ELF transmissions. Freeland points out in 1994, the Secretary of Defense was extremely excited about the capabilities with the Ionospheric Research Instrument (IRI), "VHF-UHF 3GHz (billions)" and the "earth-penetrating tomograph (EPT)" package; subsequently petitioning congress to increase HAARP's funding to "$75 million."[18] Also, she mentioned these HAARP sites are not just in America. There are over 50 situated around the world from "High-power Auroral Stimulation Observatory (HIPAS) in Fairbanks, Alaska (17MW. 64.8378° N, 147.7164° W); SuperDARN (Dual Auroral Radar Network) in Saskatoon, Saskatchewan (52.1311° N, 106.6353° W); China HAARP Array (43° 04'51.75" N, 92° 48'26.85" E)," to name a few.[19]

What is interesting about these systems, ionospheric heaters are known transmitters while the observatories are classified as receivers resigned to synthesize active data.[20] To further prove HAARP does work in conjunction with cloud seeding, the CCP successfully created snow during the 2008 Beijing Olympics. And in the Middle East, remarkably it was reported that "five WEATHERTEC ionizers units with 20 emitters" created precipitation "52 times" in one Abu Dhabi hottest summers yielding "rain, hail, gales, and lightning in the eastern Al Ain region."[21]

Science writer Colin Baras, wrote in the *New Scientist*, about a "laser" used in Germany to generate clouds that amazed their Government. Baras wrote:

Nothing could be seen with the naked eye, but weather LIDAR/ LADAR [Light Detection and Ranging / Laser Imaging Detection and Ranging], which uses laser to measure light scattering in the atmosphere, confirmed that the density and size of water droplets spiked when the laser was fired.[22]

Foreign nations protest to chemtrails

There is overwhelming evidence surrounding geoengineering practices, particularly when it comes to sovereign nations having reservations about the dangers of chemtrails and cloud seeding. We will not hear mainstream media report on these events due to the pursuit of the American, some foreign governments and global elites. In fact, it has been reported that chemtrails have been investigated by Croatia, Greece, Belgium, Africa and India over the past 20 years.[23] It is important to note, though there is great danger from the dumping of chemtrails as our children and pets breathe in these toxic metals daily, as these chemicals are extremely harmful to humans and the environment. Why would people running around screaming climate change, climate change, as though their hair is on fire? Yet these hypocrites pursue practices of spreading radiation and chemicals, thus polluting the world? In no way am I a tree hugger, nor, am I a climate alarmist. The bottom-line – I call it as I see it. Nevertheless, I waited to save the best news for last. Guess who is an investor in geoengineering since the mid-2000s? It is uncle Bill Gates.

In February 2012, John Vidal, wrote in *The Guardian* about this business venture consisting of "a small group of leading climate scientist, financially supported by billionaires including Bill Gates, are **lobbying governments and international bodies to back experiments into manipulating the climate on a global scale** to avoid catastrophic climate change (emphasis added)."[24] Do you now believe this insane weather dating back to Dark Winter, to include December 11, 2021, might as well be man-made like coronavirus is not natural, but man-made? Do you think the globalists, like Bill Gates and Klaus Schwab could be desperate enough to create one crisis after crisis? Perhaps, even "do whatever it takes," by "any means necessary" to finally handcuffed and shackled the globe to their Great Reset? I believe these men has the mental state to engage in this type of scandal. And I would not underestimate their psychology to engage in such wicked schemes because a man's heart is wicked above all things.

Russia (Bear) and CCP (dragon) smell weakness

In December 2021, we have witnessed Russia stage close to 200,000 troops at the Ukraine borders for an invasion. Within the months of this book goes to print, I suspect, based off my military experience, Ukraine will become occupied by Russian forces. Russian President Putin knows Washington is weak when there is a Democratic president in tandem at the White House. He also understand that NATO will sit idle without American leadership. Germany's hands are tied because of the energy deal made with the Kremlin. Well – France... I do not know about France as this nation is unpredictable. Russia is aghast by NATO invitation for Ukraine to join the alliance. And an imminent war is the solution to have NATO abandon that deal. Realistically, Putin does not want a large war. Right now, his approval rating is in the low sixty percentile. He is popular but not untouchable if a war breaks out and the European Union map is redrawn into Russia. He understands such risks, thereby is watching and waiting to see how Washington will respond before moving his chess pieces.

China is likely to invade Taiwan after the Olympics. For one, we have to remember the CCP feed off of propaganda and hype. To invade the little nation could draw undesirable attention and pushback, as far as, nations boycotting the Olympics would embarrass Beijing. The CCP war doctrine has them currently at war with America. Since the summer of 2021 their military has been practicing tactics to sink our Naval vessels in the event, Biden miraculously gives Commanders a green light to defend Taiwan. It will not happen. I could be wrong, and the old Biden shows up to give the CCP a reality check on their capabilities against our more proven force. Either way, there is no good solution to this crisis because over the past 30 years China has been like a bulldozer to become the dominant global leader. And Biden, along with his leftist party will capitulate to the pressure from Beijing all the way leading up to the 2024 election and beyond.

I could be wrong about this statement – if Biden and the Democrats are unsuccessful in passing the HR 1 and HR 4 bill (to make official the election process during 2020 permanent) through the Senate, and COVID is losing its sting with quarterly new variants appearing, then expect a short, deadly war with China, that will get carried away with possible nukes being delivered from both sides; or an electromagnetic pulse (EMP) to send America back 150 years to establish the Great Reset. I'm just making this assessment from following the media coverage of the possible war climate, my military experience and the end-times. My assessment could be wrong; I hope so.

Everything points to socialism

It seems no matter the direction we turn, socialism and communism is there. On one side, there is Klaus Schwab's intention to impose a Marxist Great Reset upon the world. But most importantly, destroy Western culture as it is a threat to their endeavors. Marxist real objective is to erase the Christian institutions of faith – the Church. On another side, the Democratic Party is aggressive to take and maintain control in perpetuity, as one Senator exclaimed, "to change America." The final observation, the children today are growing fonder about socialism. I'm a member of Gen. X, and we have to clinch some blame for the psychology our children embrace. I'm not sure, people in my generation remember the 1980s when communism was still active in the U.S.S.R. and South Africa's racist past stemmed from communism. Exactly what the leftist, mostly Democrats, are wanting to deceive the world in accepting again. Remember the pig with lipstick? However, our children born in the 1990s and early 2000s have no clue of the pain and suffering people, at the bottom, had to endure. And you better believe someone has to be at the bottom of the barrow. The question is who will it be? Whites? Hispanics (particularly those from South America)? Blacks? The *Herald of Hope*, shared a story about a high school economics teacher taught his class a valuable lesson called "An Impractical Theory" about socialism – communism. I think this should be shared with as many people as possible for them to gain understanding about a poison that is being delivered to the children of this great nation:

When the teacher in a high school class in economics found that his pupils were in favor of the theory of taking from those who had more than enough and giving it to those in need, he announced that beginning immediately he would put the system in operation in the class. He would subtract from the grades of the top students and add it to the grades of the poorest students so all would get an average grade. The first month the system worked pretty well. The grades of the best students were high enough to offset the deficiency of the lower ones, and the class average was above the passing mark, then the situation changed. The top students saw no reason to put forth extra effort required to get good grades with which they would not be credited. The average students put forth less effort, for they were assured passing grades. The dullards did not work at all, since they would pass with the aid of the grades from the others. So, when at first the system provided passing grades, for all, within a very short time the entire class was failing. They then realized that this socialist – communistic theory was impractical.[25]

What an amazing experiment for children to experience socialism, and how bad it is for people who desire to become successful. It is like dominos that gradually collapse as does people's lives gradually decline into a deep pool of poverty. Those believing in the risen Christ will become targets. We are learning about all of believers whom are worshipping in underground churches in China, India, and Nigeria in the name of the Lord. It is possible that we may live to see believers being hunted like wild game because of Christ is standing in the way of a fictitious, upside down world.

Again no one knows how much "crazy" the church will endure before Christ returns for His beloved Church. As the shadow of the Tribulation draws closer, I would like to leave you with the words from our Lord and Savior, Jesus Christ, "These things I have spoken unto you, that in me ye might have peace. In the world ye shall have tribulation: **but be of good cheer, I have overcome the world**" (John 16:33, emphasis added).

God made you to bend not to break. He said, "be of good cheer;" whenever it appears life will never return to normal – "be of good cheer;" you lost a family member due to COVID – "but be of good cheer;" your husband or wife of 20 years seeks a divorce – Jesus said, "but be of good cheer." How can I be of good cheer, when everything has sucked the life out of me? Jesus said, this is why – "**I have overcome the world.**" Right now, this is a good place to stand up; lift up your holy hands, and raise your voices and shout – thank you, Jesus! Hallelujah anyhow!

The Word of God says, you and I are more than a conqueror; and for you to "Rest in the Lord and wait **patiently** for Him: **fret not thyself** because of him who prospereth in his way, **because of the man who bringeth wicked devises to pass**" (Psalm 37:7, emphasis added). You may even have to suffer a little while, but know this, "But the God of all grace, who hath called us unto his eternal glory by Christ Jesus, after that **ye have suffered a while**, make you perfect, stablish and strengthen, settle you. To him be glory and dominion for ever and ever. Amen" (1

Peter 5:10-11, emphasis added). Remember: stay prayed up, word up, so the devil won't mess you up!

NOTES

Introduction: A Watchman's Warning

1. Stephen D. Renn, *Expository Dictionary of Bible Words,* (Peabody, MA: Hendrickson Publishers, 2005), 1029.

2. James P. Boyd, *The Practical Bible Dictionary and Concordance,* (Uhrichsville, OH: Barbour Publishing Inc, 1952), 90.

3. Verlyn D. Verbrugge, *New Testament Dictionary of New Testament Theology*, Grand Rapids, MI: Zondervan, 2000), 515.

4. Ibid. 515

Chapter 1: The Key to Biblical Interpretation

1. R.C. Sproul, *The Soul's Quest for God: Satisfy the Hunger for With Spiritual Communication with God,* (Wheaton, IL: Tyndale, 1992), 47.

2. Henry A. Virkler and Karelynne G. Ayayo, *Hermeneutics: Principles and Processes of Biblical Interpretation,* (Grand Rapids, MI: Baker Book House Company, 2007), 218.

3. Ibid., 77.

4. Ibid., 16.

5. Ibid., 16.

6. *The Webster New Collegiate Dictionary* 9th ed., (Springfield, MA: Merriam-Webster, 1986), 943

7. Ayayo, *Hermenertic,* 168.

8. William Mounce and Robert Mounce, *Greek and English Interlinear New Testament (KJV/NIV),* (Grand Rapids, MI: Zondervan, 2008), 931.

9. Ibid., 931

10. Paul N. Benware, *Understanding End-Times Prophecy*, (Chicago, IL: Moody, 2006), 23.

11. Ayayo, *Hermeneutics,* 27

12. Ibid., 27-29

13. "Bible Readers Want Accuracy, Word-For-Word Translation," *Lifeway Research*, October 01, 2011, https://lifewayresearch.

com/2011/10/01/bible-readers-want-accuracy-word-for-word-translation/.

14. Benware, *Prophecy*, 28.

15. Ibid., 29.

16. Ibid., 30.

17. Ibid., 31.

18. Gary M. Burge, and Gene L. Green, *The New Testament Antiquity: A Survey of the New Testament within its Cultural Context*, 2nd ed. (Grand Rapids, MI: Zondervan, 2020), 550.

19. Mounce, *Greek and English Interlinear New Testament*, 935, 1018.

20. Amir Tsarfati, *The Last Hour: An Israel Insider Looks at the End Times*, (Bloomington, MN: Chosen Books, 2018), 124.

21. Ibid., 124.

22. Verlyn D. Verbrugge, *New Testament Dictionary of New Testament Theology*, (Grand Rapids, MI: Zondervan, 2000), 766.

23. Benware, *Prophecy*, 111.

24. Mounce, *Greek and English Interlinear New Testament*, 625.

25. Benware, *Prophecy*, 106.

26. Burge and Green, 417.

Chapter 2: Systematic Theology: Unlocking Biblical Prophecy

1. A.W. Tozer, "Quotes," *Sword of the Lord,* June 16, 2017, A. 20.

2. https://www.barna.com/research/sotb-2021/.

3. https://www.lifewayresearch.com/2014/10/28/americans-believe-in-heaven-hell-and-a-little-but-of-heresy/.

4. Ibid.

5. https://www.barna.com/research/sotb-2021/.

6. Ibid.

7. Ibid.

8. David Horton, *The Potable Seminary,* (Bloomington, MN: Bethany House Publishers, 2006), 96.

9. https://lifeway.com/wp-content/upload/2014/10/bigchart-overview.pdf.

10. Gregory R. Lanier and William A. Foss, *Septuaginta*, 2nd ed. (Peabody, MA: Hendrickson Publisher, 2005), 697.

11. Stephen D. Renn, *Expository Dictionary of the Bible Words*, (Peabody, MA: Hendrickson Publisher, 2005), 697.

12. Lanier and Ross, *Septuaginta*, 7.

13. A. Boyd Luter, *Study Notes: Galatians 4:4,* (Nashville: Holman Bible Publishers, 2012), 1964.

14. Joachim Jeremia, *Jerusalem in the Time of Jesus*, 4th ed. (Gottingen, Germany: Vandenhoech and Reprecht, 2019), 367.

15. Ibid., 367.

16. Ibid., 367.

17. Ibid., 360.

18. Ibid., 362.

19. Ibid., 363.

20. Ibid., 369.

21. William Dyer, "Sin Message," *Sword of the Lord*, June 2, 2017, 18.

22. www.lifewayresearch.com. (Retrieved August 10, 2021).

23. Ibid.

24. Elder Nathaniel Day, He was a dear friend who would share the pulpit during our Bible meetings.

25. Lanier and Ross, *Septuaginta*, 6.

26. *The Oxford New Desk Dictionary and Thesaurus,* 3rd ed. (New York: The Berkley Publishing Group, 2009), 428, 835.

27. "Pastors Uphold Christianity Exclusivity Poll Finds," *Lifeway Research*, https://lifewayresearch.com/2012/03/30/pastors-uphold-christian-exclusivity-poll-finds/.

28. Ibid.

29. Ibid.

30. https://www.thegospelcoalition.org/article/survey-a-majority-of-american-christians-don't-believe-the-gospel.

31. Ibid.

32. Ibid.

33. Renn., 849.

34. William D. Mounce, *The Analytical Lexicon to the Greek New Testament,* (Grand Rapids, MI: Zondervan, 1993), 479.

35. *Webster's New World Dictionary, 3rd ed.* (New York: Simon and Schuster, 1988), 1214.

36. Verlyn D. Vernugge, *New International Dictionary of New Testament Theology,* (Grand Rapids, MI: Zondervan, 2000), 27.

37. William D. Mounce and Robert Mounce, *Greek and English Interlinear New Testament (KJV/NIV),* (Grand Rapids, MI: Zondervan, 2008), 399.

38. "Eternal Security," *Sword of the Lord*, October 24, 2014, 7.

39. Ibid.

40. https://www.pewresearch.org/religion/2021/11/23/views-on-the-afterlife

41. Ibid., https://www.thegospelcoalition.org/.

42. Ibid.

43. Ryan Pitterson, "Endtimes Embrace of Evil," ed. Terry James, *Lawless: Endtimes War Against the Spirit of Antichrist*, (Crane, MO: Defender, 2020), 184-185.

44. William Falk, "Revelation," *The Weekly*, June 5, 2020, 6.

45.https://news.gallup.com/poll/27877/americans-more-believe-god-than-devil-heaven-more-than-hell-aspx. (Retrieved: August 10, 2021).

46. Ibid.

47. Renn, *Expository Dictionary of the Bible Words*, 850.

Chapter 3: Matthew 24: A Near Prophetic View

1. Joachim Jeremia, *Jerusalem in the Times of Jesus*, 4th ed. (Gottingen, Germany: Vandenhoech and Ruprecht, 2019), 10, 21.

2. Ibid.

3. Ibid.

4. Ibid., 22, 23.

5. Gary M. Burge and Gene L. Green, *The New Testament in Antiquity*, 2nd ed. (Grand Rapid, MI: Zondervan, 2020), 59.

6. Ibid., 60.

7. Ibid., 60-62.

8. Ibid., 62

9. Ibid., 62.

10. William Mounce and Robert Mounce, *Greek and English Interlinear New Testament (KJV/NIV)*, (Grand Rapids, MI: Zondervan, 2008), 961.

11. *The Oxford New Desk Dictionary and Thesaurus*, 3rd. (New York: The Berkley Publishing Group, 2009), 894.

12. Ibid., 891.

13. Stephen D. Renn, *Expository Dictionary of the Bible Words*, (Peabody, MA: Hendrickson Publishers, 2005), 984.

14. "Third Temple Blueprint Campaign Exceeds Funding Target," *Jewish Voice.org* accessed October 2, 2014, https://www.jewishvoice.org/read/article/update-building-thrid-temple.

15. Amir Tsarfati, *The Last Hour: An Israeli Insider Looked at the End Times*, (Minneapolis, MN: Chosen Books, 2008), 151.

16. *Jewish Voice.org*

17. Ibid.

18. Ibid.

19. "Pope and Grand Imam Sign Historical Pledge of Fraternity in U.A.E.," *The Guardian*, https://www.theguardian.com/world/2019/feb/04/pope-and-grand-imam-sign-historical-pledge-of-fraternity-in-uae.

20. Ibid.

21. Ibid.

22. Ibid.

23. *Jewish Voice.org*.

24. Ibid.

25. Ibid.

26. Joshua Peace, "You've Been Conditioned to Believe Conspiracy Theories. Or Have You?," *Popular Mechanics*, (New York: Hearst Magazine Media, 2021), 27-30.

Chapter 4: Deceived People Deceive People

1. "Competing Worldviews Influence Today's Christians," *Barna Group*, accessed: May 9, 2017. https://www.barna.com/research/competing-worldviews-influence-today's-christians/.

2. Ibid.

3. Ibid.

4. Ibid.

5. Ibid.

6. Ibid.

7. Ibid.

8. Ibid.

9. David Mclellan, "Marx, Karl Keinrick," *Encyclopedia Americana*, (Grolier Inc., 2003), 385.

10. Ibid., 386.

11. Israel Wayne, "The Schoolroom Seducers," ed. Terry James, *Deceivers: Exposing Evil Seducers & Their Last Days Deception,* (Green Forest, AR: New Leaf Press, 2018), 111.

12. Ibid.

13. Robert V. Daniels, "Marxism," *Encyclopedia Americana*, (Danbury, CT: Grolier Inc., 2003), 388.

14. Ibid.

15. George Orwell, *1984*, (Orlando, FL: Penguin Group, 1950), 206.

16. Daniels., 388.

17. Ibid., 389

18. Ibid., 390.

19. Ibid.

20. Lawrence W. Reed, "How Germany's 'Deal With the Devil' Backfired and Changed History," *The Epoch Times,* April 28, 2021, B5.

21. Donald W. Treadgold, "Bolshevik," *Encyclopedia Americana,* (Danbury, CT: Grolier Inc., 2003), 179.

22. Reed., B5.

23. Ibid.

24. Ella Kiatlinska and Joshua Philipp, "Socialist Revolution is Underway in U.S.: Author, Filmaker Loudon," *The Epoch Times,* May 12, 2021, A8.

25. Ibid.

26. Ibid.

27. Brad Jones, "California Teacher Moves to Florida After Exposing Critical Race Theory in Ethnic Studies," *The Epoch Times*, July 13, 2021, A4.

28. Ibid., A5.

29. Bowen Xiao, "Antifa, Other 'Far-left Groups' Exploit Protests for 'Revolution'." *The Epoch Times*, June 10, 2020, A4.

30. Jean Chen, "A Mom's Research: Who Are the Real Racists?." *The Epoch Times*, March 23, 2021, A20.

31. Dennis Prager, "The Denial of Evil: The Case of Communism," *The Epoch Times*, March 9, 2021, A20.

32. Ibid.

33. Bowen, A4.

34. Ibid.

35. *Webster's New World Dictionary*, 3rd. College ed., (New York: Simon and Schuster Inc., 1988), 1078.

36. Ibid., 394.

37. Ibid., 867.

38. "3 Ways America's Mainstream Media Resemble Communist Media," *The Epoch Times*, (December 15, 2020), A15.

39. Jean Chen, "A Mom's Research," Ibid.

40. "America's Critical Point In time: The Decade-long Communist Assault on America is Reaching a Climax," *The Epoch Times*, December 8, 2020, A15.

41. "This Audit Farce Must Stop if We Want Our Vote to Count in Arizona," *The Epoch Times*, May 18, 2021, A20.

42. Ibid.

43. Ibid.

44. David Horowitz, *The Enemy Within: How A Totalitarian Movement Is Destroying America.* (Washington D.C.: Regenery Publications, 2021), 130.

45. *The Epoch Times*.com

46. Jonah Goldberg, "Parties Don't Really Represent 'The American People'," *The Dispatch*, Quoted from St. Louis Post-Dispatch, June 27, 2021, A17.

47. Nelson Oliveira, "Survey Looks at Sex During Shut Down," *New York Daily News*, November 11, 2020, A24.

48. Catherine Yang, "The Growing Pains of Public Discourse," *The Epoch Times*, October 28, 2020, B6.

49. Ibid.

50. Ibid.

51. Joshua Pease, "Conspiracy Theory: You've Been Conditioned To Believe Conspiracy Theories. Or Have You!," *Popular Mechanics*, (New York: Hearst Magazine Media Inc, May 2021), 30.

52. Tod Strandberg, "Media Manipulators," ed. Terry James, *Deceivers: Exposing Evil Seducers & Their Last Days Deception*, (Green Forest, AR: New Leaf Press, 2018), 214.

53. Ibid.

54. Ibid., LBJ referred to Blacks as "niggers"; which he was very comfortable addressing African-Americans.

55. Terry James, 223-224.

Chapter 5: Cancel Culture Is Cultural Marxism

1. Mimi Nghyen Ly, "Cuba Accused of Using Chinese Tech to Block Internet Access Amid Protest," *The Epoch Times*, July 20, 2021, A10.

2. Ibid.

3. "$6.1 million," *The Epoch Times*, July 20, 2021, A2.

4. *Webster's Collegiate Dictionary*, 9th ed., "Cancel," (Springfield, MA: Merriam-Webster, 1986), 2000.

5. David Horowitz, *The Enemy Within: How A Totalitarian Movement is Destroying America*, (Washington, D.C.: Regenery Publishing, 2020), 154.

6. Ibid.

7. Tod Strandberg, "Media Manipulators," ed. Terry James, *Deceivers: Exposing Evil Seducers & Their Last Days Deception*, (Green Forest, AR: New Leaf Press, 2018), 216.

8. Horowitz, *The Enemy Within*, 132.

9. Joshua Pease, "You've Been Conditioned To Believe Conspiracy Theories. Or Have You?" *Popular Mechanics*, (New York: Hearst Magazine Media, Inc, 2021), 30.

10. Ivan Pentchoukov, "Biden's First 100 Days: A Radical Transformation of America," *The Epoch Times*, April 28, 2021, A7.

11. Julie Musto, "Carrie Severino Slams Schumer's Totally Unacceptable Attack On Justices Kavanaugh and Gorsuch," *Fox News*, March 7, 2020, https://www.foxnews.com/media/carrie-severino-chuck-schumer-threatening-comments-totally-unacceptable-issues question.statement., quoted in David Horowitz, *The Enemy Within*, 127.

12. Ibid., 142.

13. George Orwell, *1984*, (New York: Penguin Group, 1949), 28.

14. Ibid., 16.

15. "3 Ways America's Mainstream Media Resembles Communist Media," *The Epoch Times*, December 15, 2020, A15.

16. Ibid.

17. Ibid.

18. Ibid.

19. John Mac Ghlionn, "The Great Reset: Social Justice With Chinese Character," *The Epoch Times*, A18.

20. Dinesh D'Souza, "State-Sponsored Censorship," *The Epoch Times*, July 27, 2021, A18.

21. Ibid.

22. Ibid.

23. Ibid.

24. Ibid.

25. Ibid.

26. Ibid.

27. Ibid.

28. Ibid.

29. Ibid.

30. Klaus Schwab and Thierry Malleret, *COVID-19: The Great Reset*, (Geneva, Switzerland: World Economic Forum, 2020), 40.

31. D'Souza, State-Sponsored Censorship, A18.

32. Ibid.

Chapter 6: The Great Reset: Beast System Rising

1. Ida Aukin, "Welcome to 2030: I Own Nothing, Having No Privacy And Life Has Never Been Better," *World Economic Forum*, November 10, 2016, https://www.forbes.com.

2. https://en.wikipedia.org/wiki/klaus Schwab. (Retrieved: September 20, 2020).

3. Beware The 'Great Reset' New World Order, *The Epoch Times*, November 25, 2020, A17.

4. John Mac Ghlionn, "The Great Reset: Social Justice With Chinese Characteristics," *The Epoch Times*, July 27, 2021, A18.

5. Klaus Schwab, *The Fourth Industrial Revolution*, (New York: Penguin Random House, 2020), 67-68.

6. Ibid., 68

7. Ibid., 1

8. Ibid., 2-3.

9. Mac Ghlionn, *The Great Reset*, A18.

10. "Webster's New World Dictionary" 3rd ed., (New York: Simon and Schuster, 1988), 274.

11. Ibid., 207.

12. George Orwell, *1984*, (New York: Penguin Group, 1949), 206.

13. Schwab, *The Fourth Industrial Revolution*, 66.

14. Ibid., 6.

15. Ibid.

16. Ibid., 106.

17. Ibid., 12.

18. Ibid., 30.

19. Ibid., 36.

20. Ibid., 37.

21. Ibid., 38.

22. Ibid.

23. Kenan Kolday, *In 2030, You'll Own Nothing and Be Happy About It*, https://medium.com/illumination/in-2030-youll-own-nothing-and-be-happy-about-it-abb2835bd3d1. (Last Updated: December 8, 2020).

24. Ibid.

25. Schwab, *The Fourth Industrial Revolution*, 66.

26. Ibid.

27. Orwell, *1984*, 206.

28. Ibid.

29. Ibid.

30. Peter Svad, "Governor Fear Land Grab Over Biden's Conservative Plan: Impossible To Almost Triple Conservative Land Without Infringing On Private Property, Governors Says", *The Epoch Times*, July 20, 2021, A1.

31. Ibid., A4.

32. Ibid.

33. Ibid.

34. Ibid.

35. Mark Tapscott, "Senate Bill to Test taxing Americans For Each Nile Driven", *The Epoch Times*, August 10, 2021, A6.

36. Ibid.

37. "Beware the 'Great Reset' New World Order", *The Epoch Times*, November 25, 2020, A17.

38. Klaus Schwab and Thierry Malleret, *COVID-19: The Great Reset*, (Geneva, Switzerland: World Economic Forum, 2020), 119.

39. Nicole Hao and Cathy He, "China's Boast Deliberate Plan To Take-over Steps To Prevent Steps to Overthrown America", *The Epoch Times*, March 31, 2021, A1.

40. Twitter, *Associated Press*, June 2020, Quoted in *St. Louis Post-Dispatch*, June 14, 2020, A24.

41. Swab and Malleret, *COVID-19*, 107.

42. Ibid.

43. Ibid., 106.

44. Ibid., 103.
45. Ibid., 104.
46. Ibid.
47. Alex Newman, "Concern Surround IMF Plan to Flood World With Liquidity", *The Epoch Times*, July 27, 2021, A6.
48. Ibid.
49. Ibid.
50. Ibid.
51. Ibid., A7.
52. Ibid.
53. Andrew Zaleski, "GE's First Parts Take Flights, Fortune," May 12, 2015, https://fortune.com/2015/05/12/ge-3d-printed-jet-engine-parts/, quoted in Klaus Schwab, *The Fourth Industrial Revolution*, (New York: Currency, 2017), 163.
54. Ibid., 164.
55. Loren Grush, "Boy given A 3D Printed Spine Implant", *Popular Science*, August 26, 2014, http://www.popsci.com/article/science/boy-given-3-d-printed-spine-implant, quoted in Klaus Schwab, *The Fourth Industrial Revolution*, (New York: Currency, 2017), 165.
56. Kristen Leign Painter, "Cargill Tries Fitting Cows With Methane-Absorbing Masks", *The Star*, quoted in *St. Louis Post-Dispatch*, July 11, 2021, A6.
57. May Anne Copper, "Oregon's IP-13 Would Destroy Oregon's Livestock Industry", *Oregon Farm Bureau*, http://oregonfb.org, June 5, 2021.
58. Agnieszka De Sousa and Ivan Livingston, *Fake Meat or Faux Meat*, *Bloomberg News*, 2021, quoted in *St. Louis Post-Dispatch*, February 28, 2021, A2.
59. Ibid.
60. Aaron Earls, "Most Protestant Pastors See human Activity Behind Global Warming", *LifeWay Research*, https://lifewayresearch.com/2020/04/21/most-protestant-pastors-see-human-activity-behind-global-warming/, April 21, 2020.
61. Ibid.
62. Schwab and Malleret, *COVID-19*, 141.
63. Ibid.
64. Ibid.
65. Ibid., 142.

66. Ibid.

67. Ibid.

68. Cheng Xiaonong, "Why has "Global Warming" Disappeared?," *The Epoch Times,* May 19, 2021, A15.

69. Ibid.

70. Ibid.

71. *Global Volcanism Program: Current Euruptions,* https://volcano.si.edu/gvp-currentertuptions.cfm, March 12, 2020.

72. Cheng Xiaonong, *Why Has "Global Warming" Disappear?,* A15.

73. Jean Chen, "A Mom's Research: Texas Freezing and Global Warming", *The Epoch Times*, February 24, 2021, A17.

74. Ibid.

75. Ibid.

76. Ibid.

77. H. Sterling Burrett, "IPCC And Skeptics Agree Climate Change Is Not Causing Extreme Weather", *The Epoch Times*, July 7, 2020, A17.

78. Ibid.

79. Jonathan C. Bretner, "Who Are The Real Deniers?" ed. Terry James, *Lawless:End-Times Wars Against The Spirit of The AntiChrist,* (Crane, MO: Defender, 2020), 227.

80. Ibid. 228. Quoted in James Edwards Kamis, *Discovery of Massive Volcanic CO2 Emissions Put Damper On Global Warming Theory,* Climate Dispatch, November 6, 2018, https://climatechangedispatch.com/massive-volcanic-emissions-warming/.

81. Ibid., Jonathan C. Bretner, "Who Are The Real Deniers?."

82. Ibid., 230. Quoted in David Kupelian, *The Democratic Party's Ultimate Coup D' etat,* WND, December 1, 2019, https://www.wnd.com/2019/12democratic-partys-ultimate-coup-detat/.

83. James Rodger Fleming, *Fixing the Sky: The Checkered History of Weather And Climate Control,* (New York: Columbia University Press, 2010), 179.

84. Ibid., 4.

85. Ibid., 228.

86. Ibid.

87. Ibid., 230.

88. Cyrus A. Parsa, *The Great Reset: How Big Tech Elites and The World's People Can Be Enslaved By China CCP or AI,* (La Jolla, CA: The A.I. Organization, 2021), 70-71.

89. James Rodger Fleming, *Fixing the Sky,* 146.

90. Ibid.

91. Ibid., 147.

92. Elana Freeland, *Chemtrials, HAARP, and The Full Spectrum Dominance of Planet Earth,* (Port Townsend, WA: Feralhouse, 2014), 95. A book one must have with a lot of evidence and sources.

93. Rosalie Bertell, "Background of The HAARP Project," *Earthpulse.com.*

94. Clifford E. Carnicom, *Contrail Distance Formation Model,* March 22, 2001.

95. "Unilateral Geoengineering: Non-technical briefing Notes For A Workshop At The Counsel On Foreign Relations," Washington D.C., May 5, 2008.

96. James Rodger Fleming, *Fixing the Sky,* 2.

97. https://futurism.com/the-byte/uae-rainstorms-cloud-seeding-drones. (Retrieved: September 3, 2021).

98. James Rodger Fleming, *Fixing the Sky*, 180. .

99. Ibid., 178.

100. Ibid., 180

101. https://medium.com/illumination/in-2030-youll-own-nothing-and-be-happy-about-it_8bb2835b3d1.

102. William D. Mounce and Robert Mounce, ed. *The Zondervan Greek and English Interlinear New Testament,* 779.

103. Abir Ballan, "Question Everything," *The Epoch Times,* July 27, 2021, A16.

104. Melanie Hempe, "How Blind spots and Biases hurt Our Kids", *The Epoch Times*, October 5, 2021, C1.

105. Mounce, 781.

106.https://www.atlasobsobeura.com/places/georgia-guidstones, May 14, 2020.

107. B. Mole, *Plant Based Burgers Will Make Men Grow Boobs,* Ars Technica, https://arstechnica.com/. (retrieved: April 10, 2021).

108. Jonathan C. Bretner, "Who Are The Real Deniers?" ed. Terry James, *Lawless:End-Times War Against The Spirit of Antichrist,* (Crane, MO: Defender, 2020), 238.

109. Peter M. Burfeind, *Gnostic America*, (USA, Pax Domini Press, 2014), 97.

110. Webster's Nineth New College Dictionary, *Science*, (Springfield, MA: Merriam-Webster, 1986), 1051.

Chapter 7: The Great Deception: Take Heed No Man Deceives You

1. Courtney Linder, "After You Die Be Resurrected As A Chatbot. That's A Problem*", Popular Mechanics,* (New York, NY: Hearst Magazine Media, Incs, 2021), 21-23.

2. Ibid.

3. Nathan E. Jones, "Exposing Evil Seducers And Their Days Deception", ed. Terry James, *Deceivers: Exposing Evil Seducers & Their Last Days Deception,* (Green Forest, AR: New Leaf Press, 2018), 193.

4. Ibid., 198.

5. Walter Martin, *The Kingdom of Cults* 6 ed. (Minneapolis, MN: Bethany House, 2019), 444.

6. Ibid., 445.

7. Ibid., 446.

8. Ibid., 448-449.

9. Ibid., 452.

10. Elizabeth Montgomery, *A Grant Shape Shifting Statue That Talks Could Be Coming To Phoenix. Here's What We Know,* azcentral., https://www.azcentral.com/story/entertainment/arts/2021/05/06/the-giant-worlds-tallest-moving-statue-phoenix/4947964001/.

11. Cryus A. Parsa, *The Great Reset: How Bib Tech Elites And The World's People Can Be Enslaved By China CCP Or A.I.,* (La Jolla, CA: The A.I. Organization, nd), 70.

12. Ibid., 121.

13. Ibid.

14. Aesop, "The Wolf in Sheep Clothing," *The Epoch times,* April 20, 2021, B11.

15. Mounce, *Greek and English Interlinear New Testament*, 919.

16. Evgeny Afineevksy, "Francesco," Absamorema Entertainment, October 21, 2020, www.francescofilm.com.

17. Mike Gendron, "Pontif Proclaims All Go To Heaven," ed. Terry James, *Lawless: End-Times War Against The Spirit of Antichrist.* (Crane, MO: Defender, 2020), 322.

18. "Mainline Pastors Drive Growth In Pastoral Support For Same-Sex Marriage," *Lifeway Research,* https://lifewayresearch.

com/2020/02/11/mainline-pastors-drive-growth-in-pastoral-support-for-same-sex-marriage/.

19. Verlyn D. Verbrugge, *New International Dictionary of New Testament Theology*, (Grand Rapids, MI: Zondervan, 2000), 17. Also identified as NIDNTT.

20. Ibid., 1022.

21. Ibid., 1192.

22. Ibid., 1025.

23. Michael Gryboski, "Catholic High School Can Fire Staff In Same-Sex Marriage Cout Rules," *Sword of the Lord*, September 3, 2021, 6.

24. Ibid., Mike Gendron, "Pontif Proclaims All Go To Heaven," 323.

25. Norman Geisler, *Systematic Theology* vol. One (Grand Rapids, MI: Bethany House Publishers, 2011), 953.

26. Ibid., 964.

27. Mike Gendron, "Pontif Proclaims All Go To Heaven," 323.

28. R.A. Torrey, "questions Answered," *Sword of the Lord*, August 20, 2021, 9.

29. Mike Gendron, "Pontif Proclaims All Go To Heaven," 320.

30. Tod Robberson, "Prophecy vs. Heresey: Calling Out Right-Wing Preachers Who Miscalled Trumps Election Victory," *St. Louis Post-Dispatch,* July 25, 2021, A16.

31. Ibid.

32. Ibid.

33. "Competing Worldviews Influence Today's Christians, *Barna Group*, April 5, 2021, https://www.barna.com/research/competing-worldviews-influence-todays-christians/.

34. Ibid.

35. Richard Rorty, *The Encyclopedia Americana*, Vol 14. C.v. "Materialism" (Danbury, CT: Grolieri Inc, 1986), 485.

36. Ibid.

37. Geisler, *Systematic Theology*, 726.

38. Ibid.

39. Klaus Schwab, *The Fourth Industrial Revolution*, (New York, NY: Currency, 2016), 4.

40. Geisler, *Systematic Theology*, 726.

41. Barna Group, Ibid.

42. Ibid.

43. "Court Strikes Down 'Preferred' Pronoun Law, *Sword of the Lord,* August 20, 2021, 2.

44. https://en.wikipedia.org/wiki/woke.

45. Barna Group, Ibid.

46. Martin, *Kingdom of the Cults,* 319.

47. "Competing Worldviews Influence Today's Christians," *Barna Group*, Ibid.

48. Ibid.

49. Ryan Pitterson, "End-Times Embrace of Evil," ed. Terry James, *Lawless: End-Times war Against The Spirit of the AntiChrist,* (Crane, MO: Defender, 2020), 175.

50. Ibid., 174.

Chapter 8: Wars and Rumors of Wars: Unrestricted Warfare

1. "Vast Majority of Pastors See Signs of End Times In Current Events," *Lifeway Research,* https://lifewayresearch.com/2020/04/07/vast-majority-of-pastors-see-signs-of-end-times-in-current-event/.

2. Ibid.

3. James P. Boyd, *The Practical bible Dictionary and Concordance,* (Uhrichville, OH: Barbour Publishing Inc., 1952), 96.

4. Ibid.

5. Amir Tsarfati, *The Last Hour: An Israeli Insider Looks At The End Times,* (Minneapolis, MN: Chosen Books, 2018), 190.

6. Ibid.

7. "China's Secret War Against America: Method of Subversion and Unrestricted War Used To undermine The United States," *The Epoch Times,* June 10, 2020, A1-A7.

8. Ibid.

9. Ibid.

10. "Chinese Propaganda Outlet Paid Millions To Washington Post, Wall Street Journal," *The Epoch Times,* June 17, 2021, A2.

11. China's Secret War Against America, A6.

12. Ibid., 20.

13. Frank Fang and Cathy He, "China's 'Wolf Warrior Diplomats Use Political Warfare Against US." *The Epoch Times,* April 28, 2021, A1 & A10.

14. Ibid.

15. China's Secret War Against America, A6-A7.

16. Jonathan Watts, "Chinese General Warns of Nuclear Risks to U.S.," *The Guardian,* quoted from *The Epoch times,* July 15, 2021.

17. China's Secret War Against America, Ibid.

18. Andrew Thornebrooke, "CCP Anti-Satellite Weapons Present Complex Challenge For U.S.: Experts," *The Epoch Times,* September 7, 2021, 19.

19. China's Secret War Against America, Ibid.

20. China's Military Scientist, *The Epoch Times,* May 12, 2021, A10.

21. Jeff Carlson and Hans Mahnck, "Intelligence Community Assessment On COVID-19 Origins Ignores Readily Available Information," *The Epoch Times,* September 15, 2021, A15.

22. Ibid.

23. Ibid.

24. Ibid.

25. "CCP Collects America's DNA," *The Epoch Times,* April 20, 2021, A4.

26. Ibid.

27. Ibid.

28. Ibid.

29. Ibid.

30. Ibid.

Chapter 9: The Great Betrayal

1. *The Oxford new Desk Dictionary and Thesaurus* 3 ed. s.v., "Ethnic", (New York: The Berkley Publishing Group, 2009), 270.

2. Verlyn D. Verbrugge, *New International Dictionary of New Testament Theology,* (Grand Rapids, MI: Zondervan, 2000), 161.

3. Ibid.

4. Natalie Bazile, "The Indelible Legacy of Land," *National Geographics,* April 2020, 17.

5. Ibid.

6. Ibid.

7. Paul Davidson, "Trump's Tulsa Rally Calls To Minds 1921 Race Massacre: Oklahoma City's 'Black Wall Street' Destroyed By White Mob," *USA Today,* June 16, 2020), 2B.

8. Ibid.

9. Ibid.

1-. Jean Chen, "A Mom's Research: Who Are The Real Racist," *The Epoch Times,* March 23, 2021, A20.

11. Ibid.

12. Ibid.

13. Davidson, *Trump's Tulsa Rally Calls To Minds 1921 Race Massacre,* Ibid.

14. Ibid.

15. Sean Murphy, "Black Freemen Struggle For Recognition," *Associated Press*, n.d., quoted in *St. Louis Post-Dispatch,* May 9, 2021, A25.

16. Ibid.

17. Ibid.

18. Roman Star, "Rising Star, Young Bull Rider Could Add To Mostly Forgotten Legacy Of The Black Cowboy," *Washington Post,* n.d., quoted in *St. Louis Post-Dispatch*, May 2, 2021, D8.

19. Ibid.

20. Ibid.

21. Ibid.

22. Charles Butt, "Enter Black Lives Matter, Or They Don't! Black "Baby Lives Matter!." *Onenewsnow.com,* quoted in *Sword of The Lord*, September 3, 3031, 5.

23. Secular Democrat PAC Aims For Policy Changes In A Biden Administration, *Decision Magazine*, December 21, 2020, https://www.decisionmagazine.com/category/news/. Also see 28 – page document at https://seculardems.org/wp-content/upload/2020/.

24. "Chinese Regime Burns Religious Books, Jails Believers In Way Against Faith, *The Epoch Times*, March 3, 2021, A10.

25. Ibid.

26. Frank Fang, "Chinese Authorities Raid Church In Shenzhen City, Detain 10," *The Epoch Times,* April 28, 2021, A10.

27. Frank Yue, "More House Christians Detain In Southwest China," *The Epoch Times*, May 11, 2021, A8.

28. Ibid.

29. Anugrah Kumar, "Hindu Leader Issues Call For AntiChristian Violence," *Christianpost.com,* quote in *Sword of the Lord*, September 3, 2021, 2.

30. Ibid.

31. Anugrah Kumar, "Radical Islamic Jihadist Killed Over 1400 Nigerian Christians In First Four Months of 2021," *Christianpost.com*, quoted in *Sword of the Lord*, June 25, 2021,6.

32. Emily Wood, "Mozambique Radical Jihadist Extremist Behead Children," *Christianpost.com*, quoted in *Sword of the Lord*, July 23, 2021, 8.

33. Ryan Foley, "MSNBC Host Jay Reid Compares Christian Right To Taliban Militants," *Christianpost.com*, quoted in *Sword of the Lord*, September 17, 2021, 4.

34. "FBI Tells Americans To Report 'Family Members And Peers In Tweet," *The Epoch Times*, July 20, 2021, A3.

35. Alex Newman, "Echoes of Mao: Weaponing Schools With 'Critical Race Theory," *The Epoch Times*, April 27, 2021, A20-21.

36. Ibid.

37. Ibid., A21.

38. Ibid.

39. "The Chinese Communist Party Has Destroyed The Best Of China," *The Epoch Times*, July 13, 2021, A1.

40. Leonard Pitts, "Republicans Stoke White Right Fears With Latest 'War'!," *Miami Herald*, quote in *St. Louis Post-Dispatch*, July 11, 2011, M1.

41. Ryan Foley, Black Civil Rights Activist Says America Has A "Grace Problem," Not a "Race Problem," *Christianpost.com*, September 2021, quoted in *Sword of the Lord*, September 3, 2021, 21.

42. Alex Newman, "Rise of 'Fed Ed' Accelerated Demise Of Real Education," *The Epoch Times*, June 18, 2020, A19.

43. Robert Knight, "A Parents' Revolt From Coast To Coast," *Sword of the Lord*, July 23, 2021, 6.

44. Marx and Engels, "*The Communist Manifesto* (Chapter II. Proletarians and Communists), https://www.marxist.org/archive/marx/works/1848/communistmanifesto/cho2.htm.

45. Israel Wayne, "The Schoolroom Seducers," ed. Terry James, *Deceivers: Exposing Evil Seducers And Their Last Days Deception*, (Green Forest, AR: New Leaf Publishing Group, 2018), 118.

46. Ibid., 115.

47. Ibid.

48. Alex Newman, "Rise of Fed Ed," A19.

49. Ibid.

50. Israel Wayne, "The Schoolroom Seducer," 113.

51. Tony Perkins, "Public School Wokeism Brainwashes And Indoctrinates Children," quote in *Sword of the Lord,* July 9, 2021, 16.

52. Sandhya Rama, "Pandemic Hampers reductions of Sexually Transmitted Infection," *St. Louis Post-Dispatch,* April 14, 2021, A20.

53. "50s Sexual Research Still Causing A Stir," *WebMD,* https://www.webmd.com/sex-relationships/features/50s-sexuality-research-still-causing-stir.

54. Dr. Judith Reisman and Leslee Unruh, *The Causalities of Kinsey: The Truth About The Founder Of Sexual Decay In America,* https://www.parentsrightsined.org/uploads/1/1/8/8/118879585/truestoriesthecasualititesofkinsey/.pdf.

55. Ibid.

56. Ibid., "50s Sexuality Research Still causing A Stir.":

57. Ibid. Reisman and Unruh, *The Causality of Kinsey.*

58. Perkins, "Public School Wokeism Brainwashes And Indoctrinates Children," Ibid.

59. Ibid.

60. Ibid.

61. Charlies Butts and Bily Davis, "Public Libraries Bringing Back Drag Queen Story Hour," *onenewsnow.com,* quote in *Sword of the Lord,* July 23, 2021, 16.

62. Jeff Minick, "Innocence Lost: Our Children And Pornography," *The Epoch Times,* May 18, 2021, C6.

63. Adriana Brasilerio, "New Florida Mosquito Species 'very aggressive,'" *Miami Herald,* quote in *St. Louis Post-Dispatch,* February 21, 2021, M1.

64. Susanne Rust, "Blood-Thirsty Ticks On The Rise At California Beaches," *St. Louis Post-Dispatch,* A22.

65. "China Monkey B Virus," *The Epoch Times,* July 27, 2021, A10.

Chapter 10: #There Are 'Woke' Pimps In The Pulpit

1. Sarah Pulliam Bailey, "Post-Trump, Some U.S. Pastors Are Ditching The Label Of Evangelicals," *The Washington Post,* n.d. quoted in *St. Louis Post-Dispatch,* October 24, 2021, A9.

2. Ibid.

3. Ibid.

4. Ibid.

5. Ibid.

6. Ibid.

7. Ibid.

8. Ibid.

9. Ibid.

10. https://www.arcgis.com/apps/cascade/index.html?appid=7b33d5df643842a8875ff9f675cebae2.

11. Claire Gecewicz, "'New Age' Beliefs Common Among Both Religious and NonReligious Americans," *Pew Research Center*, October 1, 2018, https://www.pwersr.ch/2Nr7Bme.

12. Ibid.

13. https://www.PewForum.org/Religious-LandscapeStudy/#Religious.

14. Leo Lyon Zagami, *Invisible Master: Puppeteers Hidden Power,* (Consortium Collective Consciousness Publishing, 2019), 69.

15. www.arcgis.com, Ibid.

16. Jan Markell, "Globalist Declare War On Sovereignty" ed. Terry James, *Lawless: End-Times War Against The Spirit Of AntiChrist,* (Crane, MO: Defender, 2021), 19.

17. Jackson Elliot, "CDC Points People to Transgenderism, Teen Sex Websites," *The Epoch Times,* August 9, 2022, A6.

18. Jim Townsley, "How To Become A Liberal," *Sword of the Lord,* October 22, 2021, 11.

19. A Good Laugh, *The Sword of The Lord,* September 17, 2021, 5.

Chapter 11: Finish Strong

1. Frederick William Danker, *A Greek-English Lexicon of The New Testament And Other Early Christian Literature* 3d ed (BDAG), (Chicago, IL: The University of Chicago Press, 2000), 793.

2. Oswald J. Smith, "You Can't Get There Unless You Start Here," *Sword of The Lord,* February 10, 2017, 3.

3. Ibid. Danker, *DBAG*, 256.

4. "Epiphyllum Oxypetalum," *Wikipedia*, Last modified: November 15, 2021, https://em.wikipedia.org/w/index.php?title=Epiphyllum_oxypetalum&oldid+1055410537.

5. Josh Shepherd, *Survey Finds Only 9% of Self-Identified Christians Hold To Biblical Worldview,* https://julieroys.com/george-barna-survey-biblical-worldview/.

6. Ibid.

7. William Mounce and Robert Mounce, *Greek and English Interlinear New Testament (KJV/NIV),* (Grand Rapids, MI: Zondervan 2000), 1645.

8. Verlyn D. Verbrugge, *New International Dictionary of New Testament Theology,* (Grand Rapids, MI: Zondervan, 2000), 1645.

9. Danker, BDAG, 287.

10. Minister Walter Graham, Interview with the author, November 17, 2021. Used with permission.

Conclusion

1. Sarah Taylor, "Studies Find Aspirin Can Significantly Cut COVID Risks And Every Death," *TheBlaze.com,* quoted in *Sword of the Lord,* November 19, 2021, 16.

2. Ibid.

3. Seymour Morris Jr., *American History Revised* (New York, NY: Broadway Books, 2010), 147.

4. Ibid.

5. "Transforming Our World: the 2030 Agenda For Sustainable Development," *United Nations,* 16, https://sustainabledevelopment.un.org/content/documents/21252030%20Agenda%20for%20sustainable%20development%20web.pdf.

6. Dr. Ronald Hoffman, "What Do Bill Gates, Eggs and "Soylent Green" Have in Common?", *Intelligent Medicine,* October 4, 2013, https://drhoffman.com/article/what-do-bill-gates-eggs-and-soylent-green-have-in-common/.

7. Mark Prigg, "Let Them Eat Fake – 'Artificial Egg' Made From Plants Backed By Bill Gates Set To Revolutionize Cooking Goes On Sale At Whole Foods," *Daily Mail UK,* September 10, 2013, https://www.sott.net/article/266209-Let-them-eat-fake-artificial-egg-made-from-plants-backed-by-Bill-Gates-set-to-revolutionize-cooking-goes-on-sale-at-Whole-Foods.

8. Transforming Our World, Ibid.

9. Micaiah Bilger, "Hope Heralding Hippos Hideous," *Lifenews.com,* quoted in *Sword of the Lord,* November 19, 2021, 9.

10. Ibid.

11. Chem May Yee, "Malaysia To Battle Smog With Cyclones," *Wall Street Journal*, October 2, 1992.

12. Bob Fitrakis and Fritz Chess, "Stormy Weather," *Columbus Alive*, December 6, 2001.

13. A.K. Johnstone, *Defence Tactics: Weather Shield To Chemtrails*, Hancock House, 2002.

14. Elana Freeland, *Chemtrails, HAARP, and The Full Spectrum Dominance of Planet Earth*, (Port Townsend, WA: Feralhouse, 2014), 259.

15. Freeland, 37.

16. Ibid., 63.

17. Bernard J. Eastlund, "Patent #4,686,605," www.scribd.com/doc/27704690/US-Patent-No-4-686-605-HAARP.

18. Freeland, 51.

19. Ibid., 55, 57 & 113.

20. Ibid., 54.

21. Ibid., 96.

22. Colin Baras, "Laser Creates Cloud Over Germany," *New Scientist*, May 2, 2010.

23. Freeland, 107.

24. John Vidal, "Bill Gates Backs Climate Scientists Lobbying For Large-scale Geoengineering," *The Guardian*, February 5, 2012.

25. "An Impractical Hope," *Sword of the Lord*, November 19, 2021, 13.

ABOUT THE AUTHOR

Dr. D.A. Kelly, Sr. is a former pastor, military officer and educator, and has led an evangelical ministry to stand in the gap as a Watchman. God has given him the ability to discern end-times prophecy through current events in ways others struggle to ascertain. Dr. Kelly is a graduate from a Baptist seminary and anointed Bible teacher dedicated to end-times prophecy, soul-winning, discipleship, and leadership development. Dr. Kelly is the founder of Razor wire Faith, a prison discipleship ministry, as the Lord placed in his heart a "message for the men."

Contact the author at:

515 Edwardsville Road
P.O. Box 223
Troy, IL 62294-9998

or visit his website at:

drdakellysr.com